The Encyclopaedia
of Girls' School Stories
Volume One

Sue Sims and Hilary Clare

Edited by: Tig Thomas
Consultant: Lyn Dodd

Girls Gone By Publishers

Published by
Girls Gone By Publishers
The Vicarage, Church Street, Coleford, Radstock, Somerset, BA3 5NG, UK

First published by Ashgate in 2000
This new edition first published 2020
Text © Sue Sims and Hilary Clare 2020
Design and Layout © Girls Gone By Publishers 2020
Cover photograph taken by David Hirst © Girls Gone By Publishers 2020

The moral right of Sue Sims and Hilary Clare to be identified as the author of this book has been asserted by them in accordance with the Copyright, Designs and Patents Act 1988.

All rights reserved.
Without limiting the rights under copyright reserved above,
no part of this publication may be reproduced, stored in or introduced into a retrieval system, or transmitted, in any form or by any means (electronic, mechanical, photocopying, recording or otherwise), without the prior written permission of the above copyright owners and the above publisher of this book.

Neither Girls Gone By Publishers nor any of their authors or contributors have any responsibility for the continuing accuracy of URLs for external or third-party websites referred to in this book; nor do they guarantee that any content on such websites is, or will remain, accurate or appropriate.

Edited by Tig Thomas
Cover design by Ken Websdale and Sue Sims
Typeset in England by GGBP
Printed and bound by Short Run Press, Exeter, EX2 7LW

ISBN 978-1-84745-257-3

Contents

Volume One
Preface	5
Acknowledgements	9
Typesetting the *Encyclopaedia*	13
Introduction	17
The Critical Response	35
Researching the *Encyclopaedia*	53
Apologia and Explanation	59
Authors A-F	A 67, B 75, C 131, D 161, E 181, F 193
Adult School Fiction	209

Volume Two
Authors G-M	G 231, H 251, I 275, J 281, K 287, L 291, M 313
Annuals	369
Ballet and Stage School Stories	389
College Stories	409
Convent School Stories	415
Early School Stories	425
Evangelistic School Stories	441

Volume Three
Authors N-Z (NB there are no entries for the Letters Q, X or Z)
N 455, O 465, P 485, R 509, S 523, T 543, U 557, V 563, W 573, Y 591

The Girl's Own Paper	595
Girls' School Story Papers	599
Guide School Stories	603
Historical and Fantasy School Stories	611
Little Folks	627
Modern School Stories	631
Pony School Stories	651
Scottish School Stories	659
General Bibliography	669

" ' Aren't you aware that we've been looking for you everywhere for the tennis practice? ' Yvonne exclaimed." *(See page 44.)*

The frontispiece from *Joan and the Scholarship Girl* by Brenda Page

Preface

The first edition of *The Encyclopaedia of Girls' School Stories* was published by Ashgate in 2000 as one of a pair, its companion being *The Encyclopaedia of Boys' School Stories*, edited and mainly written by Robert Kirkpatrick. *The Encyclopaedia of Girls' School Stories* was popular enough to go into a second impression within six months, but there were no more impressions after that, and for many years it has been available only on the second-hand market, generally at very high prices.

This was the first and only encyclopaedia devoted to English-language girls' school stories. It covered British and Commonwealth school stories, their histories, critical reception, authors, topics, and critical analyses of the works themselves, together with bibliographical details of all examples of the genres known to the editorial team, and of writing about school stories and their authors. It was a pioneering work for many reasons.

Many of the biographical details of school-story authors appeared in print in its pages for the first time. In the case of those authors who had received some critical attention in the past, previously published errors and omissions were corrected; in the case of the vast majority, light was shed on hitherto ignored or unknown lives and a substantial body of information unearthed about their work. Many bibliographies, even of recognised writers, were presented for the first time complete and, it was hoped, accurate.

School stories had long suffered from critical dismissal and public derision and it is only recently that their influence and merits have begun to be re-valued. But, as with any literary genre, all school stories are not alike and not all are of equal worth. The critical assessments in the first edition which accompanied all but the most minor contributions to the genre made it possible to distinguish the variations in style and approach of different authors and books, as well as to appreciate the sheer scope of the genre's achievement. While the editorial team deplored the tendency to lump all school stories together as mindless trash, they recognised that some authors wrote better stories than others (though there are differences of opinion here) and that some books in a writer's oeuvre are undoubtedly better than others, especially if they enjoyed long writing careers.

But the 'better' books are not necessarily the most popular, and the study of school stories and their readers yields many fascinating insights not simply into the values and customs of each era but into the possibility of 'oppositional' readings which may subvert the expressed messages.

We all have our favourite books and our pet hates and while the contributors to this *Encyclopaedia* are all sincere devotees of the genre, that does not mean that we love them all uncritically or esteem them all equally. It means, indeed, that we can even laugh at them on occasion—not the undiscerning laughter of contempt but in sympathetic recognition that some of these novels *are* unintentionally funny and that some, in truth, do not deserve too serious consideration. Conversely, some school stories are really good, and our contributors do not hesitate to name the ones they think merit literary or popular acclaim.

This second edition, published in three volumes by Girls Gone By, has been many years in the making. It includes authors and books discovered since 2000, and also the biographies of many writers of whom little or nothing was known at that time. The genre has not remained static: books set in girls' schools have continued to be written, so we have updated the relevant articles and bibliographies, and added an essay covering girls' school stories written since the first edition. We hope that this edition is up to date at the time of writing, but realise that, try as we may, there will be errors and omissions: we welcome corrections and additions from our readers.

Many people had a hand in compiling the information in this book. Writers are credited at the end of individual articles; where there is no attribution, the article is by Hilary or Sue. Tig Thomas has done a magnificent job in editing the three volumes, and Clarissa Cridland of GGBP has spent untold hours preparing them for publication. Grateful acknowledgements are also due to Rosemary Auchmuty, who oversaw the first editions of both *The Encyclopaedia of Boys' School Stories* and *The Encyclopaedia of Girls' School Stories*, and who has maintained her interest and encouragement throughout; and to Lyn Dodd, who has given valuable assistance in so many ways.

Finally, we would like to dedicate the second edition of this *Encyclopaedia* to the memory of Joy Wotton, whose untimely death prevented her from editing these volumes as she had edited the first edition.

Hilary Clare and Sue Sims 2020
Based on the original preface of 2000 by Rosemary Auchmuty

The frontispiece from *Hot Water* by Joan Butler-Joyce

The frontispiece from *How Damie Found Herself* by Mary Martin

Acknowledgements

Much of the work for this book has been done in the British Library and the Bodleian Library, Oxford, to whose staff we owe thanks for their constant assistance and patience. This is especially true of John Slatter of the Bodleian's Nuneham Repository, who suffered our visits with unfailing good humour and helpfulness.

Our particular gratitude is also due to Selina Corkerton, of Edinburgh, who nobly pursued numerous writers at Register House and has added very greatly to our knowledge of their lives. Thanks too to Alicia Ash and Avis Whyte, research assistants in the School of Law, University of Westminster.

We are indebted to the authors, editors and publishers of the many books on children's literature whose research we have used in the preparation of this volume. These works are all cited in the General Bibliography and/or in individual bibliographies.

We are grateful for help and information from the following, though we regret to record that many of the valued contributors in this list have died since the first edition:

Schools: The Cheltenham Ladies' College; Clifton High School for Girls; Croydon High School; the High School of Glasgow; Godolphin School, Salisbury; the Harrogate Ladies' College, especially Mrs R Silverman; the Kingsley School (formerly Leamington High School); Oxford High School; Queen Anne's, Caversham; Roding Valley School (formerly Loughton High School); St Leonard's School; South Hampstead High School; Sutton High School; Sydenham High School; Truro High School; Wycombe Abbey School, especially Fiona Mather of the Wycombe Abbey School Seniors; Sandwell Department of Education;

Colleges: Corpus Christi College, Cambridge; Girton College, Cambridge; Lucy Cavendish College, Cambridge; Newnham College, Cambridge; Royal Holloway and Bedford New College; St Anne's College, Oxford; St Hugh's College, Oxford; Trinity College of Music; the University of Liverpool; Canon David Smith, Chaplain of Bromley and Sheppard's Colleges;

Archives and Record Offices: The staff of the Record Offices of Hampshire, East Sussex, Oxfordshire and Warwickshire; Dr Iain Brown of the National Library of Scotland; Margaret Courtney, Archivist of the Guide Association; Peter Foden, formerly Archivist at OUP; Kate Hutcheson and her staff at the Business Records Centre, University of Glasgow (Blackie archives); John Lenton of the World Methodist Historical Society; Alison Lindsay of the Scottish Record Office; Dr Martin Maw, Archivist at Oxford University Press; Joy McCarthy of the Royal Historical Society; Kristin Thomas, Librarian at Deakin University Library, Geelong;

Individuals: Terry Adams, Mabel Esther Allan, Ruth Allen, Mr and Mrs R Allden, Jane Badger, Norah Baker, Jenny Balston, Carol Ann Barnett, John Baxter, Nancy Bayes, John Beck, Polly Beidas, Louise Bendall, Gill Bilski, Nora Blacklock, Gladys Bland, Fiona Bradley, Lewis Braithwaite, Gretchen Breary, Sarah Burn, Mary Cadogan, Diana Channon, Sophie Cleverly, Eleanor Coggin, Belinda Copson, Julia Courtney, Pamela Cox, Alex Daborn, Thelma Dawkins, Barbara de Foubert, Carolyn Denman, Lyn Dodd, Robert Dougan, Ann Dowker, Esmé Engleheart, Jean Finch, Godfrey Fitzhugh, Jan Frisby, Anne Froggatt, Griselda Fyfe, Bertha Galliford, Dr Katie Gilchrist, Regina Glick, Monica Godfrey, Miss D Griffin, Elly Griffiths, David Grugeon, Pat Hanby, Rodney Harris, Margaret Heaton, Di Henley, John Herrington, Phyllis Hunt, Michael Jeans-Jakobsson, Paul Joyce, Christine Keyes, Alison Lindsay, Bill Lofts, Margot Louis, Patricia Lowe, Marcia McGinley, Muriel  McIntosh, Janet Maconie, Neville Masterman, G M Milne, Sue Mongredien, Sir John Mortimer, Mr and Mrs Paul Mossop, Lin Murison, Shirley Neilson, Joyce Norris, Phyllis Norris, Kate Nwume, Mary O'Kill, Barbara Penrose, Arthur Plunket, Tom Pocock, Imogen Purkiss, Sheila Ray, Barbara Robertson, Chloe Rutherford, Helen Schinske, Lynda Singleton, Marion Smith, Sarah Stanfield, Sarah Sneddon, Robin Stevens, Dorothy Stewart, Aishwarya Subramanian, Tony Summerfield, Sue Surman, Judith Thomas, Scott Thompson, Eileen Tranaker, Hilary Turner, Kate Tyler, Jocelyn de Horne Vaizey, Helen Vincent, Judith Waite, Joy Welch, Kay Whalley, Jessica Wilson, Penny Wilson, and Barbara Worthington; the readers of *Folly* and the magazines devoted to individual writers, the subscribers to the Girlsown Google group, and the many Facebook groups that have sprung up since the first edition of this *Encyclopaedia* for their continued help, support and suggestions.

Finally, we must thank those, each expert in her field, who contributed an entry or entries to this *Encyclopaedia of Girls' School Stories* on their specialist areas: Mary Cadogan, Jean Garriock, Alison Lindsay, Eva Löfgren, Margot Louis, Helen McClelland, Sheila Ray, David Rudd, Jennifer Schofield and Kate Tyler.

Sue Sims
Hilary Clare

The frontispiece from *Lowanna* by Castleden Dove

"That's a clever dodge for making us talk German."
Page 10

The frontispiece from *A Girl Among Girls* by E A Gillie

Typesetting The Encyclopaedia

Typesetting is the process of putting the text and illustrations together so that the book is ready to send to the printers. Typesetting the *Encyclopaedia* is one of the most challenging jobs I have ever done. Typesetting a normal Girls Gone By book, even one with illustrations, usually takes about eight to twelve hours. I have lost count of the number of hours I have spent typesetting the *Encyclopaedia* but it is probably nearer 300! During the process I have learnt a lot, although things were not helped when I had got as far as half-way through the letter B and the whole document jammed. I had to cut my losses and start again. I have worked through holidays in order to finish it, and I have to say that there is a silver lining in every cloud—during the almost total isolation I am in because of Covid-19 I have managed to finish the book. I say 'book', but actually there are three volumes. We had originally anticipated two, but the extra material and the many illustrations prevented that.

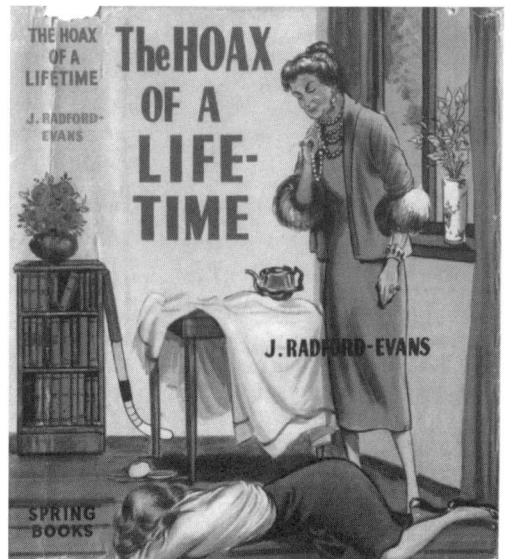

While there are three volumes, we do actually think of the *Encyclopaedia* as being one book. So you will find that the first volume finishes on page 224, the second starts on page 225 and finishes on page 448, and the third starts on page 449 and finishes on page 672.

When front and spine show a continuous design, I have reproduced the entire picture; when there are discrete images on front and spine, they may be reproduced in different places in the text. I have not asked Sue to re-scan pictures already sent, even if they had continuous designs.

I took the decision to start each chapter on the right-hand side, and in almost every case I have been able to include a frontispiece on the opposite page to the opening. And sometimes where the text finishes on the left-hand side, there is a frontispiece on the right as well. Sometimes a chapter will end half-way up a page, and in that case we have included an illustration from the stock Sue collected to illustrate *Folly*: all originally came from annuals, but the individual source was never recorded, so they cannot be credited.

It has been especially pleasing to be able to include in each volume eight pages of illustrations in colour—that is 32 colour illustrations per volume, which makes a total of 96! Many of these have also been used in black and white in chapters of the *Encyclopaedia*, but not all.

Although most of the illustrations have come from Sue, she was not able to supply everything. Lyn Dodd, who also has an amazing collection of school stories, supplied many, especially during a time that Sue had (ordinary) flu. Christine Ward was also incredibly helpful and sent a number which neither Sue nor Lyn had. When it came to the chapter on annuals, Sue could supply very few illustrations and Lyn does not have room for annuals in her flat! So I appealed in my Friday email (if you do not know about this, please go to https://www.ggbp.co.uk/, scroll down the page and sign up). I had a terrific response, and Kate and Mark Blackadder, Jennifer Hill, Christine Ward, and Judy and Richard Wright supplied me with more than I could need, which was wonderful. Judy and Richard also supplied me with illustrations for Girls' Story Papers. As well I had one or two illustrations from each of the following: Hilary Clare, Mary Evans, Susanne Harper, Marcia McGinley and Kristen Thornton. There were others who offered to supply, but whom I had to decline because by that stage I had enough. I hope I have not missed anyone off this list, but a huge huge thanks goes to you all, and especially Sue and Lyn.

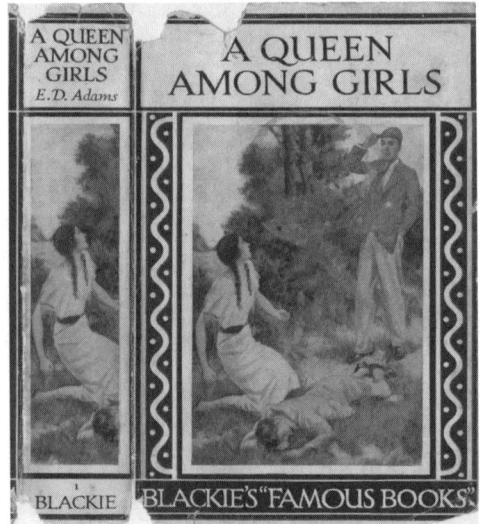

After I typeset, every single chapter has been proof-read by two people, before being finally checked by Sue, Hilary, Lyn and editor Tig (as well as myself). Those who did this were Sheryl Burke, Linda Buckingham, Katherine Bruce, Amanda Brunt, Georgia Corrick, Sonja Crosby, June Edwards, Amy Fletcher, Susan French, Julie Gleeson, Hilary Hartley, Mia Jha, Sara Jones, Jane Lee, Adrienne Lingard, Moira Lott, Marcia McGinley, Penny McMahon, Inez Meadows, Susan Merskey, Alison Oliver, Pat Olver, Elizabeth Oxbury, Elizabeth Roberts, Carol Royston-Tonks, Pam Stanier, Mark Taha, Judy Wright, and Marie-Claire Wyatt. Once again, huge thanks to you all.

I should also like to thank Tig Thomas for being such a superb editor, not only editing so sensitively Sue and Hilary's text, but replying to all my queries so quickly.

The illustrations on this page and pages 12 and 13 have been chosen because I like them. However, rather than include another frontispiece opposite, I have chosen the most extraordinary illustration for a school story which I have been sent. This is the front board for the first edition of *What Katy Did at School* by Susan Coolidge: the insect (on the leaf, roughly above the W) is a Katydid (also known as a Bush Cricket and a Leaf Bug). It was sent to me by Christine Ward, to whom I am most grateful.

As I look back over the typesetting of the *Encyclopaedia*, in spite of the setbacks and challenges, I have actually enjoyed working on it very much indeed. I hope you will enjoy reading it as much.

Clarissa Cridland, Publisher, Girls Gone By

The front boards of the first edition of *What Katy Did at School* by Susan Coolidge
(please see opposite for further details)

The frontispiece from *First Term at Malory Towers* by Enid Blyton

INTRODUCTION

To spare the reader continual references to other articles, in the following pages authors in upper case **BOLD** have their own entries in the alphabetical section.

In general, revising any work of non-fiction for a new edition is a reasonably straightforward (if time-consuming) task. One corrects the errors that sneaked into the previous edition despite the dedicated and rigorous supervision of the authors, editor and copy-editor; adds the new information which gallant readers have provided in the interval; and provides necessary updates. All these elements are present in this book.

However, with *The Encyclopaedia of Girls' School Stories*, it is also necessary to rewrite a large portion of this Introduction because, while completely correct at the time of writing, the situation has most happily altered. In the first edition, we complained somewhat bitterly that, while boys' school stories were generally regarded as respectable, the girls' variety was anything but. We quoted Elizabeth Bowen and Margery Fisher, both of whom despised the genre: the former, commissioned to write an introduction to the 1957 reissue of Antonia White's *Frost in May* (see **Adult School Fiction**), laid it down that '[school stories] for boys are infinitely better than those for girls. The curl-tossing tomboys of the Fourth at St Dithering's are manifestly and insultingly unreal to any girl child who has left the nursery; as against this, almost all young schoolgirls devour boys' school books, and young boys, apparently, do not scorn them'. Margery Fisher, normally a responsive reader and a generous critic, acknowledged that 'some [boys' school story] writers were genuinely creative' and described **ANTONIA FOREST**—whom she did admire—as 'cutting across the silliness and triviality which resulted from half a century of Angela Brazil and her imitators' (*Intent upon Reading*, revised edition 1964). Both women, it will be noticed, assumed that boys' school stories are worth at least considering; girls' school stories could be lumped together without distinction and tossed in the waste-paper bin reserved for silly, trivial, curl-tossing tomboys.

We also described in some detail the cringing embarrassment which tended to overcome literate and well-educated females when caught reading a girls' school story in public. We ascribed this partly to the chronological snobbery which makes adults ashamed of seeming childish, but more to the sense that in reading girls' school stories they were endorsing a type of writing which had been almost universally condemned as rubbish.

THE CHALET SCHOOL DOES IT AGAIN

ELINOR M. BRENT-DYER

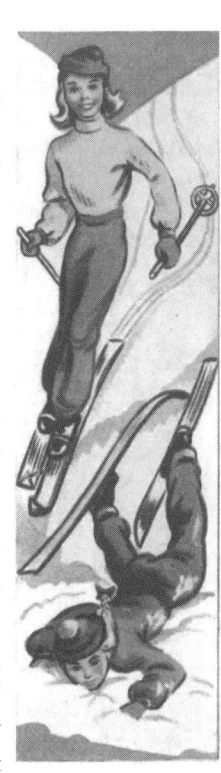

Even in the late 1990s, however, the situation was beginning to change. We noted the existence of fan clubs for authors such as **ELINOR M BRENT-DYER** and **ELSIE JEANETTE OXENHAM**, and the constant trickle of articles, academic studies, and books on girls' stories and girls' writers (see **The Critical Response** and **General Bibliography**). Since then, the rise of the internet and the immediacy of online communication has greatly lessened the embarrassment factor—there are so many other like-minded individuals in the online communities and on social networks—and few people wish to be thought 'judgemental', so even if school story readers are still commonly despised, we are at least no longer aware of it.

There remains one problem, however, for a book of this type which the passage of time has not, alas, removed. Although critics, academics and fans have a very clear idea of what they mean by 'girls' school stories', defining what is meant by the term is very difficult. A working definition might focus on the following characteristics: the story will be wholly or largely set in a girls' school; it is intended for girls, rather than adults, to read; it is written mainly from the point of view of one or more of the girls; school overall is seen in a positive light, although any given school, house or form may need reformation; there is no central heterosexual love interest, and no overt lesbian material; and the school community is the focus of the story. Of course there are exceptions to all these criteria: **MABEL ESTHER ALLAN**, **ENID BLYTON** and **LYDIA GRAHAM**, among others, set stories in mixed schools; a number of writers such as **NETTA SYRETT, MARGARET MASTERMAN** and **LUCY KINLOCH** wrote books which must be classified as school stories

but which (because of their autobiographical inspiration) raise issues normally only confronted in adult novels; **BRENT-DYER**'s *New Mistress at the Chalet School* tells the whole story through the eyes of the eponymous New Mistress; and several of **ELSIE OXENHAM**'s school stories point to a future marriage between a boy or a girl who are currently just 'chums' (for example, the 'Swiss' series, beginning with *The Two Form Captains*). Even the last exclusion, that there should be no overtly sexual content, has been breached in some recent books which in all other respects must be called girls' school stories—see **Modern School Stories**. Still, when all necessary exceptions have been made, a definition of this nature does exclude many well-known books set in wholly or partly in girls' schools which are not perceived by fans of the genre to be girls' school stories: *Frost in May* (Antonia White: see **Adult school fiction**) is intended for adults, not for girls; Miss Minchin's seminary (cf **FRANCES HODGSON BURNETT**) is an appalling institution that no girl would ever wish to attend—nor is it ever suggested that Sara Crewe should try to reform it.

Perhaps the most important single criterion is the idea of *desire*. Stella Waring made the point well in 'Before the School Story' (*Folly* 15 & 16): one cannot have school stories as we know them until girls see school as a desirable place. For that reason alone, few school stories earlier than (roughly) the 1880s fit snugly into our concept of 'the girls' school story'. Many of the themes and motifs that preoccupied later generations of writers can be traced back through the 19th century; some even to the 18th century; but the schools portrayed are not tempting places of fun and 'japes', nor even institutions where clever girls could get an academic education. They are either frivolous, snobbish and worldly establishments, intended to test the patience and virtue of the heroine (such as **EMILIA MARRYAT NORRIS**'s *Theodora*, 1870) or schools where girls spent most of the day learning pages of textbooks by heart and preaching to their less virtuous comrades (**EMMA J WORBOISE**'s *Grace Hamilton's School Days*, 1856, is a case in point). That these choices were based on the education actually available to middle-class girls is indisputable; the fact remains that neither of them is very attractive to a young reader.

Certainly a handful of schools such as North London Collegiate—institutions focusing on offering girls an academic education as good as that given to their brothers—had been established before 1870, but they had not so far affected the education of the enormous majority of girls. It was not until the Taunton Commission validated the work of the girls' schools pioneers in their 1868 report, and Maria Grey and her sister Emily Shirreff established the Girls' Public Day School Company, that a High School or public school education came within range of more than a small minority of British girls. Only then could the full-blown school story develop—not, as is commonly assumed by those who have never read them, as a frilly imitation of the male variety, but based on the realities of female education. (See **Early School Stories** for a fuller discussion.)

Nevertheless, it would be wrong to depict the girls' school story as leaping fully formed from the head of the Taunton Commission. The changes in girls' education affected a type of book already being written; it was not actually called 'a girls' school story' until the 1880s, but it fulfilled many of the criteria listed above. Most of the 'school stories' written from around 1850 until the turn of the century have certain characteristics in common. They are moral, and generally religious in tone: they focus on temptation and purification through suffering, even death (as in *Ruth and Rose* or *Lily and Nannie at School* (see **Early School Stories**), though on the whole it is the good who die—frequently causing the bad to see the error of their ways. The message largely concerns duty, holiness, even temperance (*We Girls* by **M A PAULL**, 1890, is an explicitly temperance school story), although this lessens as the century moves on: books like **HANNAH MACKENZIE**'s *Kitty's Cousin* or **GRACE STEBBING**'s *That Aggravating Schoolgirl* (both 1885) eschew overt preaching and present lively schoolgirls who ultimately realise that seriousness is also necessary.

These schools are generally small (between 10 and 40 pupils); thus the rivalries are all personal, rarely if ever between different age groups or classes. There is no hierarchy—the title of 'Head Girl' is normally used for the oldest and (in general) most learned girl in the school—and no prefects, though older girls may be expected to have a motherly function (one of **L T MEADE**'s school stories, published in 1907, is actually called *The Little School-Mothers*). Insofar as these stories were thought of as part of a genre, they were family stories, with school as the replacement family. It is interesting to note how many early heroines are orphans or motherless (later school stories tend more towards fatherless families); the scene where the repentant pupil weeps on the lap of the motherly but stern Head recurs throughout this era. Pupil teachers sometimes appear at this period; they are rather in the position of later prefects, with only their personality to wield authority. The Headmistress (and proprietress) is often a widow, an elderly lady whose wisdom and understanding is recognised by all her girls. The resident teaching staff, generally between two and five in number, are untrained governesses (Queen's College in London, for the training of governesses, only opened in 1848, and trained comparatively few governesses) plus, in some schools, a 'Mamzelle' or 'Fräulein'.

'Masters' are brought in for certain subjects, generally music and art. There are no public examinations (which girls were not allowed to sit until 1867, even had these seminaries encouraged such pursuits) though some of the girls are described as 'scholars'; and since most girls are there to acquire accomplishments, a great deal of time is spent on French, music, drawing and the social graces. Many of these books, though by no means all, depict intense friendships which are expected to involve kissing and other physical contact. (This seems, like most of the cultural details in these books, to have been based purely on fact. Such behaviour continues with no comment until the turn of the century, when writers such as **EVELYN SHARP** and **DOROTHEA MOORE** start to create boyish heroines more influenced by brothers than by female friendship.) There are few games, if any, at the beginning of this period, when exercise is provided by a once- or twice-daily walk, with small girls using hoops or balls. As the 80s turn into the 90s, hockey and tennis are mentioned occasionally, although they are still very much recreational; gymnastics and drill (with clubs) become popular.

The characteristic plot of these early school stories involves a girl (generally the heroine) being wrongly suspected of an evil action, such as stealing an (internal) examination paper, cribbing, cheating on a prize essay or reading forbidden novels. Sometimes it is merely circumstances which lead to suspicion; more frequently, it is the malice of an enemy, such as Bertha in *The New Girl* (**M E GELLIE** 1879). Interestingly, we rarely see that internal conflict, common in later school stories, where the heroine has to choose between telling the truth and betraying another girl, or keeping silent and taking severe punishment: in these early books, the accused does not usually know who has got her into trouble, and the suffering she endures is given to her not to show her honourable nature but either to lead the villainess to repentance at the heroine's near death-bed, or to purge the latter of her madcap ways. The best-known British girls' school story of this period, **L T MEADE**'s *A World of Girls* (1886), is an excellent example of this, with 'wild, naughty, impulsive' Annie, 'the most popular girl in the school' needing to be put through the refiner's fire of false accusation before she can shed her 'moral weakness [which] was not observed by these inexperienced young eyes'.

It is clear that these early school stories differ from their descendants in several ways, but one is crucial. Although there are plenty of attractive madcaps and harum-scarums, they always incur authorial disapproval for that quality. Writers are not against liveliness *per se*, but they will tolerate no rebellion against authority, even when (as in Grace Stebbing's *That Aggravating Schoolgirl*) authority, in the shape of the hard young governess, Miss Rowe, is herself presented as unChristian and unjust. The message is very much that of the first Epistle of St Peter:

'Submit yourselves to every ordinance of man for the Lord's sake ... Servants, be subject to your masters [or here, mistresses] with all fear; not only to the good and gentle, but also to the froward' (1 Pet.2: 13 & 18).

Insofar as madcappery is seen as rebellion, it has to be crushed; though at this period, over-harsh or unreasonable ('froward') governesses are almost invariably converted by the sight of innocent suffering bravely born.

By the turn of the century, however, this attitude was fast altering. It is always dangerous to assign influence to any single work, but it is very tempting to see this change as at least partly due to an American book published in 1873. This volume cannot, by and large, include American school stories, and Susan Coolidge's *What Katy Did at School* is no exception, but so influential was that book that it needs to be discussed here. Its predecessors, like those in Britain, had been mainly from the evangelical tradition. Susan Warner ('Elizabeth Wetherell') was perhaps the best known of these writers, with *Melbourne House* (1868, later retitled *Daisy*) having a long school episode, and *The Two Schoolgirls* (a novella-length story) being entirely set at school: the stories are concerned either with conversion, or with a Christian girl's efforts to be 'in the world but not of the world'. *What Katy Did at School* changed all that.

Admittedly, if summarised, *What Katy Did at School* could not be told apart from its British contemporaries: two girls go to a school which has a sizeable element of silly, frivolous and worldly girls, including a popular madcap, and which is mainly staffed by unsympathetic teachers. The heroines enact a reformation of the school by the nobility of their natures and the elevated tone of their moral principles; this despite the elder of the heroines being unjustly accused of correspondence with a young man. This is a fair outline of the plot: yet few readers of *What Katy Did at School* would recognise it from that description, which omits almost everything which has made the book a favourite with girls for over 140 years.

The importance of *What Katy Did at School* for future school stories, British even more than American, lies in the author's attitude. There is an implied moral lesson (live up to your principles and you will win through) but the book is almost completely undidactic, and makes its point through lively humour and excellent characterisation. Katy and Clover do not preach, but their personalities attract their schoolmates, and they are able to effect reform through laughter and good fellowship.

Vain, empty-headed Lilly is not criticised directly at any point; but 'the girls [do] not break their hearts' when she refuses to join the 'Society for the Suppression of Unladylike Conduct'—the moral, that the Lillys of this world are not popular with the girls *really* worth knowing, does not need to be stressed. Even more significantly, Rosamond Redding (Rose Red), whose 'eyes [sparkle] with fun and mischief' is most certainly a madcap; but although her wilder exploits are slightly toned down by association with Katy and Clover, she remains her bewitching impetuous self to the end. She is not falsely accused (indeed, she manages to escape many correct accusations), and she does not reform; and throughout we enjoy her as much as Coolidge does. *What Katy Did at School* is at least the harbinger of a gradual movement away from the heavy-handed approach which had hitherto characterised the girls' school story.

What Katy Did at School seems to have set the pattern very quickly for subsequent school stories, in Britain (which here includes the Empire) and America: but it was to be a different pattern in each country. In the US, late 19th- and early 20th-century school stories tended to divide into two types. Some could be classified as *bildungsroman*, following a girl throughout childhood and adolescence: clearly, school was a part of this, but no more. *Ten to Seventeen* (J D Bacon, 1906) or *Helen Grant's Schooldays* (A M Douglas, 1910) fall into this category: but this type of book was extremely fissile, and tended, like the Katy books, to become an entire series, with one or more books devoted to the heroine's schooldays and perhaps to her life at college, and the rest made up of a whole raft of adventures, as with Annie Fellows Johnston's *The Little Colonel* series (where one title is *The Little Colonel at Boarding School*). The other type (more common up to World War I, less so afterwards) is a single school story; but it patterns itself on *What Katy Did at School* in that the protagonist tends to be an older girl, sixteen or seventeen, often with a strong vein of humour; and the story itself is far more likely to be episodic than the British variety, which normally have strong central plots. *A Nest of Girls* (1901) by Elizabeth Weston Timlow and E Jordan's *May Iverson Tackles Life* (1912) are two of many; the best known of this type in Britain is probably the pair of books by Jean Webster (author of *Daddy-Long-Legs*) about Patty and her friends at school and college: *Just Patty* and *When Patty Went to College* (1903: retitled *Patty and Priscilla* in Britain).

By Mrs. George de Horne Vaizey

In Britain, the lightness of touch which characterises *What Katy Did at School* can be seen in **EVELYN SHARP** (from 1897) and **MRS GEORGE DE HORNE VAIZEY** (from 1901), followed by **OLIVIA FOWELL** (1905) and **E L HAVERFIELD** (1906). The very attractive *Teens* (1907), by the Australian writer **LOUISE MACK** must also be mentioned; Australian, New Zealand and the small number of Canadian school stories developed along very much the same lines as British ones, and will be discussed in the alphabetical section without distinction. All use humour to convey moral messages (though by no means always the same moral); all have a strong sympathy for the madcap, who is socialised but not reformed by the end of the book. At this period we also see educational changes gradually filtering into the school story. The first High School story seems to be **MRS HENRY CLARKE**'s *The Ravensworth Scholarship* (1894). As Amy Key, Mrs Clarke had been the first headmistress of Truro High School, and seems (along with her Truro colleague **MARY BRAMSTON**) to have been the first of many High School and public school mistresses to write school stories. Other writers follow the trend established by Mrs Clarke. **L T MEADE** has a very early public school story in *Girls New and Old* (1895); **MRS GEORGE DE HORNE VAIZEY**'s *Tom and Some Other Girls*, also set at public school, follows in 1901, **RAYMOND JACBERNS**' *A School Champion*, set at 'Lyndhurst College', appears in 1904 and **MAY BALDWIN**'s *Dora: a High School Girl* in 1906.

It may be noticed that the name of **ANGELA BRAZIL** has so far not appeared in this list. Despite her high profile, she is not, on the whole, a pioneer in the genre: her appeal is more in the wholeheartedness with which she throws herself into schoolgirl experience than in any innovations. She is not the first to avoid didacticism, use humour or affirm the madcap, and in educational terms lags considerably behind her peers. Her first book, *A Terrible Tomboy* (1904) has a heroine who attends a large High School, but the book is influenced more by *Little Women* than by any school story, and the only portion set in school is very reminiscent of Amy March's dreadful day in the chapter called 'Amy's Valley of Humiliation'. From *The Fortunes of Philippa* (1906) until World War I, Brazil's school stories are set in private schools of between 20 and 100 girls, save for two of her 1912 books, *A Pair of Schoolgirls* and *The New Girl at St Chad's*, where she does introduce large public schools, reverting afterwards to the small school for the majority of her books.

However, Brazil's books bring us firmly into the period of the archetypal school story—the books about Elizabeth Bowen's 'curl-tossing tomboys of St Dithering's' (*op.cit*). This is the golden age of the school story. Roughly speaking, we are looking at the inter-war years, although, as we have seen, there are many pre-war examples, and the genre certainly does not come to an end in 1939. This is the period when school is (fictionally, at least) at its most desirable, even glamorous; partly because the school stories are reflecting the actual situation (or the situation when many of the writers were themselves pupils) where the High School or large boarding school is an escape and an opportunity for the huge number of girls who would previously have been educated under governesses or at small 'family' schools, à la **L T MEADE**.

It is also seen as a privilege. In real life, universal secondary education after the age of fourteen was not available on the state till 1944; although local authorities were establishing secondary schools from the late 19th century, they were too few to cater for the number of girls who could have profited from them. Nor did they have the glamour of the boarding schools, which took only girls from wealthier families—and, of course, occasionally scholarship girls, featured in many inter-war school stories. Interestingly, the heroines of these tales are almost always middle-class girls whose families have lost money; often father has been killed or seriously injured in the Great War. When a girl is from a working-class background (like **BESSIE MARCHANT**'s eponymous Millicent Gwent) she turns out more often than not to be a mislaid aristocrat who finds her true family by the end of the book. Nevertheless, the scholarship girl plot stresses the fact that education is seen as both a privilege and an empowerment.

The typical school in fiction has grown enormously during the inter-war years. The average size

is between 100 and 200, and many schools have over 300 girls—very large for the period. Where authors choose to create this type of establishment, the action generally focuses on a smaller unit: a house or a form. Girls are no longer (save in the books of **MAY WYNNE**, who never quite caught up with the 20th century in this respect) taught by 'governesses', and 'teachers' are limited to 'Board Schools' (the older version of what became Local Authority or maintained schools); girls in school stories have 'mistresses' and 'staff', who are mainly young and enthusiastic with a university degree, though there may still be a few unpopular elderly staff around. Book after book describes the astonishment of the new girl on finding that the Head is young and pretty—though just as wise as those of the previous generation, and a better disciplinarian. (This was partly based on fact: Oxbridge graduates were highly sought after, and many took up posts as heads in their 20s or early 30s.) Music and art are still important, but generally only because girls are working for examinations or scholarships in those areas. Academic lessons may be delivered by subject specialists, although the old 'form mistress' who taught all the 'English subjects' (grammar, literature, history and geography) will be around for some time to come. There is a conscious contrast in many books between the older 'family' style schools (often despised by the author as well as the girls) and modern 'public' schools on the model of Cheltenham Ladies' College, Roedean and Wycombe Abbey, or the High Schools. **DOROTHEA MOORE** is particularly interested in this contrast, with books such as *Tam of Tiffany's* (1918) and *The Wrenford Tradition* (1930).

The school has also become hierarchical. The Head Girl (often now known as 'School Captain', to distance her from the old version) is no longer simply the best scholar; she is the Head's vicereine, and a personage of huge importance. She is supported by a troop of prefects with all manner of privileges and sanctions; a games captain of terrifying mien; house captains with their own house prefects; sometimes junior captains, leaders of the Middles, form captains, dormitory heads … the list could be lengthened. School discipline is no longer motherly, as in the older stories, but imposed by a theoretically impartial authority, impervious to pleas. Fagging is not unknown, but is far less frequent than in boys' schools (whether real or fictional); when it occurs, it is often informal, with older girls sending messages via any younger girl who happens to be available. Where fagging is institutionalised, it is often justified on the grounds that older girls can look after the younger ones and keep an eye on their progress: that this is, on the whole, a rationalisation is clear from books like *Alison—the Sport* (**CONSTANCE HARVEY**, 1934).

But the biggest change from the 19th-century school story may be summed up in a single word: games. One can almost count on the fingers of one hand the golden age writers who do not foreground games to some extent. This is one of the features which, according to the critics, has been imitated from boys' school stories; in fact, the books are again imitating life. The walks and backboards of the 19th-century seminary had, by 1900, given way to organised drill, gym, hockey, lacrosse, cricket and tennis, initially as healthy exercise and spontaneous recreation, and then (as the girls' public schools consciously started to imitate the boys' equivalent) as a focus of 'team spirit'. What began as fun had become central to the whole idea of school life. The school stories simply pick up this idea and reproduce it.

By the 1920s, school has become an institution with institutional values which are not necessarily those of society. It can be given loyalty, devotion and all the energy of its pupils. In some stories it is actually capitalised: one only has to read **ETHEL TALBOT** to realise how 'School' is personified and given almost divine attributes, particularly the ability somehow to create its devotees, and thus deserve the lives of its girls in return. It is significant that titles, which in earlier books very frequently foregrounded a girl's name (*Wild Kitty, Little Violet*) now focus on school, even when there is a girl's name in the title (*Gerry Goes to School, Pat's Third Term*). School stories have become a genre, and the titles are coded to show this, replacing the subtitles and bylines provided by older books, such as 'a School Story for Girls' or 'a School and Home Story'. Publishers in the interwar period preferred titles which conveyed their genre even to the untrained eye. The Juveniles editor of the Oxford University Press wrote to **EVELYN SIMMS** on 17 January 1929, accepting the MS of the story she had called *Heritage House*: 'There are some doubts about the title. Generally speaking, we find that the title of a school story should indicate at first glance that it is a school story. It should not depend upon the subtitle in this respect.' Miss Simms wrote back suggesting *Trouble in the Upper Fifth*; ultimately the book was published as *Stella Wins the School*. School, not the individual, has become central, something epitomised in **DORIS POCOCK**'s 1926 title, *Self or School?* (hint: School wins).

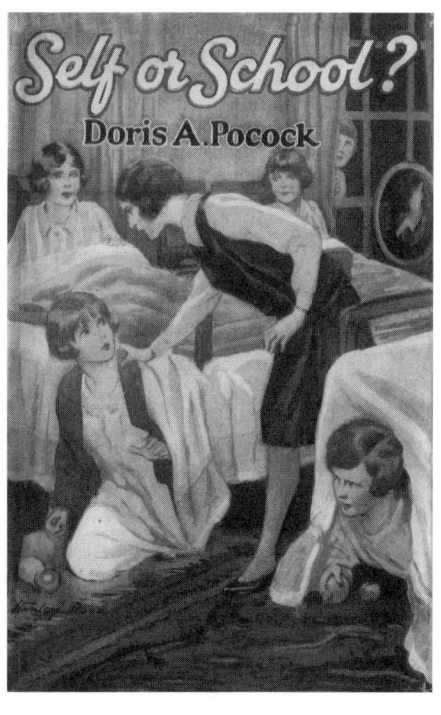

One of the main consequences of this deification of School can be seen in the decline of any specifically religious emphasis. Many school story writers were sincere Christians, but the pervasive piety found throughout the 19th century is largely lacking, although most girls pray when cut off by the tide. The 1920s is the period when evangelistic books gradually separate from the general run of school stories, and become the preserve of specialist publishers: see **Evangelistic School Stories**. Where life is not threatened, religion is replaced by a new concept (new, that is, to the girls' school story): that of 'honour'.

'Honour' in the school story is not an easy concept to define, though the reader gains a very clear idea of its connotations. It is an amalgam of two almost opposite ideals. The first is the code of behaviour largely derived from the boys' public school code, which itself goes back to pre-Arnoldian days when discipline was brutal and conditions harsh, as depicted in the first part of *Tom Brown's Schooldays*. This code is twofold: one does not complain; and one does not betray one's friends (conceived as one's entire peer group—liking is irrelevant). The second ideal seems to be a later addition, and, the cynic might feel, imposed on children by their elders, whether parents, teachers or writers: in this, 'honour' implies an extraordinarily strict adherence to truth—not just the letter, but the spirit. Not 'owning up' is thus considered to be 'acting a lie', and is not 'straight'. Clearly the two ideals cannot co-habit with any ease, since 'owning up' may mean involving other people: this implicit contradiction in the code of honour provided the impetus for the vast majority (or so the jaded critic may feel) of girls' school stories in the golden age.

There is no doubt that the boys got there first: 'honour' first appears in a boys' school story title in 1861 (*Schoolboy Honour: A Tale of Halminster College* by Rev. H C Adams, and the girls only arrived on the scene nearly 40 years later in 1902, with *On Honour* (**ELLINOR DAVENPORT ADAMS**—the coincidence of names is interesting, though presumably meaningless). Girls were very aware of the priority of the masculine claim, and spent many books proving that girls could be just as 'honourable' as boys; ironically they managed it so well that, long after the boys' school story had decided to concentrate on sport and feuds, the girls were still agonising over problems of honour. It must be said that 'honour' has acquired ramifications far beyond the basic code. Honourable people put the community above the individual, in school and on the playing field;

they take responsibility for their actions, particularly when they are 'put on their honour' so that when they break rules, they will often own up even before they are challenged; they are utterly honest and trustworthy. But still the most important factor is the original one: an honourable schoolgirl will not betray anyone else, even when that person has brought them to the brink of expulsion or beyond (**ELSIE J OXENHAM**'s *Expelled from School*, 1919, is typical); nor will they complain about their plight, whatever their interior agonies.

The classic girls' school story reached its peak both in quality and quantity in the mid-20s. Quantitatively, the major publishers of children's books (Chambers, Collins, OUP, Cassell, Blackie) had greatly expanded their girls' school story lists from 1920, and a number of publishers were entering the field for the first time: the Epworth Press published its first girls' school story in 1922, Sampson Low in 1925, and the National Sunday School Union, a very minor player up till 1925, changed its name to the Pilgrim Press and threw out school stories at an enormous rate until 1935, when it disappeared as suddenly as it had emerged. 1924 was the peak, taking school stories as a proportion of all girls' books published: in that year, 43% of all new girls' books were school stories, calculating from the accession lists of the Bodleian Library. Publishers began to put out cheap editions, always a sign of popularity and, indeed, competition. The archives of the Oxford University Press cast light on this process. C J L'Estrange, one of their Juveniles Editors (see **Annuals**) had proposed to bring out **DORITA FAIRLIE BRUCE**'s new book, *That Boarding School Girl*, in their new series of large printed board format at two shillings and sixpence, rather than the standard cloth cover at five or six shillings. Miss Bruce's reply, dated 12 February 1925, runs, in part 'I am quite willing to accept the terms you propose (a 5% royalty up to 15,000, rising to 10% afterwards) because it seems to me, at such an attractive price, the sales ought to increase, so in the end it may be as broad as it is long—or even broader, for many people tell me they buy the cheaper Dimsie books to give as presents, when they cannot afford to buy the later ones. Also, the 2/6 price would bring it within the means of Guildry companies, who would probably give it as a prize, being a Guildry tale.'

Nor was it merely in quantity that the 20s may be considered a golden age. Many of the most innovative writers and those who established the inter-war paradigm started publishing full-length school stories between 1918 and 1925 (**ELINOR M BRENT-DYER, DORITA FAIRLIE BRUCE, E M CHANNON, CHRISTINE CHAUNDLER, WINIFRED DARCH, JOSEPHINE ELDER, KATHARINE L OLDMEADOW, DORIS POCOCK, EVELYN SMITH, ETHEL TALBOT** and **MAY WYNNE**) or reached their peak in quality at that time (**DOROTHEA MOORE, ELSIE J OXENHAM**). **ANGELA BRAZIL** wrote what many would think her best books slightly earlier, between 1914 and 1919; we can hypothesize that the popularity of Brazil and (possibly) **L T MEADE** and **MAY BALDWIN** may have encouraged many of these slightly later writers to try their hand at school stories, particularly those who had been at High School or boarding school themselves (Chaundler, Bruce, Smith and Elder) or were teaching (Brent-Dyer, Smith, Darch and Talbot). This is also the period which sees the huge popularity of the schoolgirl story papers such as *School Friend* (from 1919), *Schoolgirls' Own* (from 1921) and *Schoolgirls' Weekly*: these magazines made no attempt to present school realistically—their appeal lay in the humour and liveliness of their characters and the fantastic, thrilling or ridiculous events—but they relied on their readers already having a basic concept of the girls' public school which had been established by the hardback writers (*see* **Girls' School Story Papers**).

What of the women who wrote these books? Individual biographies may be found in the alphabetical section, where facts are discoverable; but some generalisations may be made. They tended to come from the professional middle classes, and the large majority of them had been educated at school rather than by governesses; many were among the first generations at High School or public school, though comparatively few went on to higher education. Only a small number of the major writers married (two of the writers in the lists above), though the less prolific writers were frequently married women with children: those of us with families will find no difficulty in postulating a direct correlation here. Interestingly, many of the unmarried writers were professional women, though sometimes living with their family: commonly they were teachers, one (Josephine Elder) a doctor, and one (May Wynne) a worker in an East End mission. The 1920s boom in the girls' school story meant that it was quite possible to earn one's living, as Christine Chaundler and Evelyn Smith did, by writing children's books. Chaundler actually had a house built in Fittleworth, Sussex, with the proceeds of her writing; she shared her expertise in *The Children's Author*, published by Pitman in 1934. One needed, however, to be an astute businesswoman and hold out for royalty agreements. A literary agent, such as Chaundler employed from 1923, was a useful acquisition. Many publishers were only too happy to take advantage of unworldly ladies like Doris Pocock; in a writing career lasting from 1919 to 1954, she appears to have sold almost all her copyrights outright, receiving no royalties despite many of her books being reprinted until the 1960s.

The popularity of the genre during the 1920s continued during the next decade. The 1930s found plenty of school story writers beginning to publish, but on the whole very few innovations. Many of the writers who began publishing in the very late 20s or 30s, such as **RITA COATTS**, **NANCY DELVES**, **CONSTANCE HARVEY**, **BERTHA LEONARD**, **WINIFRED NORLING** and **MARY LOUISE PARKER**, picked up the ideas of their predecessors and turned them into formulae, bringing nothing new to structure, plot or characterisation. Certainly there were others, such as **E M DE FOUBERT**, **MARY GERVAISE**, **IRENE MOSSOP** and **IERNE L PLUNKET**, who were more original, and definitely better writers. Nevertheless, by the 1930s the sense of excitement and novelty had dissipated. This may well reflect girls' actual experience; the middle classes were sending their daughters to High Schools and large boarding schools in greater numbers, and County High Schools were far more numerous, so that most working-class girls who reached the academic standard and whose parents were willing could obtain a place at such a school. The opportunity was, in theory, there for everyone; so it was viewed as less of a privilege and more of an expectation. School had lost its glamour; school stories followed in its wake.

But there is another possible reason for the lack of innovations in plot and theme: almost every combination of motifs imaginable had already been tried out. New girls being reformed or reforming the school or house; captains, prefects and head girls making good; false accusations and honourable girls refusing to betray the guilty party; success through games; finding lost sisters, mothers, fathers, grandfathers, cousins and heirs; identical twins pretending to be each other; the list could go on and on: but every element has been used and re-used by the time the 30s writers come along.

There was, however, a small but significant movement towards a slightly ironic approach; something which probably could not have taken place when the genre was developing, since one can only mock successfully an established institution. In the first half of the 1930s, **JESSIE McALPINE**, **JOANNA LLOYD** and **VERONICA MARLOW** are all writing superficially straightforward school stories which nevertheless do not idealise the schools or the pupils. To some extent, they mock the traditional school story by presenting, for instance, new pupils who do not fit in or, to quote **ETHEL TALBOT**, 'become School'. The values of the school story are not denied, but the girls and staff are not idealised; in each case the writer has based her books on the school which she attended. These books are very funny; the idealism and moral seriousness of many of the 20s books are gently held up to ridicule. This is not simply a matter of dates: one may contrast the account of the lacrosse match in Brent-Dyer's *Ruey Richardson, Chaletian*, with its earnestness and careful account of play, with that in Marlow's *The Lower School Leader*, where staff are ruthlessly mocked, and the whole event is an occasion for slapstick comedy. *Ruey Richardson* dates from 1960, *The Lower School Leader* from 1935; but the values of the Chalet series are still those of 1925, when the ethos of the school story was, so to speak, pure.

This combination of humour and greater realism was clearly the way ahead for the school story in the 40s and 50s. **NANCY BREARY** and **JANE SHAW** picked up the humour and made it their own, while **OLIVE C DOUGAN**, **MARY K HARRIS**, **CLARE MALLORY** and **ANTONIA FOREST** emphasised realism and focused on character. Established writers, such as Brent-Dyer, Bruce and Oxenham, continue to mine the traditional seam; and some writers who began in the late 30s and 40s imitate the older formulae, although obviously bringing to the genre their own individual style and more contemporary settings. Such are **JANET GREY**, **JUDITH GREY**, **OLIVE L GROOM** and **PHYLLIS MATTHEWMAN**, and, more famously, **ENID BLYTON** in her St Clare's and Malory Towers series (though her Naughtiest Girl trilogy is rather more original in its portrayal of a co-educational progressive school).

In the 40s, we begin to see the fusion of school stories with other genres. Individual writers had always been prone to introduce thriller elements into their school stories—**MAY WYNNE**, whose penchant for secret passages and evil 'Chinamen' was second to none, and **RITA COATTS** and **J PATERSON MILNE**, who were clearly bored by school and preferred kidnappers, revolutionaries and miscellaneous villains, are notable examples of this—but in the 40s and 50s it sometimes felt as though every school in the country was either ballet-mad, pony-mad, spy-mad or full of criminals chasing concealed loot (see **Ballet and Stage School Stories** and **Pony School Stories**, though we haven't provided a section on Black-Hearted Moustachio'd Evildoer school stories). The criminal fraternity's interest in girls' schools may have been helped by World War II with all its spy scares: certainly **GWENDOLINE COURTNEY** took her initial inspiration from the opportunity that spies offered her, and went on to gangs of thieves and schoolgirl robbers (as well as the occasional duchess). We also see school stories which herald the end of the 'girls only' culture: occasional books featuring boys and girls at the same school had appeared previously, but **MABEL ESTHER ALLAN** and **ENID BLYTON** both wrote several books set in co-educational 'progressive' schools, and **ERIC LEYLAND** under all his many aliases depicted schools which, though single-sex and often boarding, allow unrestricted mixing between boys and girls outside school hours.

It has to be said that the attempt to revitalise the school story by mixing genres and sexes failed. School stories continued to be written throughout the 50s, but by 1957 publishers were consciously withdrawing from both new and established school story writers and refusing any more girls' school stories. Both **CONSTANCE M WHITE** (Hutchinson) and **PATRICIA CALDWELL** (Chambers) testify to their publishers rejecting school stories after 1957; White was told that she should in future concentrate on the teenage market and give her stories a career slant; Caldwell could publish nothing further until the rise in fanzines and internet communities encouraged her to self-publish several further books in her Vivians series, later published professionally by Girls Gone By. Chambers continued to publish Brent-Dyer's money-spinning Chalet series until her death in 1969, and Blackie kept Breary going until 1961 and accepted Bruce's 'Sally' series (1956-61); the OUP published no traditional girls' school stories after 1951, and since the late 1940s had been moving over to 'quality' fiction with (occasionally) some school interest, such as **ELFRIDA VIPONT**'s *The Lark in the Morn* (1948) and its sequels, or **A STEPHEN TRING**'s 'Penny' series. Symbolically, Bruce's final school story was rejected by all publishers (private correspondence with Sheila Ray).

The question must arise: *why* did school stories go into such a steep decline? There are many possibilities. Did the rise in professional criticism of children's books (generally unfavourable to school stories—see **The Critical Response**) help to cause the decline; or was the quality already declining, and the adverse criticism due to the poverty of the books? Sarah Sneddon has suggested that the innovative ideas of the 20s had attracted girls, and that the books ceased to attract because the genre lost its cutting edge: the radicalism of many of these writers (for instance, the criticism of staff and the presentation of strong, career-minded women) had by the 1960s become part of society's normal outlook (unpublished PhD thesis, 1997). It is also possible that the conscious attempts to introduce boys into the world of girls actually discouraged potential readers.

Surveys of girls' reading habits show school stories gradually sliding down the popularity lists: those from the 20s and 30s show that school stories formed around 40% of books read by girls; in 1942, a survey shows that adventure stories and mystery stories had easily overtaken the school story in popularity, and the latter seemed to be read by somewhat younger girls on average (see *Popular Reading and Publishing in Britain 1914-50*, Joseph McAleer, Clarendon Press,1992); in 1981, girls aged 13-15 are reading almost no school stories at all (Pauline Heather's *Young People's Reading: a Study of the Leisure Reading of 13-15 year olds*: CRUS Occasional Paper 1981). Certainly by the late 50s and early 60s the publishers (who presumably were in the business to make money) were not printing as many copies of new school stories as they had in earlier years; any collector who has tried to get hold of first edition hardbacks of the later school stories of **NANCY BREARY, ELINOR M BRENT-DYER, DORITA FAIRLIE BRUCE** or **GWENDOLINE COURTNEY**, to name but a handful, will confirm that.

But by this period, new hardbacks tended to be bought by libraries, rather than by children or their parents. Did the libraries have something to do with the publishers' rejection of school stories? Many were beginning to follow the trend begun by librarians such as the New Zealander Dorothy Neal White, who states her policy quite openly in *About Books for Children* (Wellington 1946): 'In Dunedin from 1937 we steadily withdrew the second-rate books, the Westermans, the Brent-Dyers, and the Hadaths from our shelves. We deliberately maintained a high standard of book selection. Nothing was bought unless it had some literary merit and some originality, unless it was a contribution to modern children's literature'. She is quite certain that this category includes no school stories, which she dismisses as 'The Fourth Form at St Bunkum's'. The factor of what is now called 'political correctness' may also have been important: most school stories relate to upper-middle-class girls, something which became extremely unfashionable during the 1960s. It is interesting that books by **ANTONIA FOREST** were not stocked by Birmingham libraries in the 1980s because they were 'too middle-class' (Sue Sims' interview with chief Children's Librarian, Central Birmingham Library, 1983). Publishers are not going to produce what they cannot sell, and if libraries were no longer buying, they had to react.

Clearly any adherence to a single theory is dangerous—'truth' in such matters cannot easily be established, and all these factors and others may have worked together in a complex interaction to destroy the girls' school story. Its decline is undeniable. Initially it was kept alive to a small extent by the evangelistic books published by Christian publishing houses, most notably Pickering and Inglis. Judging by the labels inside these books, they were almost invariably handed out as

Sunday school prizes, and considering the immaculate condition of those which come on to the second-hand market, largely unread. In this way writers such as **OLIVE L GROOM** and **HELEN S HUMPHRIES** continued to write school stories from the 40s or 50s onwards, and new writers like **DIANA GREEN** entered the market (see **Evangelistic School Stories**). There were reprints from Collins, whose cheap, often abridged, Children's Press editions are now a feature of second-hand bookshops and charity shops, and during the 1960s Blackie continued to reprint **ANGELA BRAZIL** in hardback, and Chambers reissued the earlier Chalet books (also in hardback). Collins (now HarperCollins), whose Armada paperback imprint took a large share of the market when introduced in the 1960s, gradually reprinted all the Chalet School series and a handful of Angela Brazils. Puffin Books, whose editor Kaye Webb had been consistently hostile to girls' school stories, acknowledged the quality of **ANTONIA FOREST**'s writing and obtained the rights from Faber for her four school stories in the early 1970s; and **ENID BLYTON**'s Malory Towers and St Clare's series have never gone out of print.

All the same, reprints, however numerous, are no substitute for new writing. If the reader can bear more statistics, the figures for new school stories are most instructive. There were roughly 250 girls' school stories published during the 1950s, and around 75 during the 1960s; of the latter, 55 appeared between 1961 and 1965, and only 20 between 1966 and 1970, most of these being evangelistic. During the entire 1970s, only around 15 books appeared which could remotely be described as girls' school stories, and most of these are borderline, not really fitting into the genre. (Figures are compiled from the holdings of the copyright libraries, listings in contemporary *Books in Print* and Sue Sims' collection, and do not include reprints of older school stories, such as Blyton, Brent-Dyer and Brazil.) In many ways, the posthumous publication in 1970 of **ELINOR M BRENT-DYER**'s last Chalet book (*Prefects of the Chalet School*) was the end of an era. The public libraries almost all divested themselves of stocks of girls' schools stories during the late 70s and 80s: many collectors are grateful to those library sales, although they may deplore the reason for them.

Had lovers of the traditional girls' school story agreed with contemporary critics on nothing else, they might have agreed in pronouncing the school story well and truly dead. However, it would have been unwise to shut the coffin lid too firmly. Even in 1998, when we completed the research resulting in the first edition of the *Encyclopaedia*, there were indications that school stories were rising from the grave, although somewhat transmogrified. In fact, the girls' school story has (if we may be allowed to mix metaphors) sprouted so many new shoots in the later 20th and 21st centuries that a separate essay was needed to address the topic. Space, alas, makes it impossible to provide entries in the alphabetical section for every writer who has produced relevant books between 1970 and 2019, but we attempt to outline developments over the last half-century in **Modern School Stories**.

Finally, mention should be made here of one major innovation since the *Encyclopaedia* appeared twenty years ago: the rise of the small independent publishers who have brought so many of these books back into print—admittedly for a largely adult readership nostalgic for the books of their youth, but nevertheless ensuring that the girls' school story and associated genres remains part of our culture. Bettany Press, Books to Treasure, Fidra, Margin Notes, The Elsie J Oxenham Society and, above all, Girls Gone By, who have published the volume you're now reading—without them, most of these books would have disappeared irrevocably into the past, to our great loss. They deserve our thanks.

Sue Sims

The frontispiece from *The Girls of St Olave's* by E L Haverfield

"It seems I'm to have a bad time," laughed Helen

An illustration from *Dunham Days* by M I Little

THE CRITICAL RESPONSE

British children's literature criticism has gone through several different phases from its bibliographical beginnings between the wars to its current status as a respected academic discipline, but its attitude to girls' school stories remained remarkably constant until the end of the 20th century. With very few exceptions, girls' school stories were ignored, dismissed, ridiculed or despised by adult critics, whether teachers, librarians, or literary scholars. When you have read account after account condemning girls' school stories for repetitive plot-lines, stereotyped characters, false values, lack of reality and so on, it is a relief to encounter the late 20th century's small body of criticism (often

influenced by feminist approaches) which not only found things to praise in many girls' school stories but refocused our attention on the books' significance in girls' and women's lives. Alongside these, however, more mainstream books continued to peddle the old messages or (not uncommonly) to ignore them altogether, all combining to suggest that, if thousands of girls and women have loved these books, there must be something wrong with us.

The earliest studies of British children's literature were historical accounts intended for the bibliophile. Florence V Barry's *A Century of Children's Books* (1922) devoted some attention to Sarah Fielding's *The Governess* (1751) and other early school stories but was not concerned with contemporary fiction. Percy Muir's *English Children's Books 1600-1900* (1954), largely intended for collectors of first editions, has a line on **LT MEADE** (see her *A World of Girls*, left) but nothing else of relevance. Only F J Harvey Darton, whose *Children's Books in England: Five Centuries of Social Life* was published by Cambridge University Press in 1932, noted the rise of the 'school-tale for girls' which 'in the past decade [ie the 1920s], it is said, has been in considerable demand'. Darton explained that the genre had inevitably emerged later than the boys' school story because modern girls' schools were a later phenomenon and needed a generation to establish an 'ethos'—a community sense—before they could be represented in print. He hazarded no assessment of the stories' worth, nor did one appear in later editions of an essentially descriptive work.

Even in the inter-war years, when the girls' school story was in its heyday, there were signs of a mounting reaction against the genre. In 1934 **CHRISTINE CHAUNDLER**, one of the school story's most prolific and successful authors, published a handbook for aspiring writers for children called *The Children's Author: A Writer's Guide to the Juvenile Market*, in which she warned of critical antagonism:

> There has been a tendency, in recent years, for reviewers of children's books to ridicule school stories, especially school stories intended for girls, and to deplore their popularity—as though the mere fact of their *being* school stories was enough to put them beyond the pale, quite irrespective as to how they were written.

In 1936 the Carnegie Medal, for excellence in children's book writing, was established. 1936 also saw the launch of the *Junior Bookshelf*, the first British periodical devoted to children's books. Its policy of not reviewing school stories provided a foretaste of the attitude which was to dominate literary criticism of children's books from then on. The new journal was aimed at the specialist children's librarian whose rise was marked by the formation, in 1937, of the Association of Children's Librarians, the School Library Association, and the Schools section of the Library Association. These librarians, not (at least initially) specifically trained for work with children, were guided in their selection policies by such works as Kathleen Lines's *Four to Fourteen: A Catalogue of Books for Boys and Girls*, a list of recommended titles for librarians published by the National Book Council in 1938 and revised and expanded in subsequent years. It never recommended a girls'

school story. Even as **ELINOR M BRENT-DYER** was urging her fictional heroine Jo Bettany to write school stories for girls (in *Jo Returns to the Chalet School*, 1936), librarian-critics were doing their best to stop girls from reading them.

Book People

While Roger Lancelyn Green's *Tellers of Tales* (1946) was the first critical study of writing for children, the first full-length work which encompassed girls' school stories was Geoffrey Trease's *Tales out of School* (1949). Trease, a distinguished writer for children, reflected the new critical concern with 'quality' in children's books. Opposing the views of some other writers, notably Captain W E Johns and **ENID BLYTON**, he argued that children's enjoyment was not the sole or even the main criterion of a good children's book, and that, since children are influenced for better or worse by what they read, they should be provided with the 'best' (in the eyes of the adult critics) and discouraged (if not actually prevented) from reading the 'worst'.

These views led Trease to praise travel stories and career novels, which combined useful instruction with entertainment, and to criticise those types of book which he perceived as being out of touch with 'reality'. The school story was the worst offender here. Yet he felt that the genre had potential. School formed a big part of children's lives, and treatments of *real-life* dilemmas would surely be helpful to modern schoolgirls. 'But if the literary form is to develop it must begin to reflect the new conditions'.

Trease was particularly concerned about girls' school stories because they were read by many more children than boys' school stories. A recent survey had revealed that fifty per cent of 'club girls' (that is, working-class city girls who had left school at fourteen and belonged to clubs aimed at improving their lives and their morals) read school stories at the age of fourteen. Girls who stayed on at school tended to give them up by the age of eighteen but twenty per cent of shop assistants of that age and ten per cent of office-workers and 'factory-girls' were still avid fans.

In contrast to Trease's view that the school story could move forward, Frank Eyre's attractive-looking pamphlet produced for the British Council, *20th Century Children's Books* (1952), confidently predicted its death. Artificiality had already killed the boys' school story and the girls' school story was now on the way out. Despite this diagnosis he noted that the stories continued to be popular in Commonwealth countries, particularly Australia and New Zealand, 'largely, it would seem, because the absolute unreality of the stories (in countries where boarding-schools are almost unknown) turns them into an exciting form of escapism'—as if that were not true for most British readers, too.

The 1950s saw the first official recognition of the role played by children's libraries and librarians. The Library Association started to train Youth Librarians; schools were ordered by the Ministry of Education to improve their libraries, and towards the end of the decade, a new qualification, the Teacher-Librarian Certificate, was introduced by a joint board of the Library Association and the School Library Association. There is some evidence that the growth of children's sections in public libraries caused sales of children's books to fall, since children could now borrow all the stories they wanted. But the libraries may have affected publishers in another way. The newly recognised profession took itself very seriously, and its strictures seem to have influenced not simply which books were made available to young people in libraries but also which books were actually published—since no publisher wanted to produce books that libraries boycotted. Where such books continued to be published, as did the work of Enid Blyton and Elinor M Brent-Dyer, for example, it was only because the publishers knew the books would sell well anyway and could afford to ignore official disapproval. The high point of critical arrogance was reached in the 1956 edition of Kathleen Lines's *Four to Fourteen* which, while resolutely continuing to ignore girls' school stories including those by **ANTONIA FOREST** and **MARY K HARRIS**, included some 'books of undoubted quality about whose appeal to children I am uncertain'!

This emphasis on quality, together with the critical assumption that school stories were almost bound to be poorly written, helped to accelerate the decline of the girls' school story; this was exacerbated by the growing fashion for books that brought the sexes together. The 1960s was the era of mixed-sex adventure and family stories, together with 'career' novels (a trend begun during the previous decade); few girls' school stories were produced. Starting with Boris Ford's anthology

Young Writers, Young Readers (1960), which laid into Enid Blyton and W E Johns and ignored school stories altogether, the decade produced a series of influential critical studies which found little of worth and much to deplore in most of the books that children actually read by choice.

One of the most influential was Margery Fisher's *Intent upon Reading: A Critical Appraisal of Modern Fiction for Children*, published in 1961. Fisher dealt with school stories (along with pony and ballet stories) in a chapter entitled 'Fossils and Formulas'. Most of her attention was devoted to stories for boys, as was usual, and she found something of value in the work of Talbot Baines Reed, Anthony Buckeridge and William Mayne. She condemned 'the silliness and triviality which resulted from half a century of **ANGELA BRAZIL** and her imitators' and considered that only Antonia Forest was capable of keeping the school story alive. 'It is a relief to turn from the wooden unrealities of Angela Brazil and her descendants to the fresh and vigorous life of a girls' day school,' she concluded, drawing particular attention to a novel by **ALICE LUNT** about a secondary modern school. She also praised Mary K Harris.

The following year Fisher established her own magazine, *Growing Point*, a 'regular review' of juvenile literature. As with the *Junior Bookshelf*, the quest for social realism dominated her recommendations for teenage girls so, for example, there is room for Nancy Martin's *Probation Officer*—'a story which is very much of our times'—and for *Janet, Young Rider* by Patricia Leitch, but none for any school stories, whether by Elinor M Brent-Dyer or Antonia Forest.

Marcus Crouch's *Treasure Seekers and Borrowers: Children's Books in Britain 1900-1960* (1962), produced by the Library Association, was less judgemental and more inclusive. Crouch was keen to include all levels of literature in his survey, from the critically acclaimed to the merely popular, because 'Children ... do not confine their reading to the best any more than do their elders. Their minds are formed by Harry Wharton as well as by Stalky'. Thus he chronicled the rise of the girls' school story from 'The Edwardian Age' when it 'came into its own' with the novels of Angela Brazil, through its 'heyday' in the 1920s—'the great age of the "Reward"'—to the present. He distinguished, however, between the 'better' examples of the genre—here he cited **DORITA FAIRLIE BRUCE**'s Nancy and Dimsie books, **JOSEPHINE ELDER**'s *Evelyn Finds Herself*, and (in contrast to most of his fellow-critics) Elinor M Brent-Dyer's Chalet School books—and the run-of-the-mill formula stories:

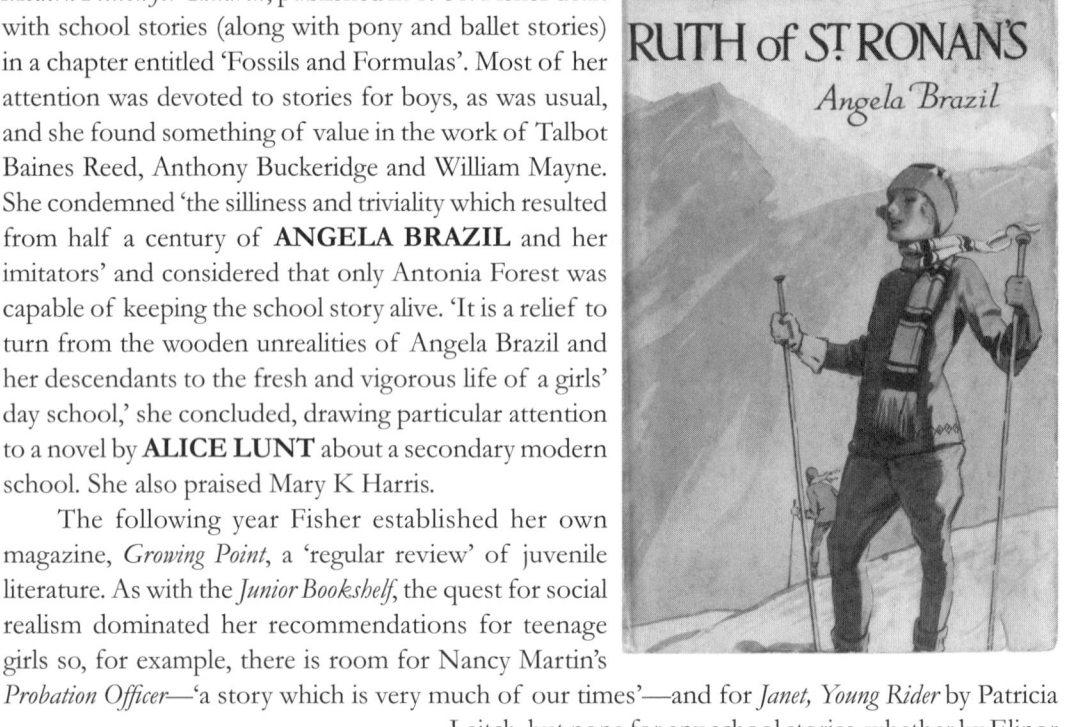

Such books stand out so brightly from the great mass of school-stories that it is tempting to exaggerate their excellences. They are in fact the shallowest of steps towards Elfrida Vipont, but at least they lead upwards.

In the 1930s Crouch detected a new and praiseworthy degree of 'naturalism' but by 1941, he asserted, the school story had become 'an anachronism'. Of post-war writers, **OLIVE C DOUGAN** and Antonia Forest were 'by far the best', and he also liked **A STEPHEN TRING** (Laurence Meynell), one of the few male writers of girls' school stories.

It is fascinating to compare the first and second editions of John Rowe Townsend's *Written for Children: An Outline of English Children's Literature*, published in 1965 and in 1974. The 1965 edition offers two whole chapters on school stories, the first devoted to the 19th-century boys' school tale, the second dealing with 20th-century books for boys *and* girls. 'No author of the first rank was writing school stories for boys or girls in the 1920s and 1930s,' Townsend opined, dismissing in two subsequent lines the combined contribution of Angela Brazil, Elinor M Brent-Dyer and **ELSIE J OXENHAM**. Of post-war work, he devoted a respectful page to Antonia Forest. Interestingly, however, it was the characterisation rather than Forest's 'excursions into difficult territory' such as religion and divorce that most impressed Townsend: 'These are far and away the best girls'-school stories I know'. **ELFRIDA VIPONT**'s *The Lark in the Morn* (1948) and Mary K Harris's school stories also received praise.

By the time of the second edition of *Written for Children*, published nine years later, school stories had been confined to one chapter (Chapter 9: 'The World of School') which was essentially a re-working of the text devoted to the 19th-century boys' stories with the addition of some American and Australian comparisons. Girls' school stories had disappeared entirely; gone from the index were Blyton, Brazil, Oxenham, and Brent-Dyer, not to speak of Forest, Vipont and Harris! If this did not indicate critical disapproval of the girls' school story it was certainly an example of scholarly sexism, surprising in a work of the 1970s.

Wallace Hildick's *Children and Fiction* (1970) devoted two pages to the popularity of the school story but offered no examples except his own Jim Starling books, which are set in a secondary modern school. In 1971, however, Frank Eyre published a much expanded version of his 1952 pamphlet, re-titled *British Children's Books in the Twentieth Century*. Here his dismissive remarks about Angela Brazil, Elinor M Brent-Dyer, Dorita Fairlie Bruce and Elsie J Oxenham were repeated, but he was forced to modify his earlier claim that 'by 1950 the girls' boarding school story seemed well on the way to extinction'. Praise was then heaped on the work of Antonia Forest and Mary K Harris, whose *Autumn Term* and *Seraphina* seemed well on the way to becoming canonical texts in the genre. Eyre's surprised observation that Harris never won the Carnegie medal for children's writing, though in his view her work was 'at least as good' as many who did, throws new light on the baleful influence of the librarian-critics: 'One wonders whether a subconscious prejudice against the school story may have influenced the librarian judges against awarding it to her in 1960 for *Seraphina*?' Harris was runner-up for the Carnegie Medal in 1965, as was Antonia Forest no fewer than three times (in 1957, 1961 and 1963); but not for any of their school stories.

In 1972 Marcus Crouch's second important study, *The Nesbit Tradition: The Children's Novel in England 1945-1970*, appeared. It was a very different book from his *Treasure Seekers and Borrowers* of 1962, reflecting the changes in publishers' output and the increased critical interest in children's literature that had taken place in the intervening decade. School stories now occupied only a few pages in a composite chapter entitled 'School—Home—Family', while 'Work' had a chapter all to itself. But the underlying message was the same: *quality* was what counted. 'I come more and more to the conclusion that there *are* no children's books. ... If you must have a classification, it is into good and bad'.

As Eyre had done in 1952, Crouch closed off critical analysis of the school story by pronouncing it dead. 'It died many years ago of exhaustion and social change,' he asserted.

> ... Indeed, even without a social revolution the school story was doomed from within. The possible variations of school, playing-field, bullies, friendship, were arithmetically predictable, and they had been used up.

That said, again like Eyre, he had a few kind words to say about Mary K Harris, Antonia Forest and Elfrida Vipont, in whose books, he declared, 'school and home and family are all interdependent parts of the full life'.

By the mid-1970s the critical focus on quality, with its uncontested judgements about style, plot and characterisation, in which girls' school stories always came off badly, began to give way to new ways of looking at children's books. But quality remained, and still remains, an issue for most critics. Fred Inglis's *The Promise of Happiness: Value and Meaning in Children's Fiction* (1981), ostensibly a study of 'popular culture', actually focuses on 'quality' books: Enid Blyton is confronted, certainly, but Angela Brazil and Elinor M Brent-Dyer are, for Inglis, simply authors whose work was read indiscriminately in childhood, along with 'better' books. That many literary judgements rest squarely on personal value systems, which in turn are part of wider public ideologies, is starkly revealed in Inglis's unsolicited comments about the Women's Liberation movement:

> Taking part in its more strident and sectarian version deprives women of what the culture at large most lacks in its public places: tenderness, peacefulness, care and love, sweetness, long-suffering. If women do not look after these things, no men will.

In these remarks which, absolving men of all responsibility for moral behaviour, read as if they were penned in 1881 rather than 1981, we recognise this male critic's lack of interest in any form of fiction which, like the girls' school story, may seek to challenge, or at least extend, the range of possible 'feminine' characteristics and roles available to girls and women in our society.

In Context

Of the new approaches to children's literature which emerged at this time, one was historical and contextual, aiming to look at the books as products of the time in which they were produced. Gillian Avery's *Childhood's Pattern: A Study of the Heroes and Heroines of Children's Fiction 1770-1950* (1975) is a good example. Her aim was to answer the questions 'What in any given age do adults want of children?' and 'What are their values?'. Her outline of the reasons for the popularity of the girls' school story, and of various writers' contributions to it, was serious and insightful, but marred by an occasional fixation on sexuality which doubtless reflects the era in which she was writing. Her misreading of the 'passionate attachments' which were a feature of the early fiction is actually ahistorical ('One must assume that these authors ... had not the faintest idea in this instance what they were writing about'), and, in the end, she has nothing positive to say about Angela Brazil, May Wynne, Enid Blyton or Elinor M Brent-Dyer.

Much worse, however, is the chapter (one only) on girls' school stories in Isabel Quigly's *The Heirs of Tom Brown: The English School Story* (1984). Quigly set out to write a historical account of the development of the school story genre, but for her this means the *boys'* school story, which she admires; the girls' equivalent was for her but a poor, indeed risible, imitation:

> Like every other form of fiction, girls' school stories have a sociological interest, telling us a great deal about their time and its attitudes; but it is hard to consider them as more than (occasionally charming) kitsch.

Most of the chapter is devoted to the work and personality of Angela Brazil, whom she treats with inexcusable contempt. In traditional scholarship criticism of women's achievements has often been an excuse for criticism of the women themselves: Brazil is mocked because she did not marry, because she had no relationships with men except family, because she was 'genuinely fond' of her girl fans, and because she wrote books whose 'eye-level is that of adolescence, yet they are the work of a middle-aged woman, then of an old woman, a real-life Peter Pan'. This comment displays an odd logic: should not an author of books for children try to portray events from her audience's viewpoint? Should middle-aged women address themselves only to their peers? What of all the *boys'* school stories written by middle-aged and old men?

'Whether she was the best (or at least the most energetic) of a bad lot, or whether she killed the girls' school story stone dead before anyone else could get at it, it is hard to say,' Quigly goes on smugly, ignoring the major part of the history of the genre. Though she mentions other writers in passing—among them, Christine Chaundler, **EVELYN SMITH**, **WINIFRED DARCH** and Dorita Fairlie Bruce—who 'turned out schoolgirl stories by the dozen', she contends that their quality is so poor that 'Arthur Marshall seems to have done the only thing possible with them. His take-offs and reviews of schoolgirl stories are funnier, and almost more affectionate, than they deserve'. It would seem that Quigly based this chapter entirely on Gillian Freeman's biography of Angela Brazil, *The Schoolgirl Ethic* (1976), and there is scant evidence that she had actually *read* any of the girls' school stories she so readily condemned.

Like Avery, Quigly could not resist drawing attention to the lesbian overtones of many stories which, she declared, are 'full of girls called Freddie or Bill' and mistresses who 'are boyish hoydens with Eton crops ... Curly hair, interest in clothes or domesticity, frilliness or softness of any kind, are thought "soppy" and soon become quite unmentionable'. This passage misrepresents the books while begging the question as to whether 'frilliness' is really a better thing than tomboyishness.

As a piece of disrespectful, inaccurate and misogynistic writing Quigly's chapter is unparalleled. I feel sure, however, that Quigly had no personal grievance against girls' school stories; her hostility is simply an expression of the dominant ideology's traditional contempt for women's cultural forms. (When I met her, years later, this impression was confirmed.) Her account appeared in a study much acclaimed for its serious and largely accurate treatment of the boys' school story. Unfortunately, when it comes to girls, Quigly failed to examine the books' real values in the context of women's situations in the period when these authors were writing.

Enter Politics

Bob Dixon's two-volume *Catching Them Young* (1977) is the classic critique of sexism, racism, elitism and conservative values in children's literature. Dixon scarcely touches on girls' school stories in his unfortunately muddled chapter on 'Sexism: Birds in Gilded Cages', except to castigate Angela Brazil for the amount of 'physical restraint' to which her heroines are subjected, Elsie J Oxenham for the 'fairly strong emotional attachments between girls expressed in an open way', and Antonia Forest for her upper middle-class bias. That the first two criticisms take no account of the historical circumstances in which the books were produced doesn't bother Dixon:

> I can never see much in the argument which 'makes allowance' for the period when a book was written. If books are read now ... then surely we have to apply contemporary standards in evaluating them.

Like Avery and Quigly, Dixon can't leave sexuality alone: he refers with schoolboy relish to Brazil's 'unluckily named *Bosom Friends*' and remarks of Brent-Dyer's heroine Tom Gay, 'things get rather confused, at times, over sex roles'. It does not seem to have occurred to Dixon that depictions of heroines who do not behave in conventionally feminine ways might present the sort of challenge to sex roles he advocates elsewhere. 'In [*Althea Joins the Chalet School*], the names Len, Ronny, Ted, Jack and Sammy, all applied to girls, carry their own message', he sniggers; and perhaps they do, though it is not the message he is hinting at.

Dixon's account, like so many, is factually inaccurate—he describes the Chalet School as 'a kind of posh finishing school'—but its main fault is its inability to see that books may present positive messages among the negative, and that children may read selectively and creatively. The books he criticises most are among those which children love the best, and there must be a reason for it: girls and women are not mindless dupes.

Women's Point of View

In 1968 a disarming book on girls' education by two mothers, called *Locked-Up Daughters*, included a chapter on girls' school stories. The authors, Felicia Lamb and Helen Pickthorn, were very much of their time. They were concerned about the threat of 'emotional involvement and Lesbianism' in the single-sex school (this was the heyday of the co-education movement) and correspondingly aware of it in girls' fiction. Here the 'pash' appeared as a 'natural and harmless stage of development'; as Lamb commented cheerfully (and inaccurately) of the Chalet School books, which were still appearing at the time she wrote:

> Boys' names—Joey, Tom, Jack, Len, Ted—are common and these hybrids refer to each other as 'chaps' or say 'They knew Jack to be a man of her word'. However, with the young doctors [at the nearby Sanatorium] not far off, this stage is happily outgrown ...

Heterosexism aside, the chapter is a largely sympathetic account of the significance of girls' school stories for 20th-century girls' education in Britain. 'For the promotion of their ideals, schools owe much to school stories ... Community spirit and the unimportance of self are stressed'. Lamb, who had clearly read widely, approved of Angela Brazil's broad canvases, condemned Enid Blyton's narrow ones, and called Elinor M Brent-Dyer 'the outstanding romantic among modern story tellers'—a judgement which goes a long way towards accounting for Brent-Dyer's extraordinary and enduring popularity. At the end of the chapter Lamb revealed that the influence of the librarian-critics had not been lost on her. 'There are signs of the movement for greater realism in children's stories ...'. Nevertheless, *Locked-Up Daughters* pointed the way to a new approach to girls' school stories.

A major impetus came from the Women's Movement which began in the late 1960s. As part of a general endeavour to 'reclaim' areas of women's culture which had been devalued by mainstream scholarship, feminists named girls' reading as *important*: important to girls, important to the women they became, and important to society at large. They made it possible for readers who had loved certain books and who, indeed, had carried their ideals and role models through into adult life to acknowledge the significance of the books. 'I read them all,' wrote Bobbie Ann Mason in her study of American girl sleuths, listing the heroines of her favourite series: Nancy Drew, the Dana Girls, Cherry Ames, Vicki Barr ... 'I was an authority on each of them. But they were also *my* authorities, the source of my dreams'. In Britain, Cammilla Nightingale discussed school-stories in an article on 'Sex-Roles in Children's Literature', first published in *The Assistant Librarian* in 1972. It was not easy for these writers to reconcile their recognition of the reactionary values of many of these books with their knowledge that girls and women not only enjoyed them but also found something positive in them.

The landmark text on girls' literature was Mary Cadogan and Patricia Craig's *You're a Brick, Angela! A New Look at Girls' Fiction from 1839-1975* (1976). In its breadth of coverage, its grasp of the texts and the contexts in which they were produced, and its authors' ability to pinpoint with concise and often witty insight what they see as the essence of each writer's work, it is an unrivalled *tour de force*. It puts most earlier critical judgements of girls' literature to shame, and has been shamelessly (and often solely) relied upon by subsequent writers in the field, particularly by men who have little acquaintance with girls' books and no wish to make any. This is unfortunate, since not only does *You're a Brick, Angela!* represent a particular approach which is not always sympathetic to the genre, it also contains a large number of inaccuracies.

Cadogan and Craig devoted one chapter each to Angela Brazil and Elsie J Oxenham, and one to Dorita Fairlie Bruce and other school-story writers. Though their expressed aim was to assess each writer's contribution in the context of her time, they did not hesitate to use the language of 'quality'. Their judgements are, indeed, often quite subjective (for example, they like Dorita Fairlie Bruce but not Elinor M Brent-Dyer) but, being presented as part of a study of ideas, have often been accepted uncritically by later literary critics. Not, however, by the fans, who resent both the authors' partisanship and the authority which the book has acquired. Cadogan and Craig were writing in an era when the only acceptable mainstream approach to girls' school stories was to joke about them, and to some extent (as Mary Cadogan told me later) they felt they had to adopt this approach—hence the title. That Mary Cadogan refused to take school stories too seriously is demonstrated by her second work in the field, *Chin Up, Chest Out, Jemima! A Celebration of the Schoolgirls' Story*, published in 1989, which included a couple of her own parodies in the style of a sexualised Arthur Marshall.

Clever put-downs besprinkle the text of *You're a Brick, Angela!*:

[Rosamund] is the only Abbey girl to find the sheltered atmosphere constricting ... Not obviously 'gifted', she hankers after a life of buying and selling ... and briefly sets up a handcrafts showroom in a converted cottage. The author cannot leave her there, of course; and Rosamund, who would have settled for a tea shop and independence, is given a castle ...

And yet, of course, Cadogan and Craig are right. Oxenham's snobbery is a major stumbling-block for her readers, and the relationship of the books to reality is tenuous. What is sad is that, while Cadogan and Craig were adept at pointing out what is wrong with these books, they did not account for the fact that so many girls and women love them. There is insufficient assessment of their positive qualities, and readers who enjoy Oxenham's books are left wondering if their judgement is as flawed and their tastes as inexplicable as the critics have always claimed.

Since Cadogan and Craig, writing about girls' fiction has taken two different routes. One followed the path of literary scholarship: it is the work of professionals, latterly academics, who also appreciate the books. The other is a grass-roots response: the contribution, of enormous significance in this field, of fans—members of the many appreciation societies. The two groups overlap, since much of the 'fan' criticism is scholarly, and many of the 'scholars' are themselves fans. Gillian Freeman's biography of Angela Brazil, *The Schoolgirl Ethic* (1976), for example, was the work of a professional writer: readable, light, coolly critical of her subject. Helen McClelland's biography of Elinor M Brent-Dyer, *Behind the Chalet School* (1981, revised edition 1996), on the other hand, was a labour of love which, while never forgetful of Brent-Dyer's failings as author or human being, yet recognised and tried to account for her immense popularity with readers. It is no accident that Freeman found a mainstream publisher for her book while McClelland had difficulty getting hers published at all. Brazil's is the name most people associate with girls' school stories but it was Brent-Dyer whose stories were still selling at the rate of 100,000 a year into the 1990s and who had a fan-club of 3000-plus in her lifetime and now, fifty years after her death, has two, with hundreds of members between them. To school-story readers she is immeasurably more significant than Brazil.

Feminist Approaches

19th-century girls' literature has attracted most feminist interest so far, with studies such as J S Bratton's *The Impact of Victorian Children's Fiction* (1981), Judith Rowbotham's *Good Girls Make Good Wives: Guidance for Girls in Victorian Fiction* (1989), and Kimberley Reynolds's *Girls Only? Gender and Popular Children's Fiction in Britain, 1880-1910* (1990). All three touch on the beginnings of the modern school story and the work of LT Meade. Sally Mitchell's *The New Girl: Girls' Culture in England, 1880-1915* (1995) provides an excellent survey of girls' education and books in its stated period, bringing the school story up to the beginning of the 'golden age'. Shirley Foster and Judy Simons include a case study of Angela Brazil's *The Madcap of the School* in their *What Katy Read: Feminist Re-Readings of 'Classic' Stories for Girls* (1995).

The inter-war and post-war school story has received much less attention. Gill Frith's '"The Time of Your life": the Meaning of the Girls' School Story' (in Steedman et al. eds. *Language, Gender and Childhood*, 1985) broke new ground in attempting to address the question 'Why it is that the boarding-school story is now (and has been for the past century) such a popular form of reading for girls?'. Frith took issue with Cadogan and Craig's assumption (which they revised in the 1986 edition of *You're a Brick, Angela!*), that the books had become historical documents, no longer popular with girls. Drawing on classroom experience, she argued that:

> the school story presents a picture of what it is possible for a girl to be and to do which stands in absolute contradistinction to the configuration of 'femininity' which is to be found in other forms of popular fiction addressed specifically to women and girls.

School stories depict girls who are assertive, active and ambitious, and who put their energies into friendships with other girls instead of having to concentrate on heterosexual romance. This is very enabling for young readers: 'In a world of girls, to be female is *normal*, and not a *problem*'. Frith concluded, however, that the effect is short-lived; that the fantasy 'cannot survive the material arrival of puberty'; and that girls then put aside school stories for more adult forms of reading.

Many, perhaps most, girls do give up reading school stories at this point, but arguably this is the result of media influence and peer pressure rather than any biological imperative. Frith's thesis cannot explain, moreover, why some girls do *not* give up reading school stories at puberty, or why many women return to them in adulthood. It cannot account for the existence of adult fan clubs and fanzines and the great interest shown in girls' school stories by adult subscribers and contributors to magazines and journals devoted to children's literature. In *A World of Girls: The Appeal of the Girls' School Story* (1992) and its sequel, *A World of Women: Growing up in the Girls' School Story* (1999), Rosemary Auchmuty suggested that, in offering depictions of all-female worlds with strong role models, friendships between and among women, and a range of ways of being which went far beyond conventional prescriptions of femininity, girls' school stories provided—and still provide—an escape for girls and women from the worst pressures of patriarchal life: from the need to prioritise men, the restrictive roles, the enforced femininity and so on.

Around the same time Jan Montefiore produced an article from a psychoanalytic approach entitled 'The Fourth Form Girls Go Camping: Sexual Identity and Ambivalence in Girls' School Stories' (in Still and Worton eds. *Textuality and Sexuality*, 1993). Masters and PhD theses started to be produced on girls' school stories, a clear sign of the area's growing incorporation into scholarship. These were not all written from feminist perspectives, of course, but they owed their existence to the feminist achievement of making women's culture an acceptable subject for academic research.

The Contribution of the Fans
In a period when girls' school stories were nowhere acknowledged in print, except in deprecation, the fan clubs and fanzines which sprang up in the 1980s and 1990s provided readers with a forum in which they could air their appreciation and knowledge of the books for the benefit of others who shared their positive assessment of them. Typically, a frank exchange of views mingled with literary and biographical articles in the magazines and journals of the Friends of the Chalet School and the New Chalet Club, and in the *Abbey Guardian* (Australia), *Abbey Gatehouse* (New Zealand) and *Abbey Chronicle* (all devoted to Elsie J Oxenham), *Serendipity* (Dorita Fairlie Bruce), and *Folly* (Fans of Light Literature for the Young, the most important place for general school story criticism). Although the last two have ceased to function, the rest are alive and flourishing. Their readers are united by their love of, and interest in, school stories and their conviction that they are worth spending time on. To the fans we owe the depth and breadth of our knowledge about girls' school stories and their authors, for they, more than anyone else, have kept alive interest in a critically despised genre.

A secondary development has been the burgeoning market in second-hand books and, in recent years, inexpensive reprints of favourite classics of the genre. To meet the fans' need to rediscover and explore girls' school stories from the past, specialist dealers—mostly fans themselves—started to emerge about fifty years ago. Today, with the continued growth of fan clubs and, especially, the internet, books can be purchased not just from shops and catalogues but on eBay and Amazon, at fan events, and through the fanzines, on a scale never seen before. It is a truism that objects seen to be worth money acquire a sudden access of dignity: this certainly happened to many of the rarer girls' school stories by sought-after authors like Brent-Dyer, Bruce and Oxenham, which have sold for several hundreds of pounds, though there has been a decline in this market because of the development of reprints. Paperback reprints by small private enterprises such as Girls Gone By Publishers, Fidra, Bettany Press, the EJO Society and Books to Treasure have brought some difficult-to-come-by titles within reach of large numbers of readers and collectors, including books by writers such as **DOROTHEA MOORE**, Evelyn Smith, and Winifred Darch. This thriving market in girls' school stories—and the perception that they have monetary as well as sentimental value—is another important reason for the greater seriousness with which they are now viewed.

Mainstream Academic Work

'That thoughtless notion of the inferiority of writing for children hangs, of course, on a similarly shallow story of the inferiority of children,' observed Edward Blishen in the introduction to his edited collection *The Thorny Paradise: Writers on Writing for Children* (1975). That notion of inferiority which prevented children's books from being classed as 'literature' kept their critical study off the literature curriculum in British universities until the 1980s. Even then it entered through the back door, via disciplines such as history or women's studies, even as its earliest homes in education and library studies were being upgraded to graduate and postgraduate status.

A flurry of scholarly activity ensued: it is now respectable for academics to work in children's literature—but rarely from a purely literary viewpoint. Research is more likely to be hosted by sociology or psychology than English departments. And if children's literature in general has been thus side-lined, it is unsurprising that outside feminist scholarship, which tends to operate at the margins, the girls' school story has hardly featured. Mainstream literary criticism remains unaffected by new work on girls' school stories: it continues largely to ignore them or, when obliged to include them in general surveys, to misrepresent them. There have been some notable exceptions. Sheila Ray, whose *The Blyton Phenomenon* (1982) started life as an MPhil in Librarianship, gave serious attention to Enid Blyton's school stories which she regarded as among her best work.

But Ray was a fan as well as a scholar. Much more typical were the comments of Margaret Marshall in *An Introduction to the World of Children's Books* (2nd ed., 1988):

> Many of the plots are repetitive, the characters stereotyped, the slang outdated; there is little to do with real-life boarding-school practice in the educational sense and almost no explicit boy-girl relationships.

She concluded hopefully: 'It seems possible that that kind of school story will disappear', but was forced to concede that it showed few signs of doing so: 'girls (sic) school stories are not only still popular in the 1980s in Britain but have a wide readership in other countries, particularly in Malaysia and the Pacific areas'. The fact that her book spells Elinor M Brent-Dyer's name in two different ways, both wrong, is a clear indication of critical indifference.

A different kind of contempt is that shown in Jeffrey Richards's chapter on 'The School Story' in Dennis Butts's *Stories and Society: Children's Literature in its Social Context* (1992), which turns out to be solely concerned with *boys'* school stories ('Because of space constraints …' runs the footnote; for which read, 'lack of knowledge …'). The same approach was adopted in his book-length study *Happiest Days: The Public School in English Fiction* (1988) and P W Musgrave's *From Brown to Bunter: the Life and Death of the School Story* (1985). It beggars belief that, twenty years after feminists explained the ways in which sexist language excluded women, and most people changed their practice, Richards and Musgrave should have thought it acceptable to omit the qualifying 'boys' from their titles. The effect was to define girls' school stories and girls' public schools as, by implication, inferior imitations of the boys' versions—not the real thing—rather than separate, equally valid, developments.

Conclusion

Peter Hunt is one of the best known of the academic writers on children's books. His *Introduction to Children's Literature* (Oxford University Press, 1994) devoted only two-thirds of a page to girls' school stories, while his chapter on the inter-war girls' school story in the later coffee-table *Children's Literature: An Illustrated History* (from the same publisher, 1996), while covering Brazil, Bruce, Brent-Dyer and Oxenham, contained numerous inaccuracies. But he made up for his earlier carelessness by commissioning Sheila Ray to write the chapter on school stories in his *International Companion Encyclopedia of Children's Literature* (1996), thus ensuring a sympathetic and accurate account that gave proper attention to the girls' stories. It seemed that finally editors had come round to acknowledging the new 'experts' in the genre and drawing on their expertise in their surveys and compilations. It is hoped that increased pressure on university teachers to publish scholarly work from the 1990s onwards, because it brings not only status but financial support for their institution, will lead to a greater plurality of subject matter and perspective, in turn leading to some interesting work on girls' school stories and the disappearance of the old contemptuous dismissal. Our aim in the first edition of *The Encyclopaedia of Girls' School Stories* was to kill once and for all the old myths and untruths about girls' school stories and to reinstate them in their rightful position as a literary genre worthy, alongside boys' school stories, of serious and accurate scholarly consideration.

Update by Hilary Clare

The passage of time has served to underscore the importance of Rosemary Auchmuty's own *A World of Girls* (1992) and *A World of Women* (1999), both reprinted (2004 and 2008 respectively). These were the first books to take the girls' school story seriously, and she is still easily the best writer about them. All the substantial work on the genre since 1992 merely follows where she led. Further important contributions by her are her paper 'The School Story: from Brazil to *Bunty*' in Nicholas Tucker, ed. *School Stories from Bunter to Buckeridge* (the proceedings of a conference of the same name held at Roehampton Institute, London, on 2 May 1998), and her masterly account of the genre in *The Oxford Encyclopedia of Children's Literature* (2006), which also included entries for several well-known British girls' school story writers (Brazil, Brent-Dyer, Bruce, Forest, Laurence Meynell, and Oxenham).

There has in fact been disappointingly little work on girls' school stories in the last twenty years, though this may reflect a diminishing interest in children's literature in general. For some time Antonia Forest (who died in 2003) seemed to be gaining her properly acclaimed place in children's literature. Susan Ang has a long section on Forest in *The Widening World of Children's Literature* (1999) and the following year Victor Watson included a chapter on Forest in his *Reading Series Fiction* (2000) with the arresting title 'Jane Austen Has Gone Missing'. Depressingly, however, *The Cambridge Guide to Children's Books in English* (2001), which he edited, failed to mention Forest's school stories at all in the very brief entry devoted to her, and indeed gave only a tenth of the whole article on school stories to girls' books. Forest is now regarded, in Sue's experience as a teacher, as too difficult for most modern teenagers.

In respect of more general accounts, Pat Pinsent's substantial chapter on school stories ('Theories of Genre and Gender: Changes and Continuity in the School Story'), in Catherine Butler and Kimberley Reynolds, *Modern Children's Literature: an Introduction* (2005, 2nd ed. 2014), provides a measured account of the development of the genre from the 1930s onwards, with a welcome emphasis on girls' school stories. In 2006, in a collection on the publisher RTS (the Religious Tract Society, later Lutterworth), Hilary Clare and Sue Sims were responsible for an essay on its girls' books (Dennis Butts ed. *From the Dairyman's Daughter to Worrals of the WAAF*). *Popular Children's Literature in Britain* (Julia Briggs, Dennis Butts and M O Grenby eds. 2008) has a reasonable article by Judy Simons, 'Angela Brazil and the Making of the Girls' School Story', but M O Grenby's *Children's Literature*, in the series of Edinburgh Critical Guides (2008), is disappointing in its survey of the school story, with very little on the specifically girls' genre. There is one chapter on 'Traditions of the School Story', by Mavis Reimer, in M O Grenby and Andrea Immel eds. *The Cambridge Companion to Children's Literature* (2009), which at least devotes not much less space to girls' than to boys' books, but Reimer is more interested in the early history of the genre than the 'golden age' and does little more than mention Brazil, Bruce, Brent-Dyer and Oxenham in the single paragraph allotted to post-First World War fiction. Julian Lovelock's *From Morality to Mayhem, The Fall and Rise of the English School Story* (2018) has nothing new, and much old, to say about the genre; he deals with single works by L T Meade, Brazil, Bruce, Elder, Blyton and Forest but shows no wide knowledge and his criticism consists mainly of plot summaries.

The most recent work on the subject, Nancy G Rosoff and Stephanie Spencer's *British and American School Stories, 1910-1960* (2019), is disappointing. Its subtitle, *Fiction, Femininity, and Friendship*, defines its scope, which is to show how 'girls were informally educated into a performance of femininity' by school stories on both sides of the Atlantic. This is a reasonable enough aim, but unfortunately the authors have chosen to consider only a limited spectrum of the genre. Of UK writers they use only Bruce (oddly referred to throughout as 'Fairlie Bruce') and Brent-Dyer and, as the general index is extremely sketchy, it is difficult to pick up references to other writers. Nor is the present work mentioned in the bibliography but only in passing as evidence of 'ongoing interest in the genre'. And of course a good half of the book is devoted to US examples. It seems a sad waste of a major publishing opportunity.

A number of girls' school-story writers have entered the pages of the *Oxford Dictionary of National Biography* in its modernised, more diverse and inclusive form. These include Brazil,

Oxenham, Bruce, Brent-Dyer and Forest (under her real name, Patricia Rubinstein), in essays commissioned from established experts in the field such as Mary Cadogan, Helen McClelland and Hilary Clare. All the main school-story writers have Wikipedia entries of varying accuracy. These developments have helped to make girls' school-story literature more mainstream.

This in turn has led to the publication of some masters and doctoral theses which in the past might never have seen the light of day. As long ago as 1989 Marjorie Morris included a dissertation on Oxenham as part of her submission for the degree of Master of Arts in Children's Literature undertaken at the University of Reading (which has a large collection of children's books) under the supervision of Dennis Butts. In 1992 Ju Gosling submitted a thesis on 'A World of Girls' for her master's degree to the University of East London, and followed it with the innovative *Virtual World of Girls* (available online at her website, www.ju90.co.uk) for her PhD in Communications and Image Studies. This is principally concerned with Brent-Dyer but contains very useful sections on the history of girls' school stories, their criticism and parodies and she does at least mention some writers beyond the 'big five', though without much detail on them. Sheena Wilkinson's *Friends in the Fourth: Girls' School and College Friendships in Twentieth-century British Fiction* (2007) originated as a doctoral thesis for Durham University. It has chapters on the position of girls in society and on the critical history of the girls' school story but, although the final chapter is on Antonia Forest ('The School Story Comes of Age'), the six books considered in detail are all adult novels, albeit with considerable reference to Brent-Dyer. Judith Humphrey's *The English Girls' School Story: Subversion and Challenge in a Traditional Conservative Literary Genre* (2010), based on her 2000 PhD thesis for the Open University, presents some interesting ideas about the way girls' school stories could liberate their readers from conformity to patriarchal society.

What all the writers bring out, following Auchmuty's seminal work, is the way school stories have become important not so much to girls as to women, whether they were read in youth or later in life. None of them pays attention to the 'series factor' in encouraging the devotion of fans (especially of the Chalet and Abbey series); their angle is feminist and sociological. Their emphasis on the adult readers who are keeping the books alive goes alongside the fact that even the Chalet books are, by and large, no longer being read by the age group for which they were written. What school stories are still being produced principally belong to the stage or ballet or fantasy sub-sections (*see* **MODERN SCHOOL STORIES** for further details). The 'straight' girls' school story really does seem to have been largely a 20th-century phenomenon. It is hoped that this new edition of *The Encyclopaedia of Girls' School Stories* will encourage further serious and positive study of a genre so many of us continue to appreciate and enjoy.

Rosemary Auchmuty and Hilary Clare

"It's Fraser Harding!" Miranda exclaimed.

The frontispiece from *The Girl from 'Chinooks'* by Lydia S Eliott

'Clad in mackintoshes, they paid a visit to the garden.'

The frontispiece from *Princess Candida* by Katharine L Oldmeadow

Researching the Encyclopaedia

Like most of us, I (Sue) began as a collector. Back in the early 1970s, girls' school stories abounded in charity shops, jumble sales and the cheaper second-hand bookshops (the posh ones tended to despise them). Ever the completist, I wanted to be able to produce an authoritative Wants List I could send to dealers—but how to find out precisely what school stories were out there?

At that time, I was an undergraduate at the University of Oxford, and had already taken advantage of the resources of the Bodleian Library (one of the six copyright libraries in the British Isles, and therefore entitled to receive a free copy of every book published in the UK) to compile bibliographies of the authors I knew about. The problem, of course, was to identify authors who didn't turn up in those jumble sales and charity shops. The Bodleian was very helpful here. Like all libraries, they classify books according to topic and type; like most academic libraries, they use their own system rather than the standard Dewey Decimal System employed by public libraries. In 1883, they'd refined their classification of children's fiction in general by opening a sub-category of books for girls (the class number was 2537) and in those pre-computer days, every class number had its own 'handlist': a thick notebook in which each book was listed in order of accession, with details of author, title and date of publication (where given in the book) or of accession. I was allowed to borrow the 2537 handlist, and spent many hours in the Upper Reading Room (when I should have been translating *Beowulf* or researching Mercian vowel variation) transcribing the complete handlist. (There were no photocopiers either in those days.)

That was fine, and I eventually had a list of 5,649 books which the Bodley librarians thought were written for girls. (The last one in the list, by the way, was Antonia Forest's 1974 *The Cricket Term*.) The problem then was to identify which ones were school stories. Certainly a book called *Fifth Form Crisis* or *The Only Day-Girl* didn't pose any problem—but what about titles like *The Twins Who Weren't* or *Hazel Asks Why*? One had to look at the books themselves. But there were literally thousands of such titles, and one could only order a few at a time to the reading rooms. The only way of checking them all was to access the 'stacks'—the storerooms. At that time, the children's book stacks lived in a huge cavern under Radcliffe Square, where the Radcliffe Camera stands, and I persuaded Bodley's Librarian that Paul (my then fiancé, now my husband) and I were fit and proper people to view them. So after Finals (where I missed out on a First due to my lack of attention to *Beowulf*, etc), we were allowed to pass through a small, almost hidden door in the Camera and descend down a long and claustrophobic spiral staircase into the vaults below. If you've ever read a thriller by Michael Innes called *Operation Pax*, you'll know exactly what they were like: several floors of concrete walls surrounding apparently infinite ranks of shelves, the latter not much over six feet high (Paul, who's six foot eight, was very uncomfortable) and touching each other, with gaps every so often and a handle on the end of each shelf. In order to look at any given section, you needed to find a gap and wind the handle so that the shelves would move along runners set in the floor, and part to allow access to the shelf you wanted. (This system is now frequently found in large academic libraries and archives, but the Bodleian was one of the first—possibly *the* first—in the UK to install mobile shelving.)

Having located the 2537-class shelves, we plunged into the identification game. Once a shelf was wound open, each book had to be pulled out, skimmed for school story content and marked if appropriate in my copy of the handlist, together with any comments. Quite often, it was a tricky decision, especially with the 19th-century books, which tended to mash together school and home. But we swiftly became more cavalier about this: initially it took us five minutes to check a book, but by the end of the first day we were up to checking 80 books an hour (pull out, flick through a couple of pages in the middle of the book, and, if there was a school setting, it was a school story). It took three weeks to go through all the books in the section, and I'm still astonished that Paul was willing to marry me by the end. But by the end, we'd identified around something in the region of 1,800 books that were either girls' school stories or 'connectors' (such as the EBD holiday books). I followed this up a couple of years later, when we moved to London, and I obtained permission to carry out the same exercise in the British Library children's stacks, which in those days were stored in Cannon House in the grounds of Woolwich Arsenal. That was a slower job, as I was teaching full-time by that stage and could only go there in the holidays.

However, there was a problem. One had to assume that not only were copies of all girls' school stories held by those two libraries, but that they were actually shelved under the appropriate classification, and both these assumptions were, in fact, wrong. This started to matter late in 1994. At that point, Rosemary Auchmuty was approached by the academic publishers The Scolar Press (later acquired by Ashgate) to edit an *Encyclopaedia of School Stories*, and contacted me. I arranged with Robert Kirkpatrick, who was (and is) the great expert on boys' school stories, to write that volume, and roped in Hilary Clare to share the labours on the girls' volume. We knew that we had to include every girls' school story ever written, but were aware that our knowledge, though broad, did have gaps, so we decided to do another trawl. By this time, the Bodleian's holdings of children's books had been moved from the Radcliffe stacks and were being stored at a purpose-built warehouse at Nuneham Courtenay, a village about eight miles from Oxford. Since Hilary lives in Abingdon, just south of the city, this was our base, and for several days we drove over to Nuneham and flourished our specially-obtained passes at the site manager. From the second day onwards, we also made sure that we took jumpers: books thrive at temperatures rather too cold for researchers. And then we looked at every single book in the children's section that could possibly be a girls' school story. (Even so, over the intervening years, more have turned up—which is why there are more authors listed and longer bibliographies in the revised *Encyclopaedia*.)

All this is, of course, only half the story (though considerably more than half this article, so don't panic). The *Encyclopaedia* isn't just a list of books and analytical articles: it also, wherever possible, provides authorial biographies. Overall, considerably more time and energy has over the years been spent on investigating the lives of the writers of these books than on the books themselves. Hilary, as an Oxford History graduate and a qualified archivist, was no stranger to research, and had begun doing this many years before the *Encyclopaedia* was conceived, searching for information on writers like Violet Needham (Hilary co-founded the Violet Needham Society) and Antonia Forest; she already knew her way around archives and record offices. I, a lowly English graduate, started rather later: the first issue of *Folly* came out in 1990, and from then on, we specialised in articles that included not only critical appreciations of authors but something about their lives. Some major authors—Blyton, Brazil, Brent-Dyer, Bruce and Oxenham—had already been the subjects of biographies, but there were hundreds of writers of whom nothing was known at that stage. Hilary was brilliant at tracking them down. A few were still alive, and could be interviewed personally, such as Constance M White and Olive L Groom. Where (as was, alas, more common) the author had died, Hilary discovered relations who could provide information. Between us, we interviewed or corresponded with Christine Chaundler's nephew, E M Channon's daughter, Joanna Lloyd's sister-in-law and Olive C Dougan's husband, among many, many others. Sometimes we were lucky: I was able to talk to Nancy Breary's sister and May Baldwin's niece, both of whom were living in nursing homes and who died within a couple of months of my meeting them. Sometimes we were able to correct faulty information: Hilary discovered that Ethel Talbot wasn't, in fact, Ethel Talbot—at least, she was a different Ethel Talbot from the one previously assumed to be the school story author.

How was it done? Mostly by Hilary. In those days, there were no online records, so she had to trawl through endless microfiche indexes or (worse) manhandle the lethal quarterly indexes in the General Register Office in London; access publishers' archives (where available)—OUP and Blackie were particularly useful—look at voting registers; contact schools; and generally spend a great deal of time (and money) gathering basic information about the authors of girls' school stories. Sometimes *Folly* readers would prove to have useful knowledge which could be followed up: that's how we discovered who Winifred Norling really was. And there were serendipitous encounters: the wrong Ethel Talbot was laid to rest when Hilary bumped into the nephew of the real Talbot at a children's book conference at Roehampton.

It's all so much easier now. Census records till 1911 are online, as is the Household Register of 1939; one doesn't have to visit the General Register Office any more to obtain certificates of birth, marriage and death—and even Google can sometimes be helpful. Obviously, this has all fed into the revised *Encyclopaedia*, which now has much more detailed biographies of well-known writers plus a great deal of information on previously unresearched authors. And the work goes on…

Sue Sims

SOMETHING IN HER APPEARANCE SEEMED TO STRIKE THE GIRL.
[See p. 25

The frontispiece from *The New School and Hilary* by Winifred Darch

They remained quiet while Jan unlocked the big gates (p. 93).

Frontispiece from *Bookworm, the Mystery Solver* by Rita Coatts

Apologia and Explanation

Arrangement of Entries
The section which follows is arranged alphabetically by the writer's surname. In general, the name given at the head of the article is that given on the majority of title pages.

Where the author is known by a pseudonym, s/he will generally be listed under that pseudonym: thus the reader should look up **Josephine Elder** rather than 'Olive Gwendoline Potter', although the actual name will be given in brackets beneath the pseudonym.

Some early school stories were published anonymously; where the name of the author is known (generally from library catalogues) it is placed between square brackets. Otherwise anonymous authors appear under the listing 'Anon' in the A section.

Exceptions
(a) When a writer has written books under more than one name, the books are generally listed under the more prolific name, with a cross-reference given from the other: eg **Dora B Francis**: *see* **Dora B Chapman**.

(b) In the rare case of a writer, always it seems a man, who used a large number of different pseudonyms, and also wrote boys' school stories under his real name, cross-references are given from each of the pseudonyms to that name: eg **Sylvia Little**, **Nesta Grant** and **Elizabeth Tarrant** are all listed under **Eric Leyland**.

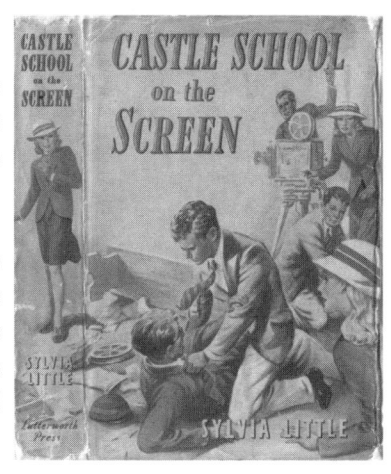

(c) Where a writer uses part of her/his name, or a married women uses her maiden name, the full name is given in brackets below, in the order: Forename(s), maiden name, married name if appropriate: eg **E M R Burgess (Esther Margaret Rooke Archibald Burgess)**.

Choice of Entries
We have tried to include in the alphabetical section and the specialist articles every British, Australian and New Zealand author between 1876 and 2020 who has written at least one full-length girls' school story published as an individual book. Where other authors have written continuations to

popular series which were originally written before 2006, these appear under the original author's entry. Recent school stories are discussed in the article **Modern School Stories**, which appears in Volume Three. The rationale for choosing 1876 as the cut-off date is given in **Early School Stories**: before that date, all school stories found are listed in the Bibliography appended to that article. American and most Canadian writers are excluded, partly because the genre developed differently in North America, and partly because it has proved very difficult to establish a comprehensive database of such school stories. Canadian writers such as Ethel Hume Bennett and Commonwealth writers such as L J Ogle or Swapna Dutta, who consciously wrote in the British tradition, are included, however. Continental school stories are also omitted; these are not particularly common, and also show variant development. Eva Löfgren's *Schoolmates of the Long-Ago* (Symposion Graduale 1993), gives an excellent account of European school stories.

Clearly we have been limited to the books which could be traced, either because they are in a private collection or in the copyright libraries; there will undoubtedly be many books which we have missed out through ignorance. We can only apologise for these omissions, and ask readers to let us know of any girls' school stories in their own collections which are not listed here.

We have not generally listed authors who are found only in annuals or in story papers (though *see* **GIRLS' SCHOOL STORY PAPERS** for a discussion of some of these) or 'Pocket Library' editions such as those published by Gerald Swan; exceptions are made for certain titles which might otherwise lead collectors to expend large sums of money on items which they assumed were straightforward school stories. A comprehensive treatment of girls' annuals would need a volume to itself, and several more years of research. This is not intended to denigrate the story papers or those writers whose only school stories are found in annuals: some, such as Alice Massie, are excellent writers, and one can only regret that none of their children's books is set in school. Nevertheless, the alphabetical section of the book confines itself in general to girls' school stories in book form.

General Articles

At the end of each volume of the *Encyclopaedia* will be found articles which attempt to bring together books which form a kind of sub-section of the school story: ponies, ballet, evangelistic stories and so on. In these articles, names in **bold type** mean that the author referred to will also be found among the alphabetical entries.

Biographies

We are only too aware of the limited amount of biographical information which we have managed to discover about the women and men who wrote these books. Boys' school story writers have been a major area of research: but until very recently, nothing was known about the majority of girls' school story writers. Enid Blyton, Angela Brazil, Elinor M Brent-Dyer, Dorita Fairlie Bruce and Elsie J Oxenham had been studied to a greater or lesser extent, but all the other significant British writers in this genre were unknown quantities, apart from those who were still with us at the time the original research was being carried out. (For some reason, far more had been written about Australian writers.) Furthermore, tracking down women is considerably harder than chasing men: many women marry and change their names; they are less frequently heads of households and thus listed in local directories; and until 1918, they did not appear on voting lists. Frustrating though the dearth of information may be, this volume represents a huge advance on what was previously known; we hope that it may stimulate readers to do their own research on those writers who have so far proved resistant to enquiries—and to let us know the results!

We have given a biographical outline wherever possible; where we have only a few details, we list those. Sources of information are given at the end of each article, where appropriate, but we have not listed the basic sources—birth, marriage and death certificates, school and college records, wills, local directories, census material and voting lists—as this would become repetitive. Where no source is listed, it can be assumed that all information comes from these areas.

Critiques

Ideally, each entry would have given a brief plot summary of every school story by that writer, together with a general assessment of style, major themes and influences. Since that would have made this book roughly twenty times as long and unpublishable, many writers have no critiques at all, merely a bibliography (see below). We have tried to follow a rule that any author who published three or more full-length school stories should be discussed, whatever the quality of the books: authors of one or two school stories may also qualify if their books are interesting in some way: many of these are excellent, and a few are egregiously awful. We apologise if your personal favourite is given a bare bibliography. In critiques of prolific authors, we have tried to draw out themes and give an idea of style and quality, rather than summarise plots.

A number of experts have contributed to this section of the book, and their names are appended to the end of their articles. Where no name is given, the article is by Sue Sims or Hilary Clare; the latter also carried out most of the biographical research, save for some major authors.

Bibliographies

Listing criteria
Readers who are interested in books other than school stories will be frustrated by many of these bibliographies, as most do not give a complete list of books by their authors. Deciding how to compile the bibliographies was, in fact, the most difficult decision we had to make.

We initially wanted to follow the demands of academic rigour, and provide a complete bibliography for every author who had written a girls' school story. However, when we realised that we had to deal with writers such as **Evelyn Everett-Green**, who wrote over 300 books among which is one girl's school story, it became clear that the task was impractical. So we took a tentative decision to list only school stories; an idea quickly modified to listing school stories plus non-school 'connectors': no **Brent-Dyer** fan is going to take kindly to a list of Chalet books which excludes *Jo to the Rescue* or *A Future Chalet School Girl*.

But this raised further problems. **Antonia Forest** wrote thirteen books: four are set in school; six concern the same family during their holidays; two focus on a Marlow ancestor. All those could go into the Forest bibliography as connectors. ('Connectors' is the usual word among fans for a book which uses one or more of the characters from a series but is not itself part of that series.) But *The Thursday Kidnapping* is unconnected with any of the others: yet to leave out a single book is clearly unsatisfactory.

In the end, we reached a compromise, which, like most compromises, will probably satisfy nobody. Where at least fifty per cent of a writer's output comprises girls' school stories, we list all her/his work; if less than fifty per cent is school-based, we list only the school stories and connectors, and try to give a brief summary of other writings at the end of the bibliography. Where a full bibliography is available, such as those in *Twentieth-Century Children's Writers*, we refer the reader to that.

Arrangement

Books are listed chronologically with the sole exception of retitled reissues (see below). As many of these authors wrote series, and on occasion wrote retrospectively, we have also listed the reading order of such series in the left-hand column. Where an author wrote more than one series, each is distinguished by a letter: thus, in the books of **Elsie J Oxenham**, 'A1' means 'the first book in the "Abbey" series'. In complex interconnecting series like these, an attempt has been made to indicate the major connections, although we cannot claim anything like completeness in this area.

In the case of writers who wrote fewer than fifty per cent school stories, the bibliographies include non-school stories if these are connected in any way with one or more of the school stories. This is the case even if the proportion of school to non-school stories is very small, as with **E E Cowper** or **Freda C Bond**. However, non-school stories are marked with an asterisk (*) to distinguish them from school stories. Some titles are marked 'part school' or 'holiday at school'; these distinctions speak for themselves.

Details

Although we have referred to 'bibliographies' throughout, we have provided only the basic details of each book: title, publisher, date of first edition and illustrator where discoverable. The intention is to give readers a checklist of a writer's output; details such as the size, number of pages, type and number of illustrations and so on will not be found here.

Title: In most cases, the full title and subtitle are given: eg *Margot's Secret: or, The Fourth Form at*

Victoria College. We apologise for any omissions here. Titles may vary within the same book: for example, the dustwrapper and the title page. Where such a discrepancy exists, we have followed the title page of the first edition where possible.

Editions: In general, only the first edition of any book is listed; the two exceptions being:

(a) where the book has been reissued under a new title. In this case, the retitled version is listed immediately below its original, thus placing it chronologically out of order.

(b) in some cases, where the book is part of an author-specific omnibus. Thus Oxenham's *The Abbey School* is listed; but Blackie's *Omnibus of Girls' School Stories*, which contains books by three different authors, is not. The books in omnibuses are by definition reprints.

(Note that later editions of some works by some authors were abridged or revised, eg Angela Brazil, E M Brent-Dyer, D F Bruce, M Edwards, L Hill, E J Oxenham. These later editions are not listed separately.)

Publisher: In most cases, the publisher's name is taken from the title page of the book. Occasionally one sees alternative names on the spine and on the title page: here, little attempt has been made at consistency. The following publishers are most frequently met with under aliases:

Epworth Press = J Alfred Sharp (or simply 'Sharp') during much of the 20s and 30s
National Sunday School Union (NSSU or SSU) = (after 1925) Pilgrim Press
Oxford University Press (OUP) = Humphrey Milford (note that up to 1916, Hodder & Stoughton and OUP published juvenile books in partnership; later reprints bore the OUP imprint)
Religious Tract Society (RTS) = Girl's Own Paper (GOP) = Every Girl's Paper = (after 1939) Lutterworth
FOCS = Friends of the Chalet School; GGBP = Girls Gone By Publishers
NCC = New Chalet Club

Date: The date may be given in one of two forms:

(a) If it appears in round brackets only, it is the date given in the book itself.
(b) If it is surrounded by square brackets within round brackets, no date is given inside the book, and we have usually taken the information from the catalogues of the Bodleian or the British Library. Since this will actually be the date of accession (ie when the book was processed and catalogued rather than when it was published) the date may sometimes be inaccurate, and caution should be exercised in this area. Roughly twenty per cent of all school stories are recorded with different dates in the British Library and Bodleian catalogues.

Illustrator: We have attempted (though not always succeeded) to give the illustrators, where appropriate, for all school stories; some illustrators are given for non-school stories, but we have felt no obligation to track these down in every case. The notation used in this section is as follows:

(a) Where the illustrator is acknowledged on the title page, his/her name is given as published eg Elsie Anna Wood.
(b) Where the illustrator is not acknowledged, but the signature on one or more of the illustrations is legible, his/her name is placed between inverted commas: eg 'Elsie Anna Wood'. This means that the same artist may appear in different guises. Occasionally we have interpreted a set of initials or a partial signature and put the artist's name in brackets; eg 'G B' [Gordon Browne].
(c) Where the illustrator's signature is semi-legible, we have made a guess at the name; in this case, a question mark is placed after the name: eg 'E Berner'?
(d) Where such a signature is partly legible only, a dash or a row of dots have been used: eg 'Hanley D...'
(e) Where the illustrator is not acknowledged, but style or other evidence makes his/her identity clear, the name is given in brackets.

In all these cases, 'signature' may be understood to mean 'initials', which many artists substituted. If none of these is present, the book is merely marked 'Illustrated' ('Illus.').

"Seated on her bed, Nancy brushed at her long, sleek hair"

An illustration from *Etheldreda the Ready* by Mrs George de Horne Vaizey

"I SAID 'GOOD AFTERNOON' TO HIM WITH A BROAD SMILE."
[*See page* 175.

The frontispiece from *Doddles* by Agnes Adams

A

Clare Abrahall, *see* **C M DRURY**

Agnes Adams
(Agnes Louise Logan Adams)
1891-1951
Agnes Adams was the daughter of the Rev. Josiah Warwick Adams. She was born in Litcham, Norfolk in 1891, and educated at Casterton School. She lived in Wall near Lichfield for a time, where her father was Vicar from 1911 to 1930. She received her LL.A (Lady Literate in the Arts) from St Andrews, and seems to have studied in Paris as well. She lived for some time at Chesham Bois in Buckinghamshire, but at the time of her death on 6 June 1951 was living in Four Oaks, Sutton Coldfield.

1   *Doddles,* OUP (1920). Illus. 'GB' [Gordon Browne]
2   *Doddles Makes Things Hum**, OUP (1927). Illus. M D Johnston

Many other children's books. Also adult novels as 'Agnes Logan'

Ellinor Davenport Adams
(Ellinor Lily Davenport Adams)
1858-1913
Ellinor Davenport Adams was the second daughter of William Henry Davenport Adams (1828-1891), journalist and author; both her elder brother and sister were also engaged in literary work. Although Ellinor was both born and died in Putney, and lived there for much of her life, her family moved around in her early years, following her father's work; from 1870 to 1878 they were in Scotland, where he founded and edited the *Scottish Guardian*. Both her father and brother have entries in the *Dictionary of National Biography* (*DNB*).

She typifies the turn-of-the-century girls' writer in many ways: her books are half-way between the Victorian tale which sought to provide moral edification and its successor which hid the pill in a very heavy coating of sugar. School appears in her stories as part of life, and not necessarily the most important. She is particularly interesting, however, in her treatment of girls (and a boy, in *A Queen among Girls*) whose natures are warped or stunted by neglect on the part of the adults who are meant to care for them. The portrait of the 'Piggies', Meg and Polly, in *On Honour*, is moving and credible. School, however, is background rather than foreground in these books, and disappears completely in *A Queen among Girls* after the first chapter.

A Queen among Girls (small part school), Blackie ([1899]). Illus. Harold Copping
On Honour, Nelson ([1901]). Illus.

Also about seventeen other children's and girls' books

Miriam Agatha
(Agatha Magdalen le Breton)
1886-1970
Agatha le Breton was born on 29 June 1886 in Maryborough, Queensland, Australia, the youngest of twelve children. Her mother was Irish, her father of English descent. The family moved to Darlinghust in East Sydney, where Agatha lived for the rest of her life. A devout Catholic, she was a teacher by profession but a writer by inclination, publishing a number of books and contributing regularly to the *Sydney Catholic Weekly*, *The Far East* (the magazine of the Missionary Society of St Columban) and other magazines. Her non-fiction works include a history of Australia for Catholic Schools, a book about the childhood of St Thérèse of Lisieux and a history of the Little Sisters of the Poor, some published under her real name and others using her pseudonym. She died on 8 May 1970.

Nellie Doran is one of the only two Australian girls' books hitherto discovered set in a Catholic convent school (the other being **M I LITTLE**'s *Dunham Days*). The book is set in Queensland, and has a preface by the (Catholic) Archbishop of Brisbane. Nellie is the youngest child of impoverished Irish immigrants in the outback of Western Queensland. A piece of good fortune enables Nellie to be sent to St Mary's High School on the coast. Her wardrobe is dreadful, and the snootiest girl in the school lives in fear that someone (especially Nellie herself) may discover that they are actually cousins. At school Nellie's extraordinary gift for the violin is discovered; she plays at a public concert and is offered the chance of studying in Germany. She chooses, however, not to leave her parents ('Love crushed down ambition in her heart'). The Queensland setting is rock solid—flying foxes, paw paws and mango trees—as is the Catholic ambience. Few school stories have passages like: 'Time passed on, and the purple shadow that is thrown from the Cloud of the Passion crept closer and closer. Lent was very near.'

Marcia McGinley and Sue Sims

The illustration on the previous page is taken from a review of this book, in *Dolour D'Arcy or The Church Between* (E J Dwyer 1915), held in the Special Collection Library, Deakin University Library, Geelong, Victoria, Australia, with thanks to the Librarian, Kristin Thornton.

Nellie Doran (Australia), E J Dwyer (1923). Not illus.

Other children's books, all concerning Catholic teaching, and an adult romance

Mabel Esther Allan
1915-1998

Mabel Esther Allan was born in Wallasey, Cheshire on 11 February 1915, of partly Scottish descent, and educated at private schools. She was a Guide, and later a keen walker and folk dancer, although congenital retinal problems prevented her from continuing to lead a very active life; ballet was another great interest. During World War II, she served in the Land Army, taught in a preparatory school and ran a day nursery; educationally, she was greatly influenced by the ideas of A S Neill, founder of Summerhill, the progressive comprehensive school. She travelled widely, and was always particularly interested in the Celtic areas and languages of the British Isles; she also spent some time in New York. She lived in Heswall in the Wirral. She was one of the most prolific of contemporary writers for young people, and also wrote under the names of Anne Pilgrim, Priscilla Hagon and Jean Estoril (*see* **BALLET SCHOOL STORIES**). Mabel Esther Allan died on 14 May 1998.

'I used to say I would have been a better author if I had liked people more,' wrote Mabel Esther Allan, adding modestly 'yet perhaps the only thing that makes my work stand out … is my ability to evoke the atmosphere of the places I have loved.' The other most strongly distinguishing feature of her stories is their embodiment of the 'progressive' ideal. An Allan school will typically be run to some degree by the pupils themselves, with all ages mixing equally; it may be co-educational; it will place little emphasis on games; it will probably have links with a farm; pupils will associate with local people, organise their own work and concentrate on subjects that interest them. Her books consciously exclude any religious reference: there are no prayers or church attendance and the only school assembly we have found occurs in her very first book.

Both the evocation of a location and the progressive nature of the books make her work stand out, and both have their drawbacks. The background of the books—Skye, the Isle of Wight, Switzerland—is always vivid; there are no long deadly travelogues in the **BRENT-DYER** mode; yet one must question whether the setting of stories in real places means as much to children as to adults. Since these are children's books, perhaps the fact that 'the background came first' (the title of two autobiographical pamphlets) is not quite a strength.

Similarly, the insistence on 'progressive' virtues provides many a good story—typically, that of a new pupil who has left a more conventional school for the unfamiliar and possibly dreaded ethos of one of Allan's 'modern' establishments (*see also* **JOSEPHINE ELDER**'s Farm School books). No Head Girls, prefects or rules! And boys! At boarding school! All this is pleasantly startling for the reader, if not for the reluctant newcomer. However, one does slightly query the author's belief in the supremacy of self-discipline and self-expression, especially as it never fails. No senior boys and girls are ever discovered doing what senior boys and girls do naturally—as Felicity in *Swiss School* insists, 'there's never any "nonsense"'. Heads and teachers are always amazingly enlightened, civilised, all-seeing and fair-minded. Nearly every pupil turns out well-balanced, talented and self-confident.

The author's own estimate of her work, that an increased interest in characterisation would have strengthened it, is a just one. But she is, nonetheless, still one of the more unusual, original and interesting writers of school stories.

Kate Tyler

Sources: *To Be an Author* and *More About Being an Author*, reissued as *To Be an Author*, Greyladies (2020); *The Background Came First*; private correspondence with M E Allan

Further Reading
Folly 24

	Cilia of Chiltern's Edge, Museum Press (1949). Illus. Betty Ladler
S1	*Over the Sea to School*[2], Blackie (1950). Illus. W Mackinlay
L1	*School under Snowdon*, Hutchinson (1950). Not illus.
	The School on Cloud Ridge[1, 5, 6], Hutchinson (1952). Not illus.
S2	*A School in Danger*[2], Blackie (1952). Illus. Eric Winter
	The School on North Barrule, Museum Press (1952). Illus.
	Lucia Comes to School[1, 4], Hutchinson (1953). Not illus.
	New Schools for Old[1, 3], Hutchinson (1954). Not illus.
(L2)	*Swiss School*[7], Hutchinson (1954). Not illus.
S3	*At School in Skye*[2], Blackie (1957). Illus. Constance Marshall
	Schooldays in Skye (omnibus of the Skye series) Blackie [1962]
	Chiltern School[6], privately printed (1990); reissued by GGBP (2011). Not illus.
	Queen Rita at the High School and Other School Stories, privately printed (1991). Not illus.
	The Two Head Girls & Other Stories, privately printed (1992). Not illus.
	The Way to Glen Braden and other Scottish, Welsh and Irish Stories, privately printed (1993). Includes several short stories set in schools from previous books

S = Skye Series (Dundonay House); L = Llanrhysydd Castle + connector book

Mabel Esther Allan wrote ballet books, family and adventure stories, teenage romances, series set in primary schools, detective novels and poetry. A full bibliography may be found in *Twentieth-Century Children's Writers* and GGBP reprints of her books. She has also published numerous short stories in annuals. She tended to re-use minor characters from book to book; the main connectors are listed below, and refer to the numbers after the books in the list above. Space prohibits listing the short stories, even the connectors.

[1] *Ann's Alpine Adventure*; *Seven in Switzerland*
[2] *Strangers in Skye*
[3] *The Glen Castle Mystery*
[4] *Holiday at Arnriggs*; *Kate Comes to England*
[5] *Return to Derrykereen*; *Mullion*
[6] *Chiltern Adventure*; Girls Gone By (2011)
[7] *Ann's Alpine Adventure*, *Drina Dances in Switzerland*; *Three Go to Switzerland*

Gwendoline Allen
The Fourth Form at White Abbey, Vawser and Wiles (1945). Not illus. Enlarged and republished as *The Fourth at White Abbey*, Featherstone Press ([1945])

Verily Anderson
(Verily Bruce Anderson, later Paget)
1915-2010
Verily Anderson was born on 12 January 1915, the second daughter of the Rev. Rosslyn Bruce and his wife Rachel Gurney. She was educated at Normanhurst School, Sussex, and married Captain Donald Anderson by whom she had one son and four daughters. After his death in 1957 she married her second husband, Paul Paget in 1971. She died on 16 July 2010.

Clover Coverdale (part-school only), Brockhampton Press (1966). Not illus.
Daughters of Divinity (autobiography), Hart-Davis (1968). Not illus.

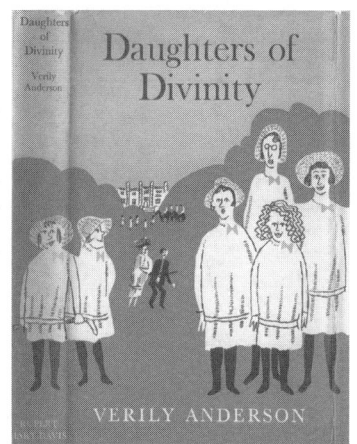

Many other children's books (including the Brownie series), volumes of autobiography, etc

Anon
Bessie Graham's School Days, RTS [1912]

Anon
Harrie, or, Schoolgirl Life in Edinburgh, RTS [1877]

Anon
May Lynwood's School Days, RTS [1886]

Thomas Archer
Miss Grantley's Girls comprises short stories, mostly romantic and historical, linked by a school setting: *The Governess* without the morality.

Miss Grantley's Girls, and the Stories She Told Them, Blackie ([1886]). Illus. 'GB'

Also many other children's books and historical novels

M Vera Armstrong
(Mary Vera Marshall Pain, later Armstrong)
1904-1992
Vera Armstrong was born in Huddersfield in 1904, one of the daughters of William Laurence Wright Marshall, surgeon; she married firstly, in 1934, Richard Shirley Pain, RE officer, and secondly (apparently following divorce), in 1946, Brigadier Edward F E Armstrong. She died in 1992 in Stroud, Gloucestershire. *See also* **VERA MARSHALL**.

As might be guessed from her published works, some written under her maiden name, she was much involved with the Girl Guide movement. She was awarded the MBE in 1974 for 'services to the Girl Guide Association', having served the movement in various capacities including (1949-52) as Division Commander in India and as editor of *The Trefoil* (1954-66).

Maris of Glenside, Warne (1953). Illus.

Other Guide stories

Mrs Arthur
(Frances Browne Arthur)
1854-1920
Mrs Browne was the daughter of the Rev. John Browne of Manorcunningham, County Donegal (d 1854); she married Professor James Arthur and lived in Edinburgh, with two daughters and a son. She was the niece of Frances Browne, author of *Granny's Wonderful Chair*. Apart from her single (part) school story she wrote books for girls and children, occasionally under the pseudonym Ray Cunningham. The first edition had pictorial boards with no author's name; Mrs Arthur was given as the author's name on the title page. Subsequent editions used the name Frances Browne Arthur.

Mother Maud (part High School), Nelson ([1904]). Illus. 'Rosa C Petherick'

The frontispiece from *A School in Danger* by Mabel Esther Allan

"I WANT A BIG BIRTHDAY CAKE MADE," SAID MIKE.

The frontispiece for *Mischief at St Rollo's* by Mary Pollock (pseudonym of Enid Blyton)

B

May Baldwin
(Mary Theodora Baldwin)
1862-1950

May Baldwin was born on 8 May 1862 in Lucknow in India, daughter of the Rev. John Richard Baldwin (a chaplain in India from 1857 to 1878) and his Scottish wife Catherine, née Rose. She was the third surviving child of the marriage, having an elder sister and brother, and a younger sister and brother. She was educated in Germany (an experience she put to good use in her first book, *A Popular Schoolgirl*), and subsequently trained as a teacher at Bishop Otter College, Chichester; we have no details of any teaching career. Her father moved back to England, on furlough from 1869 to 1871, and then permanently, to take up a living at Dewsbury from 1879 to 1881, where May joined her family. It was probably at this point that May's youngest sister, Dorothy, attended a High School—a type of institution which May wrote about in a number of books. We know that when her first book was published (1900), she was living in London; in the 1901 census she was in Cambridge 'living on own means'; in the 1911 census, she is found boarding, possibly only temporarily, in Lupus Street, Pimlico, described as 'authoress'; she moved to Bournemouth in 1914, where she had her main residence until her death.

May Baldwin was an excellent linguist, and had friends in many parts of the world. Her books on schoolgirl life in Italy, France, Germany, Russia, Singapore and various colonies are all based on visits which she made to these friends; she also spent several years during the 1920s living with her brother in Kenya. According to her family, she returned when her brother was trampled to death by an elephant. She died in Bournemouth on 3 January 1950.

May Baldwin is an acquired taste for many modern readers. Her books were slightly unusual even in their own time; class-conscious, a little stilted, with rigid principles, she may seem typically 19th century. She dislikes hoydenish behaviour, fashionable dress and make-up, and smoking; *High-Jinks at Priory School* and *A Riotous Term at St Norbert's* occasionally read like Queen Victoria's last stand. In fact, she is in many ways a pioneer, and her characters and schools cover an enormous range. She is the first prolific girls' writer to produce a majority of books dealing with school: **L T MEADE**'s 40 or so books with a school element pale into insignificance besides her 200-plus books with no school at all; **RAYMOND JACBERNS** wrote more family tales than school stories; and **ANGELA BRAZIL**'s first school story did not appear until 1907, by which time Baldwin had produced nine books, including four school stories. She is also the first major school story writer to focus on the developments in girls' education: until the Great War, all her English schools are either High Schools or public schools. Only *Spoilt Cynthia at School* and *Three Pickles in and out of School* (1918 and 1921 respectively) are set at small, family-style schools.

It would, however, be wrong to assume that Baldwin's books laid the foundations for all later development. She comes from the tradition in which school stories are a department of family stories; only six out of her sixteen English schools are boarding establishments, and the majority of the day-school stories move seamlessly between school and home—something which school stories of the 20s and 30s tended to reject. Baldwin does not see school as a closed community; nor does she see it as the ideal to which new girls must be moulded. Certainly some schools, such as Nuns' Eaton (*The Girls' Eton*), are excellent places, and self-willed or obstinate girls do change in them; but it is more usual for the new girl to mould others to her own unconventional pattern.

These heroines have been brought up outside 'normal' society, and are free from pointless shibboleths and fashionable ideas. Sometimes they have lived physically remote from 'civilisation': Alistair (*The Girls' Eton*) and Jean (*Jean and the Boys*) are from the Scottish Highlands, Rooni from 'the wilds of Africa' and Irene (*A Riotous Term at St Norbert's*) from Australia. Alternatively they may have been raised, like Barbara Bellamy, by a guardian (the majority of Baldwin's heroines have lost one or both parents) who despises modernity. In all cases, these girls—the school story equivalent of Rousseau's Noble Savage—are initially despised and excluded by many of their peers, since they are ignorant of 'correct' behaviour; but their integrity and single-mindedness eventually win over the school (sometimes converting it in the process, as in *A Riotous Term at St Norbert's*) and shame their enemies. They are courageous: Barbara Bellamy saves some younger girls from a mad dog and Rooni flies to the rescue of a party involved in a road accident. They are the standard to which the rest of the school—and society—should aspire.

Part of this standard is the sincere and unashamed practice of Christianity. Her noble savages are always *animae naturaliter Christianae*, although they may (like Barbara Bellamy) have had little experience of conventional religion. Baldwin is extraordinarily ecumenical for her period and society: Rooni, whose simple upbringing in Africa has left her ignorant of sects and divisions, takes part in a mini-pilgrimage to the shrine of the Blessed Virgin at Laghet, and is greatly moved by the Good Friday ceremonies in the local Catholic church.

This tolerance is extended even to life abroad. Any reader of Baldwin will realise very quickly that a large number of her school stories (ten out of 26) are set abroad. She is not unique in this: **ANGELA BRAZIL**, **KATHARINE OLDMEADOW**, **MABEL ESTHER ALLAN**, **ELSIE J OXENHAM** and, most famously, **ELINOR M BRENT-DYER** are among the many school-story writers who have taken advantage of exotic locations to attract young readers. But she is possibly the only prolific school-story writer who was educated abroad, and her schools are not sturdy British institutions sited in Austria, Switzerland or France but indigenous schools which take British girls. Baldwin wrote from observation, not from guide-books; and since she was more interested in people than in monuments, gives a vivid and memorable account of life in a host of different countries.

Baldwin's open-mindedness means that she never boosts the upright, honourable British at the expense of nasty foreigners. For the majority of Baldwin's peers, to come from a non-English-speaking country is to be dishonest, vengeful and sly; even Elsie J Oxenham succumbs to that mentality at times (*Expelled from School*). Baldwin certainly agrees that English girls (the phrase she most commonly uses) are generally frank and open, but they have faults to balance that, in particular the parochial mentality which sees everything foreign as inferior. They fail to take the climate into account (*Two Schoolgirls of Florence*), cannot adapt to the Russian custom of addressing acquaintances by Christian name and patronymics (*A Schoolgirl of Moscow*) and, worst of all, assume that all foreign ways are inferior to British customs (*passim*). In *Rooni*, set at a school in Nice, Baldwin actually makes an English girl, Rhoda, the villain.

Baldwin sees her mission as bringing nationalities and sects together, not by ignoring differences but by being fair to all. Contrast the anti-German sentiments in Brazil's *A Patriotic Schoolgirl* with those in *Phyllis McPhilemy*, where the Headmistress forbids any abuse of the Germans. Even Baldwin's racial comments, which by today's standards are anything but correct ('Jerogi ... is a remarkably intelligent native ... and has a very good character ...' *A Schoolgirl of the Blue*) are far more positive and objective than those of most of her peers. Many of her attitudes may be off-putting to today's readers; but her sense of justice and uncompromising allegiance to what she felt was right, regardless of others' opinions, can make her books very rewarding to read.

Source: Mrs Nora Blacklock, May Baldwin's niece

P1   *A Popular Girl* (Germany), Chambers (1901). Illus. Jessie Wilson
*A Plucky Girl**, Chambers (1902). Illus. Jessie Macgregor
P2   *Sibyl, or Old School Friends**, Chambers (1903). Illus. W Rainey
*Sunset Rock**, Chambers (1903). Illus. Harold Copping
*That Awful Little Brother**, Chambers (1904). Illus. Charles Pears
The Girls of St Gabriel's (French convent), Chambers (1905). Illus. Percy Tarrant
*That Little Limb**, Chambers (1905). Illus. Mabel Lucie Attwell
Dora: A High School Girl, Chambers (1906). Illus. Mabel Lucie Attwell
Peg's Adventures in Paris (France), Chambers (1906). Illus. W Rainey
*Mysie: A Highland Lassie**, Chambers (1907). Illus. A S Boyd
F1   *The Follies of Fifi* (France), Chambers (1907). Illus. A S Boyd
F2   *Golden Square High School*, Chambers (1908). Illus. A S Boyd
*Holly House and Ridges Row**, Chambers (1908). Illus. M V Wheelhouse
Barbara Bellamy, a Public Schoolgirl, Chambers (1909). Illus. Lewis Baumer
Muriel and her Aunt Lu (France), Chambers (1909). Illus. A S Boyd
*Sarah's School Friend**, Chambers ([1910]). Illus. Percy Tarrant
Two Schoolgirls of Florence (Italy), Chambers (1910). Illus. H C Earnshaw
The Girls' Eton, Chambers ([1911]). Illus. Percy Tarrant
A Schoolgirl of Moscow (Russia) (abridged as *An English Schoolgirl in Moscow*, 1915), Chambers (1911). Illus. W Rainey
Teddy and Lily's Adventures (Italy)*, Chambers (1911). Illus. W H C Groome
A City Schoolgirl and her Friends, Chambers (1912). Illus. T J Overnell
Corah's School Chums (South Africa), Chambers (1912). Illus. William Rainey
*Hilda's Experiences** (Australia), Chambers (1913). Illus. W Rainey
*Moll Meredyth, Madcap**, Chambers (1913). Illus. W H C Groome
*Troublesome Topsy and her Friends**, Chambers (1913). Illus. Mabel Lucie Attwell
A Ripping Girl, Chambers (1914). Illus. Gordon Browne
*A Schoolgirl's Diary** (round-the-world trip), Chambers (1914). Illus. W A Cuthbertson
Phyllis McPhilemy, Chambers (1915). Illus. W A Cuthbertson
Mrs Manning's Wards, Chambers (1916). Illus. Gordon Browne
*Irene to the Rescue** (France), Chambers (1916). Illus. J Petts
'Miss Peter', Chambers (1917). Illus. W A Cuthbertson
Spoilt Cynthia at School, Chambers (1918). Illus. Percy Tarrant
Jean and the Boys, Chambers (1919). Illus. Percy Tarrant
A Riotous Term at St Norbert's, Chambers (1920). Illus. Percy Tarrant
Three Pickles in and out of School, Chambers (1921). Illus. Molly Benatar
Only Pat (Kenya), Chambers ([1922]). Illus. Molly Benatar
*A Schoolgirl of the Blue** (British East Africa), Chambers ([1923]) Illus. Percy Tarrant
The Brilliant Girls of the School, Chambers ([1924]). Illus. W Rainey
The School in the Wilds (Kenya), Chambers ([1925]). Illus. Nina K Brisley
*Kenya Kiddies** (Kenya), Chambers ([1926]). Illus. Nina K Brisley
Rooni (France), Chambers ([1927]). Illus. T J Overnell
*The Twins Make Good**, Chambers (1928). Illus. Nina K Brisley
High-Jinks at Priory School, Chambers (1929). Illus. Molly Benatar

Not an Ordinary Girl*, Chambers (1930). Illus. Nina K Brisley
The Tarletons in Brittany* (France), Chambers (1931). Illus. Nina K Brisley

P = Popular Girl pair
F = Fifi pair

Marjorie C Barnard
(?Marjorie Calvert Barnard)
?1885-1968

This author is now thought to be Marjorie Calvert Barnard, daughter of a solicitor, born in Marylebone on 8 December 1885 but from early childhood living in Croydon; she had an older and a younger sister and three younger brothers. Her maternal grandfather was the publisher George Routledge. In 1901 she is found at home, though her elder sister was at a girls' boarding school in Folkestone. We do not know where Marjorie was educated but by 1911 she was living in Sutton, Surrey, described as an assistant mistress in a secondary school, with her employer being the Girls' Public Day School Co. (which became the Girls' Public Day School Trust)—so one assumes she was teaching at Sutton High School. By 1939, living with her mother and sister in Beckenham, she was 'assistant secretary to an educational trust', so it is tempting to think that she might have given up teaching around 1922, when her first (boys') school story was published under (if our attribution is correct) her own name.

She did not marry but continued to live in Beckenham until her death on 21 January 1968.

Marjorie Barnard's three girls' school stories are all set at Thorncliff, a small girls' boarding school about 60 strong. *'Angel Pig'* centres on the novelty of day-girl admission, and one day-girl in particular: spoilt, dishonest Angela Piggott, whose gradual reformation and socialisation is the central theme of the book. Pen, the prefect who has most influence on Angela, is Head Girl in the second and third in the series. *Mrs Noah*, which uses the substitute headmistress plot, is marginally amusing in its depiction of the firmly 19th-century replacement, but *The Twins at Thorncliff*, which uses a combination of twins, mischief and the reformation of a bad house, is unconvincing, with shadowy characters and a rather rambling plot.

1   *'Angel Pig',* Nelson ([1925]). Illus. L A Govey
2   *Mrs Noah,* Nelson ([1926]). Illus.
3   *The Twins at Thorncliff,* Nelson ([1928]). Illus. Margaret Forbes

See also *The Encyclopaedia of Boys' School Stories*, **MARJORIE C BARNARD**; Westcote Towers boys have sisters at Thorncliff.

Kitty Barne
(Marion Katherine Barne Streatfeild)
1882-1961

Kitty Barne, born in 1882, was partly educated at home, and probably then at school, but ultimately at the Royal College of Music. Her planned musical career was prevented by a damaged ear, which led to deafness, and she turned to writing children's plays and pageants. Her marriage in 1912 to Eric Streatfeild brought her to cousinship and friendship with Noel Streatfeild, who was responsible for suggesting that Kitty turn to children's books when she found her theatrical activities too strenuous.

Kitty Barne spent all her married life in Eastbourne, where she was involved with Guiding and with the WRVS; post World War II she was a frequent speaker on children's books. She died on 3 February 1961.

Kitty Barne was primarily a children's author, much loved for her stories of family life (often with a strong musical element), who won the Carnegie Medal for her 1940 evacuee story, *Visitors from London*. *In the Same Boat* is the only one of her books with a definite school-story element. It concerns the impact of Polish Antosia on staid English Bridget, when they are thrown together by being in the same boat returning to war-time UK. Bridget is keen to attend her mother's old school and keep up with tradition; Tossie is entirely focused on the fate of Poland. Barne was not interested in the school story as such, but English school life throws Tossie's pre-occupations into focus—and the impact is very funny.

In the Same Boat, Dent (1945). Illus. Ruth Gervis

Many children's books and plays, adult novels, and a history of the Girl Guides

Winifred Barnes
The Jewels and Jenny*, Schofield & Sims (1948). Illus. W Lindsay Cable
Jenny at St Julien's (college), Schofield & Sims ([1949]). Illus. W Lindsay Cable

Also other children's books and educational material

F Baron
The Flodden Rubies, Gerald G Swan (1947)
The Mystery of the Silver Statuette, Gerald G Swan (1948). Illus.

Also other works

Elizabeth Batt

An evangelistic writer, Elizabeth Batt has written an unusual story in that it is set in Jamaica; she views the people with affection, but never really ceases to see them as exotic specimens of humanity. One wonders whether she is portraying herself in the character of the English lady leading a mission in the heroine's home town.

A Jamaican Schoolgirl (Jamaica), Lutterworth Press (1962). Illus.

Also other children's books

Gillian Baxter *see* PONY SCHOOL STORIES

Barbara Beacham
While Others Dance, Kingsway (1991)

Grace Beaumont

This author's only school story is a fairly characteristic tale of the period, a religiously oriented book set partly at home and partly in 'Mrs Elder's Select Establishment for Young Ladies'. The madcap heroine ends up crippled, 'learning beautiful lessons in the school of pain'.

Aunt Judith: The Story of a Loving Life, Nelson ([1888]). Illus.

Also other semi-adult novels

Jennie Beckingsale
Pomegranate: The Story of a Chinese Schoolgirl, Morgan & Scott (1910). Not illus.

Vera Bedford
A Memorable Year: An Exciting School Story for Girls, Vawser & Wiles, London ([1946]). Illus.
Stella Black, Southern Editorial Syndicate (1947)

Ethel Hume Bennett
(Ethel Hume Patterson Bennett)
1881-1973

Ethel Hume Bennett was born in Toronto, Canada, to Joseph Patterson and his wife Isabelle Brown in September 1881. She attended the Toronto Public High School, received a BA from Victoria College at the University of Toronto, married John S Bennett in 1916, and lived in Toronto for the rest of her life, dying in 1973. She wrote a sequence of Canadian school and holiday books, set in various locations in Ontario; Judith, the protagonist of the school stories is only a minor character in the holiday books, but the main characters in the holiday books generally are (or become) Judith's schoolmates in the school stories.

Judy of York Hill, set in Toronto, is like **ELINOR M BRENT-DYER** in its celebration of school spirit, and like **ELSIE J OXENHAM** in its warmth and emphasis on emotion. Bennett depicts quite subtly the ways in which 'crushes' may inspire a girl to unusual heights or make her sink to baseness. *Judy's Prefect Year* examines crushes more disapprovingly, as Judith, now a conscientious prefect, deals with the impact on the school of a charming, influential and unscrupulous new girl. The school-story ethic is supreme in Bennett: even prefects are never allowed to 'tell' on other girls, and at moral crises when 'Top Self' (ego) wrestles with 'Deep-Down Self' (one's best impulses), Deep-Down Self is apt to produce inspiring images of the teachers and girls who stand for 'the best and finest things in York Hill'. The later books in the series are carefully constructed to show the heroines struggling against a particular besetting sin (anger in *Camp Ken-Jockety*, jealousy in *Judy's Prefect Year*, cowardice in *Camp Conqueror*).

PILLOWS WERE SORTED OUT, AND NANCY WITH THE TINY LIGHT LED THE WAY *(page 59)*

Bennett's school stories, like **ANTONIA FOREST**'s and Brent-Dyer's, show great interest in the allocation of parts for school plays and in techniques of dramatic management and costuming. The Judy books also include sports, fun, a midnight feast, anonymous letters and a flower shower with rhymes, reminiscent of *What Katy Did at School*. The books are informed throughout by the author's obvious love of English literature—Judith's housemistress, Miss Marlowe, teaches English composition and declares that that really means teaching 'Life, and it's the biggest job in the world'.

Margot Louis

Judy of York Hill, Houghton Mifflin (1922). Illus. Harold Cue
Camp Ken-Jockety*, Houghton Mifflin (1923). Illus. Harold Cue
Judy's Prefect Year, Houghton Mifflin (1925). Illus. F M Rines
Camp Conqueror*, Houghton Mifflin (1928). Illus. Constance Whittemore
A Treasure Ship of Old Quebec*, Dodd, Mead (1936). Illus. Hazel Boswell
(ed.) *New Harvesting: Contemporary Canadian Poetry**, Macmillan (1938). Illus. J M Donald
(ed.) *Thirteen Bears* (by Sir Charles G D Roberts)*, Ryerson (1947). Illus. John A Hall
(ed.) *Forest Folk* (by Sir Charles G D Roberts)*, Ryerson (1949). Illus. John A Hall

The picture at the top of the page is the frontispiece from *Judy of York Hill*. The caption reads: 'Pillows were sorted out and Nancy with the tiny light led the way.'

Note that the name on the boards (first edition) is just Ethel Hume whereas a later edition gives the author's full name.

Frederica J E Bennett
(Frederica Jane Edith Turle Bennett)
1880-1936

Frederica Bennett was born in Finchley on 29 March 1880, the youngest of the family of Dr James Turle, MOH, who died in 1905. With her mother and one of her sisters she seems to have moved around southern seaside resorts before, on 2 October 1912, in Westminster, marrying Major Charles Hugh Bennett. They had one son and eventually settled in Cheltenham, where she died on 4 November 1936.

Elizabeth and Beth, novella in *The Guides of Fairley and Other Stories of School Life and Adventure* by **DIANA PARES**, Epworth Press (1936). Illus. 'W M A'
Gillian the Dauntless, Nelson ([1937]). Illus. S J R Burgess
Harum-Scarum Jill, Wells Gardner ([1937]). Illus.

Also other children's books

Flora E Berry
(Flora Eliza Berry)
1872-1949

Flora Berry was born in Deptford on 14 February 1873, daughter of a Manchester (cotton goods) agent; the family moved to Walberton, West Sussex, then to Wimborne, Dorset, and finally (before 1911) to Swanage, where Flora died on 7 June 1949.

Monica's Choice, Partridge ([1904]). Illus. 'Malcolm Patterson'

Anna Best

School Rivals (described on the cover as 'A Bright School Story') is mainly notable for the varied athletic pursuits of these damsels, which include cricket, fencing, lassoing and boxing. The heroine performs four gallant rescues, which puts her in the *Judy, Patrol Leader* class (**DOROTHEA MOORE**). *Madge's Victory* is over her quick temper; to avoid a Victorian morality tale, Best has inserted a quite incomprehensible sub-plot with Madge's pretty stepmother being courted by a sinister man who may be a burglar who is (or possibly isn't) the villainess's uncle, or her uncle's friend, and pushes girls into ponds for reasons never explained. Unintentionally amusing.

School Rivals, Pilgrim Press ([1925]). Illus. 'FCD'
Madge's Victory, Pilgrim Press ([1926]). Illus. 'FCD'

Marjorie Bevan
(Kathleen Eleanor Marjorie Bevan Bennetton)
1900-1966

The third of the four children of Tom Bevan, schoolmaster and author, who wrote as Walter Bamfylde, Marjorie Bevan was born on 6 February 1900 in Rickmansworth, where she was still living (in Brooklyn Lodge) in 1932. In 1936 she married William Henry Bennetton, a civil servant, with whom she had one son and lived at New Milton, Hampshire. Her husband was posted overseas (Eritrea and Singapore) in the 1950s, which probably explains why she ceased writing; she certainly travelled to and from Singapore in 1960, describing herself as 'housewife' on the shipping records. She died in New Milton on 8 September 1966.

Bevan's books are not interrelated, except that her heroines, like those of **DORIS POCOCK** or **IRENE MOSSOP,** often find themselves playing tennis against characters from an earlier book. The nine books were published over a period of 22 years. The author started slowly with *Five of the Fourth*, which can be charitably described as weak, like its title, and almost plotless, being simply a succession of self-contained and trivial happenings culminating in a Devon holiday and, impossible not to mention, a stag rescued from a stag hunt when it jumps into the girls' car and is driven away from its pursuers. One wonders how big Marjorie Bevan thought stags were. However, even this first book introduces a situation common to most of them: the established 'set' is infiltrated by a new girl, although some of its members are more than reluctant to spread their friendship. *The Priory League* is not a huge leap forward, though it does have one central idea: finding a legendary buried treasure to prevent the school being sold. With *Anne of the Veld*, however, Marjorie Bevan becomes far more readable, and starts to explore several other pet themes. One is the new girl who is an outsider not merely because she's new, but because she comes from a foreign and vividly evoked background—'merely' Belinda, the Hollywood sophisticate who finds Cranleigh Abbas 'vurry odd'; Sara, the half-gypsy, at *Moorleigh*; or Bendyth Verity, whose life in the South Seas has been even more exotic than her name: 'she, who had managed a little household, disciplined two foreign servants, and been a mother and sweetheart to two big men, was now a complete schoolgirl!'

Without exception, however, these new girls are smash hits and discover all sorts of talents they had no idea they possessed. School is a warm and kindly place where nobody looks down on a gypsy, and jealous girls are conquered by the magnanimity of their rivals. Wise understanding mistresses and strict but lovable prefects nurture and guide the footsteps of the fifteen-year-old, who rarely rebels for long against their wholesome rule. Headmistresses are particularly broadminded and ever ready to forgive bounds-breaking in the cause of successful detective work or any kind of self-expression. 'We're all modern,' says Susan in *The Luck of the Veritys*: 'Everyone's decent enough to realise that we must all lead our own lives, and not be ground under heel like worms.' This during a school dance for which Bendyth has glamorised her plain friend with make-up.

(Thirty years later, at my all-girls school, people were still getting expelled for that sort of thing …)

Marjorie Bevan also demonstrates a relaxed attitude to girls meeting men—young miners, for example, in *Madcaps of Manor School*. Instead of an incoming new girl, in this book all the girls are new—new to the Welsh countryside to which their school moves from London. Some of them go down a coal-mine and are moved to new, near-Socialist ideas about working men. As in several other books, a girl discovers that she has writing ability and decides, with much emotion, to be an author.

As Marjorie Bevan's writing improved technically, the strain of morality in her books strengthened too, and this philosophy is too apt to be spelled out, usually by a schoolgirl famed for her deep thinking, instead of acted out. But the stories are good, and, after the first two, develop at least partly from the characters of the protagonists.

Kate Tyler

Five of the Fourth, Sampson Low ([1926]). Illus. 'MLP'
The Priory League, Sampson Low ([1928]). Illus. 'MLP'
The Formidable Fifth, Sampson Low ([193–]). Illus.
Anne of the Veld, Nelson ([1934]). Illus. J Phillips Paterson
The Fifth at Foley's, Sampson Low ([1936]). Illus.
Mystery Term at Moorleigh, Sampson Low ([1937]). Illus.
The Luck of the Veritys, Warne (1938). Illus. 'K W Coales'
Merely Belinda, Warne (1939). Illus. 'M Sherwin'
Madcaps of Manor School, Warne (1948). Illus. 'CPS'

Margaret Biggs
(Margaret Biggs Cadney)

Margaret Biggs was born on 9 July 1929 in Orpington, Kent (and is shown here aged 17). Her father, originally from Cambridge, was a sales manager for Chivers, covering the Kent area. In 1935 the family moved to Barnet in Hertfordshire, where Margaret attended Queen Elizabeth's Grammar School, leaving in 1946. She joined the publishing firm of Evans Brothers in Bloomsbury, and worked in the editorial department, **ENID BLYTON** being one of the authors published by Evans at this time. In 1953, she married David Cadney and moved to Finchley; they have one daughter and two sons. The family spent some time in Stevenage and Hitchin, where her husband worked in further education; her third child was stillborn (1964), and she and her husband moved away from Hertfordshire to Solihull in the West Midlands, where her youngest child was born, and where she still lives. After a break to care for her growing family, she wrote two stories set in comprehensive schools and a historical novel, none of which were published; short stories met with more success, and she has had several published in children's anthologies, as well as writing for women's magazines (sometimes under the pseudonym of Eve Gothard).

Margaret Biggs at 17, the age when she began to write the Melling stories

Triplets at Royders, (1950?) her first school story, was written in collaboration with a friend, **JACQUELINE BLAIRMAN**, who worked at Evans with her. This was followed by *Christmas Term at Vernley*, perhaps Margaret Biggs' most straightforward school story; it uses one of the standard plot devices, that of a poor house struggling to reform itself, but is never over-serious, and has a delightful central character in Philippa, the fourteen-year-old sister of the House Captain, Judy. Philippa's well-meaning efforts to help Judy continually go wrong, often to comic effect.

The writing is surprisingly mature for a first solo novel. Dramatic events are less important than the way in which characters interact. Dysfunctional families hold a particular fascination for her, and her three other non-series books are all concerned with heroines from such families: the eponymous heroine of *Bobby at Hill House*, an orphan raised by her cousin, resents the latter's new wife; *The Two Families* brings together a happy fatherless family and a miserable motherless one; and *Dilly Goes to Ambergate* is surely the most extreme example, focusing on a girl from an orphanage. The story could be saccharine, but Dilly's defence mechanism of hostility and aggression is never glossed over, and her final adoption by her best friend's family does not seem over-sentimental.

However, Margaret Biggs' best-known books are the series set in Melling school. These follow the fortunes of the three Blake sisters and their friends during a five-year period, starting from the arrival of the Blake family in the small village of Bramberley when Helen, the eldest girl, is sixteen, Roddy fourteen and Susan twelve, and finishing with Susan in the Sixth Form and Helen marrying her best friend's brother. The series was popular enough for Margaret Biggs to emulate **OXENHAM** and **BRUCE** by inserting two retrospective books—*The New Girl at Melling* and *Summer Term at Melling*—into the series.

In Melling, Biggs has achieved an unusual feat: a school of only 50 pupils, described as 'exclusive' and 'expensive', which nevertheless does not appear snobbish—perhaps because, unusually, it is a weekly boarding school. This enables the action to move seamlessly between home and family; in Margaret Biggs' work it is often hard to tell which is more important. Her interest in dysfunctional families is given full rein in the Melling books: the easy-going, tolerant Blakes are used as both a foil and a remedy for a series of unhappy domestic situations.

In the first of the sequence, *The Blakes Come to Melling*, the plot centres on the resentment of the aristocratic but poverty-stricken Lacey family towards the Blakes, who have moved into the historic Tudor house which the Laceys can no longer afford after the death of Colonel Lacey. This emotionally sterile family is remade by contact with the Blakes; the friendships between Libby and Helen, and between Susan and Laura, motivate much of the action in the earlier books. Other cold or unloving families are also affected: Anne Laurence and her aunts (*The New Girl at Melling*) and Pat Evans and her parents (*Summer Term at Melling*). One might well include Franny (*Head Girl of Melling*), another orphan who lives with an aunt and uncle: the latter, though fond of Franny, are 'the sort of people who talk in disapproving voices about the younger generation'.

Franny's problem is what modern psychologists would call lack of self-esteem, shared by Dilly, Davida (*Bobby at Hill House*) and Andrew (*The Two Families*) and most of all by Laura Lacey, perpetually in the shadow of a high-flying elder sister, and convinced of her own uselessness. *Susan in the Sixth*, where Laura is made Head Girl (much to Susan's chagrin) is a study in how confidence can be built up. Margaret Biggs never allows timid girls to leap to boldness through one heroic action, as other writers do; the most dramatic event experienced by any of these characters is Davida's winning the piano class in a music festival, and even this is unusual—the norm is for characters to change slowly through others' trust in them.

Real villains are rare in these books, and generally reform spontaneously rather than through external sanctions or punishment. Miss Whyte, the harsh substitute Headmistress in *Last Term For Helen*, is mellowed by Melling, so to speak, and ends up renting a cottage in the village; Pat Evans' new leaf is motivated by the realisation of her own unpopularity *(The New Girl at Melling)*; and Julia *(Bobby at Hill House)* and Elspeth *(Dilly Goes to Ambergate)*, who strongly resemble each other in their aristocratic disdain of social inferiors, both come to realise the error of their respective ways gradually. Only the revolting Aunt Vinny *(The Two Families)* fails to reform; but she conveniently walks out and goes to live with a friend (one of the only places where one's disbelief cannot quite be suspended—can Aunt Vinny have any friends?).

Margaret Biggs' world is warm without being too cosy, and realistic without being over-harsh. Her books stand out for their unsensational pictures of life at school and at home, of growing friendships and the gradually changing pattern of personal relationships. It is not surprising that her books are widely loved today and collected avidly.

Fifty years after *Susan in the Sixth*, Margaret Biggs published two sequels, *Kate at Melling* and *Changes at Melling*. The protagonist, Kate Lacey, is the daughter of Helen Blake and Libby's brother Matthew, thus enabling Biggs to stay with the Blakes and Laceys even though all the original family members have long since left the school. The books are still gentle and charming, and Melling fans can only regret that Margaret Biggs makes it clear in her introduction to *Changes at Melling* that she will write no more books in the series.

Further Reading
Folly 6

Triplets at Royders (with Jacqueline Blairman), Sampson Low ([1950?]). Illus.
Christmas Term at Vernley, Blackie ([1951]). Illus. W Spence
1   *The Blakes Come to Melling*[1], Blackie ([1951]). Illus. Louis Ward

2   *The New Prefect at Melling* ¹, Blackie ([1952]). Illus. Louis Ward
3   *Last Term for Helen* ¹, Blackie ([1953]). Illus. Louis Ward
    Bobby at Hill House, Warne (1954). Illus.
4   *Head Girl of Melling* ², Blackie ([1954]). Illus. Ruth Murrell
7   *Susan in the Sixth* ², Blackie (1955). Illus. Ruth Murrell
    Dilly Goes to Ambergate, Blackie (1955). Illus. Ruth Murrell
5   *The New Girl at Melling*, Blackie (1956). Illus. Ruth Murrell
6   *Summer Term at Melling* ², Blackie (1957). Illus. Ruth Murrell
    The Two Families, Blackie (1958). Illus. Ruth Murrell
8   *Kate at Melling*, Girls Gone By (2008, actually 2007). Not illus
9   *Changes at Melling*, Girls Gone By (2009). Not illus

¹Included in omnibus *Stories of Melling School* (1960)
²Included in omnibus *More Stories of Melling School* (1961)

Beverley Merton Bingham *see under* **Authors beginning with M**

Jacqueline Blairman

Jacqueline Blairman's books are amusing and in many ways original: perhaps her best creation is Gillian, an earl's daughter who goes incognito to the snobbish St Agatha's and enjoys herself cutting a swathe through the pretentious *nouveaux-riches* inmates. She is now overshadowed by her friend **MARGARET BIGGS**, who kept at the job far longer.

The Headmistress in Disgrace, Hector Kelly (1949). Not illus.
A Rebel at St Agatha's, Hector Kelly (1949). Not illus.
Triplets at Royders (with Margaret Biggs), Sampson Low ([1950?]). Illus.

Julia K Bloomfield

Glenwood: A Story of School Life, Wesleyan Conference Office ([1880]). Illus.

Rebecca Blount
(?Marion Louisa Smith Milford)
?1879-1940?

There is some very slight evidence that 'Rebecca Blount' was the pseudonym of Marion Louisa Smith, wife of Humphrey Sumner Milford, publisher to the Oxford University Press. One copy of *School Days* exists which has had 'Mrs Humphrey Milford' pencilled on the title page under 'Rebecca Blount', and while nothing has been found to confirm this, nothing has been found against the identification and there are certainly some things which suggest it could be accurate.

Marion Louisa Smith was born on 18 April 1879 in Beckenham, Kent, where the family lived throughout her youth. She was the youngest daughter of Horace Smith, a Metropolitan Police Magistrate and had three older sisters and three brothers. 'Dolores' in *School Days* has two elder sisters, one much older and one near her own age: Gertrude Smith was eight, and Janet and Dorothy four and three years older than Marion. An important episode in the book concerns a school visit to the Crystal Palace, by charabanc: this seems a perfectly possible outing for a school in Beckenham. *School Days* has an introduction by Elizabeth Wordsworth, first principal of Lady Margaret Hall, Oxford: Marion Louisa Smith was a scholar of LMH.

She married Humphrey Milford on 24 April 1902 and had three children; it seems slightly suggestive that her daughter was born in 1909, and could well have been the recipient of stories of her mother's schooldays. In 1921 the juvenile department of the Oxford University Press was just beginning to publish girls' school stories (**DORITA FAIRLIE BRUCE**'s *The Senior Prefect* is that year) and it may be that Humphrey Milford persuaded his wife to contribute a tale to the new genre—or, of course, was persuaded by her to promote her little work.

For *School Days* is a little work, small in size and only 121 pages of text. A classic borderline case for inclusion in this volume, it is a delicately-drawn vignette of the type of 19th-century school gradually being driven out of business by the 'new High Schools'—24 pupils, a charismatic but inefficient headmistress, and very little education. It certainly has the feel of an autobiography, and the introduction is rather apologetic and even cautionary ('I fear ... that the moral—if moral there be—is not a very edifying one ...'). It was the author's only work, and reasonably so, for it was certainly not in tune with the new girls' school-story genre.

If 'Rebecca Blount' was indeed Mrs Humphrey Milford (Lady Milford from her husband's knighthood in 1936) this would explain the use of a pseudonym, to hide her intimate connection with OUP and avoid accusations of favouritism. Humphrey Milford certainly did use his position to promote books in which he was interested; perhaps *School Days* was one of them.

School Days, OUP (1921). Illus. Gordon Browne

Julia Blythe
(Pseudonym for Joanna Bogle)
Intended to be the first of a series, *We Didn't Mean to Start a School* is consciously modelled on the traditional school story, partly in its plot (a school is started almost on the spur of the moment, and flourishes) but also in its ethos. Without ever appearing over-didactic, the author clearly believes that girls are happier in a structured environment with Christian values (though there is no evangelism here, and two of the pupils are Hindu). The background and setting of the book are contemporary (when burglars arrive, they are targeting computers rather than trophies), and Blythe does not succumb to idealism—there are French and German lunches once a week, but no indication that French and German days, à la **BRENT-DYER**, are a possibility; still, the atmosphere is redolent of the 1920s school story and proves a great part of the book's appeal.

We Didn't Mean to Start a School, Gracewing (paperback) (1998). Not illus.

Enid Blyton
(Enid Mary Blyton Pollock, later Enid Mary Darrell Waters)
1897-1968

Enid Mary Blyton was born on 11 August 1897, the eldest of three children, to Thomas and Theresa Blyton, in East Dulwich, South London. Her father encouraged Enid's gift for music and her interest in reading, so it was a major tragedy for her when he left the family home, by then in Beckenham, Kent, when she was twelve. Her father had hoped that, on leaving St Christopher's School, where she became Head Girl, she would take up a place at the Guildhall School of Music and pursue a musical career, but she decided instead that teaching would enable her to carry on with her writing and give her the opportunity to study the children for whom she wanted to write. She began to train as a kindergarten teacher at Ipswich High School in 1916, achieved her first professional publication, a poem, in *Nash's Magazine* in 1917 and, in 1919, began her teaching career in Bickley, Kent. Despite a number of early rejections for her creative work, she steadily increased her output while continuing to teach, moving to the post of governess in Surbiton (Surrey) in 1920. Her first book, *Child Whispers*, a collection of verse, was published in 1922. In 1924 she married Hugh Pollock, an editor at the publisher George Newnes and, in 1926, she launched a weekly magazine for Newnes, *Sunny Stories for Little Folks*, for which she wrote all the material. The birth of two daughters, Gillian in 1931 and Imogen in 1935 (besides a miscarriage in 1934), did not slow down her pace of work. She steadily moved away from publishing educational material to writing her own original stories, with her first successful novel, *Adventures of the Wishing Chair*, appearing in 1937, after being serialised in the newly retitled magazine, *Enid Blyton's Sunny Stories*. She divorced Hugh Pollock in 1943, and married Kenneth Fraser Darrell Rivers in the same year. By the end of the 1940s, Blyton had developed all her main series and characters, including the Famous Five, the Secret Seven and Noddy. She had become a household name, the most prolific and best-known writer for children in Britain and in many other countries. By the time of her death, on 28 November 1968, she had published over 600 books and, even today, remains the best-selling children's author of all time.

School stories represent a very small proportion of her total output, consisting of sixteen full-length books made up of three series, The Naughtiest Girl, St Clare's and Malory Towers. She also wrote one stand-alone novella, *Mischief at St Rollo's*, which first appeared in 1947 under the pseudonym of Mary Pollock, and has more affinity with her adventure fiction for younger children than with the other school stories.

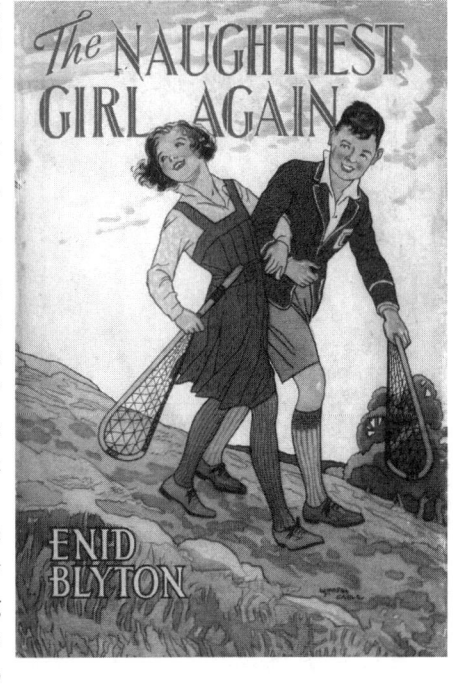

Like *Mischief at St Rollo's*, The Naughtiest Girl books are set in a co-educational school. This choice of setting may have been due to an interest in co-educational boarding schools, which were rare in the 1930s, and the theories of the educationalist, A S Neill, but is more likely due to the fact that Blyton considered herself a writer for boys and girls. All three Naughtiest Girl books had first appeared as serials in *Sunny Stories*. At the start of the first book, *The Naughtiest Girl in the School*, which was serialised between March and August 1940, Elizabeth Allen has had six governesses and her despairing parents have decided to send her to Whyteleafe School. Elizabeth vows to be so naughty that she will be sent home again. She gets away with her early rudeness because Whyteleafe is a modern, in some ways progressive, school and although the staff have things firmly under control, they are rather more tolerant of a new girl who says she has a guinea-pig with 'a face just like Miss Thomas' than many teachers would be. Whyteleafe School is governed by a School Meeting, in which all the children are involved, and which is portrayed as working admirably. It is left to the monitors and her peer group to voice disapproval of Elizabeth's bad behaviour. Although they are irritated by it, they are also quick to appreciate her good qualities, and no one is unduly surprised when she stands up at the last meeting before half-term and says she wants to stay. In the remaining Naughtiest Girl books, Elizabeth is one of the mainstays of the school and becomes a monitor, although her headstrong ways and impetuosity continue to get her into difficulties.

Throughout the series, Elizabeth remains eleven but, despite references to her as a 'little' girl, she seems much older. In contrast, the two protagonists of *The Twins at St Clare*'s (1941), although aged between fourteen and fifteen, seem much younger. This first volume of her new series was explicitly described on the title page as being 'A School Story for Girls', marking a shift in intended readership. It was new territory for Blyton and, perhaps for this reason, the book's early chapters lack Blyton's usually sure touch. The O'Sullivan twins, Pat and Isabel, are identical and are initially described as having an Irish lilt in their voices. The latter may have been due to some half-forgotten memory of a stock character of early girls' school stories, the wild Irish girl. The fact that the twins are identical obviously has potential but, although it is frequently mentioned in the series, it is used once only, early on, as a plot device; this occurs when Pat decides to go into town even though she has been expressly forbidden to do so. As for the Irish lilt, it sinks without trace after the first page.

The first three St Clare's books deal with the three terms the twins spend in the First Form; these are followed by *The Second Form at St Clare's* and *Claudine at St Clare's*. At the end of *Fifth Formers of St Clare's* (1945), the twins are about to become Head Girls as Hilary Wentworth, who has led the form throughout the school, suddenly and very conveniently becomes ineligible because she is only staying on for one more term. Although the *St Clare's* stories are well constructed, and the events of the midnight feast in *Fifth Formers at St Clare's* constitute one of the most hilarious episodes in the whole of Blyton's oeuvre, they tend to be a catalogue of reformations, and lack the focus that one strong central character might provide.

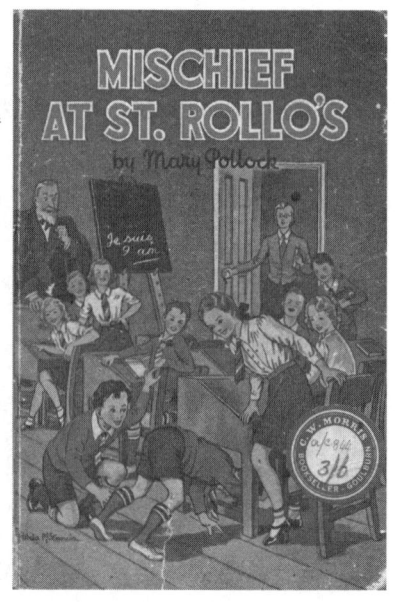

By the time *First Term at Malory Towers* (1946) was written, Blyton, who was above all a thoroughly professional writer, knew exactly what she was doing. Darrell Rivers moves steadily up the school, form by form, until she is Head Girl in *Last Term at Malory Towers* (1951). Darrell, unlike Elizabeth and the O'Sullivan twins, looks forward to going to boarding school. She learns and matures through her experiences and is one of Blyton's most successful characters (her name derives from Blyton's second husband, Kenneth Darrell Waters). The Malory Towers books represent some of Blyton's best work, with good characterisation and some convincing scenarios. By 1946, Blyton's own daughters, Gillian and Imogen, were fifteen and eleven respectively and their mother was able to draw on their experiences at Benenden School. Although Blyton lived and continued to write for some considerable time after the publication of *Last Term at Malory Towers* in 1951, she never returned to the school story.

Blyton's work has been much criticised and her school stories have perhaps not been given the credit they deserve. In particular, she should be commended for the way she avoids using some of the genre's stock devices to create a sense of excitement: there are no secret passages, captures of criminals, discoveries of lost treasure, nor even Ruritanian princesses—although these are regular incidents in her other fiction. Even the midnight feasts, fires, rescues from drowning and runnings away are used quite sparingly. Instead, most of the interest arises from the credible characters and their interplay.

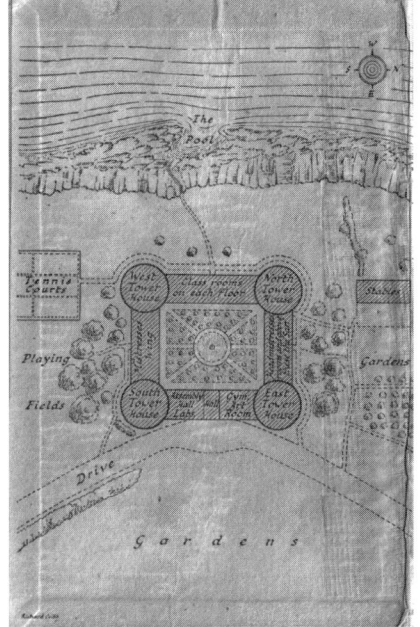

Blyton always wrote with very simple moral messages and the school stories are no exception. Good behaviour is rewarded, bad behaviour punished. If children behave badly, however, it is usually because of some external factor: treated with kindness and sympathy, they respond and behave well. Few of the characters are totally beyond redemption. Parental influence is seen as very important. Both Miss Theobald, the Head of St Clare's, and Miss Grayling, the Head of Malory Towers, shake their heads sadly over the foolish behaviour of some parents, and see education as a partnership between the school and the parents. The underlying message of Blyton's school stories is to be found in the words spoken by Miss Grayling to Darrell on the latter's first full day at Malory Towers (and twice more in the series), when she tells the new girls that the school aims to send out into the world kind, sensible and trustworthy young women, of whom the school can be proud.

Blyton has frequently been criticised for her racism and attitudes to class. These hardly surface in the school stories. She does not follow the example of earlier popular writers such as Frank Richards who introduced characters from the then colonial countries and gave them a comic style of speech. The various French teachers, who feature largely in the books, are an exception, but the humour is generally affectionate. Though they are the butt of many jokes and tricks, the Mam'zelles (one each at St Clare's and Malory Towers) and Monsieur Crozier at St Rollo's give as good as they get, and their worthy qualities are frequently emphasised. The French and American pupils also tend to be stereotypes but, again, the humour is sympathetic. Snobbery is generally seen to be undesirable, and girls are accepted for what they are, rather than because of money or social status. However, Blyton finds it difficult to shake off her intrusive authorial voice and even in her final school story, *Last Term at Malory Towers*, she is pointing out the moral message that must be obvious to even the most unsophisticated reader.

There is little sense of place in the books; Malory Towers is set in Cornwall but the reader only knows this because the fact is frequently mentioned. Certainly, the place names and the names of the schools against whom matches are played do not reflect a Cornish setting. But it is partly because of this lack of external detail that the books have survived so well. There are no references to war-time England, and the odd mention of Churchill is as valid today as when it was written. The discipline in the school is relaxed; girls are listened to and understood, and allowed much more freedom than in most fictional schools of the same period. Even midnight feasts are not regarded as a major sin, which is perhaps why there are so few. Interestingly, for a middle-aged adult reading the books in the 21st century, one thing which most obviously dates the books is the frequent reference to smacks, slaps and spanks. Apart from this shift in attitude, it is only by omission that the books appear dated: there are no televisions, no computers, and certainly no social media.

Blyton is almost as well known and as widely read in the 21st century as she was at the peak of her popularity in the 1960s when she was regularly named by children as their favourite writer. Apart from *Mischief at St Rollo's*, her school stories have never been out of print since they were first published and all are easily available; they may well be read by girls, attracted by the author's name, who never read any other school stories. The additions to the canon by **ANNE DIGBY** and **PAMELA COX**, plus titles like the more contemporary *Diary of the Naughtiest Girl* ('reimagined by Jeanne Willis') still sell extremely well, speaking to the enduring popularity of these series.

Sheila Ray, revised by David Rudd

Further Reading

Auchmuty, Rosemary, *A World of Girls*, The Women's Press (1992)
Blyton, Enid, *The Story of my Life*, Pitkin (1952)
Enid Blyton Society Journal issues 2-3, 10, 24, 41-5, 70
Ray, Sheila, *The Blyton Phenomenon*, Deutsch (1982)
Ray, Sheila, 'Enid Mary Blyton', in *The Oxford Dictionary of National Biography*, OUP (2004)
Rice, Eve, *Who's Who in Enid Blyton*, Orion Books, 2nd edition (2003)
Rudd, David, *Enid Blyton and the Mystery of Children's Literature*, Palgrave Macmillan (2000)
Stewart, Brian and Summerfield, Tony, *The Enid Blyton Dossier*, Hawk Books (1999)
Stoney, Barbara, *Enid Blyton: A Biography*, Hodder & Stoughton (1974). Revised ed. 1997
Summerfield, Tony, *Enid Blyton: An Illustrated Bibliography*: Parts 1-4, Milford (2002-5)
The Enid Blyton Society, 1995 https://www.enidblytonsociety.co.uk

N1 *The Naughtiest Girl in the School* (mixed), Newnes (1940). Illus. W Lindsay Cable
N2 *The Naughtiest Girl Again* (mixed), Newnes (1940). Illus. W Lindsay Cable
C1 *The Twins at St Clare's*, Methuen (1941). Illus. W Lindsay Cable
C2 *The O'Sullivan Twins*, Methuen (1942). Illus. W Lindsay Cable
C3 *Summer Term at St Clare's*, Methuen (1943). Illus. W Lindsay Cable
    Mischief at St Rollo's (as Mary Pollock), Newnes ([1943]). Illus. Hilda McGavin
C4 *The Second Form at St Clare's*, Methuen (1944). Illus. W Lindsay Cable
C5 *Claudine at St Clare's*, Methuen (1945). Illus. W Lindsay Cable
C6 *Fifth Formers of St Clare's*, Methuen (1945). Illus. W Lindsay Cable
N3 *The Naughtiest Girl is a Monitor* (mixed), Newnes (1945). Illus. Kenneth Lovell
M1 *First Term at Malory Towers*, Methuen (1946). Illus. Stanley Lloyd (endpapers Richard Cribb)
M2 *Second Form at Malory Towers*, Methuen (1947). Illus. Stanley Lloyd
M3 *Third Year at Malory Towers*, Methuen (1948). Illus. Stanley Lloyd
M4 *Upper Fourth at Malory Towers*, Methuen (1949). Illus. Stanley Lloyd
M5 *In the Fifth at Malory Towers*, Methuen (1950). Illus. Stanley Lloyd
M6 *Last Term at Malory Towers*, Methuen (1951). Illus. Stanley Lloyd
N4 *Here's the Naughtiest Girl!*, Hodder (1997). Illus. Max Schindler. Originally published in *Enid Blyton's Omnibus*, Newnes (1952) illus. Peter Kay

C = St Clare's series
M = Malory Towers series
N = Naughtiest Girl series

Blyton continuations

Pamela Cox
Born and brought up in Darlington, now living in Hereford, this author has, single-handedly, doubled Enid Blyton's Malory Towers series and increased her St Clare's books by half. Having written her first St Clare's filler for fun she was encouraged to produce two more, and was then commissioned by the publishers to write a new Malory Towers sequence, following the recent trend (seen in both adult and children's books) of providing sequels to popular books by deceased authors. The St Clare's books slot into Blyton's series and are here numbered to indicate their positions within it; the Malory Towers titles, on the other hand, follow on from Blyton's books and form a series focusing on Darrell Rivers's younger sister, Felicity, who made her school début in *Upper Fourth at Malory Towers*.

C4a *The Third Form at St Clare's,* Mammoth (2000). Not illus.
C4b *Kitty at St Clare's,* Mammoth (2000). Not illus.
C7   *The Sixth Form at St Clare's,* Mammoth (2000). Not illus.
M7   *New Term at Malory Towers,* Mammoth (2009). Not illus.
M8   *Summer Term at Malory Towers,* Mammoth (2009). Not illus.
M9   *Winter Term at Malory Towers,* Mammoth (2009). Not illus.
M10 *Fun and Games at Malory Towers,* Mammoth (2009). Not illus.
M11 *Secrets at Malory Towers,* Mammoth (2009). Not illus.
M12 *Goodbye, Malory Towers,* Mammoth (2009). Not illus.

Anne Digby (*see also* her own entry)
The Naughtiest Girl Keeps a Secret, Hodder (1999). Not illus.
The Naughtiest Girl Helps a Friend, Hodder (1999). Not illus.
The Naughtiest Girl Saves the Day, Hodder (1999). Not illus.
Well Done, the Naughtiest Girl!, Hodder (1999). Not illus.
The Naughtiest Girl Marches On, Hodder (1999). Not illus.
The Naughtiest Girl Wants to Win, Hodder (2000). Not illus.

Jeanne Willis
(N1) *The Diary of the Naughtiest Girl,* Hodder (2016). Illus. Alex T Smith

Also *New Class at Malory Towers,* Hachette (2019) comprising four short stories: 'A Bob and a Weave' by Patrice Lawrence; 'Bookworms' by Lucy Mangan; 'The Secret Princess' by Narinder Dhami; 'The Show Must Go On' by Rebecca Westcott. Not illus.

Freda C Bond
(Freda Constance Bond)
1894-1973
Freda Bond was born in Ipswich on 25 March 1894, the daughter of Frederick George Bond, a land agent and surveyor, and his wife Constance Eliza Hayward. She was educated at Ipswich High School and Girton College, Cambridge, where she read history, 1913-16. She was a civil servant in the Ministry of Labour from 1917 to 1933, during which time she worked abroad. In 1936-7 she was temporary manager of Church Shop, Newcastle-upon-Tyne, and in 1938-9 for short periods was in charge of investigations into the consumption of milk in South Shields. Later she worked as a freelance journalist. She died on 15 June 1973 in Henfield, Sussex. Her two series of family stories each include one school story.

L1 *The End House*,* Newnes (1943)
L2 *The Lancasters of Lynford*,* Newnes (1944)
L3 *Susan and Priscilla,* Newnes (1945). Not illus.
C1 *The Holiday that Wasn't*,* Newnes (1947)
C2 *The Week before Christmas*,* Newnes (1948)
C3 *The Carols Explore*,* Newnes (1949)

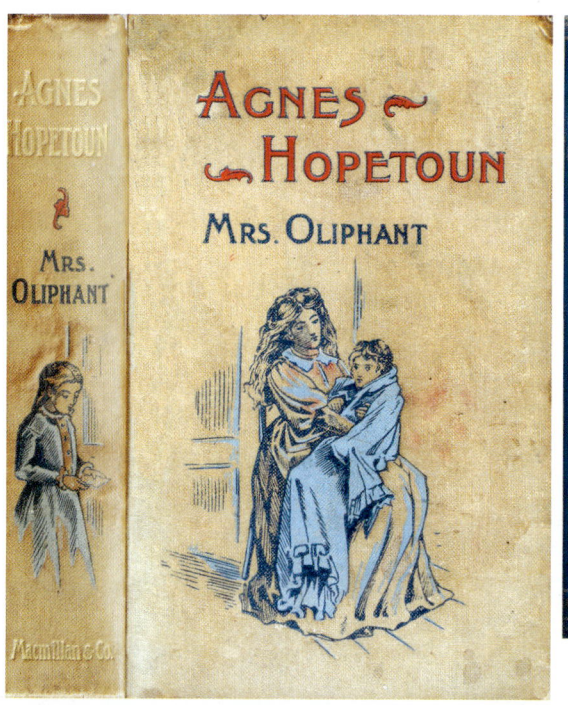

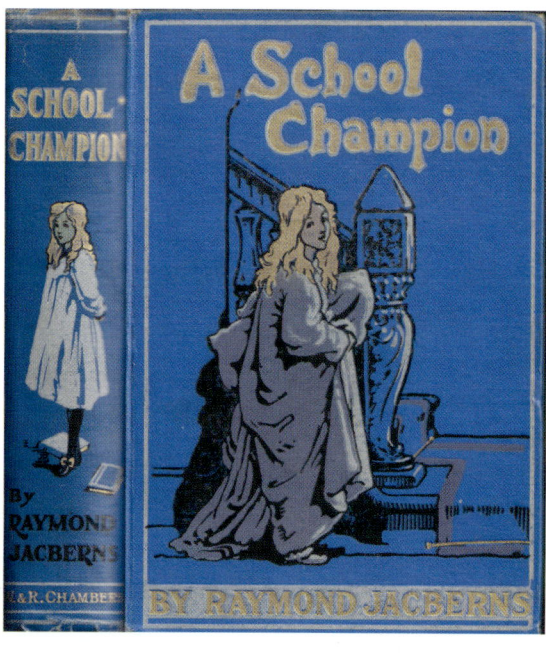

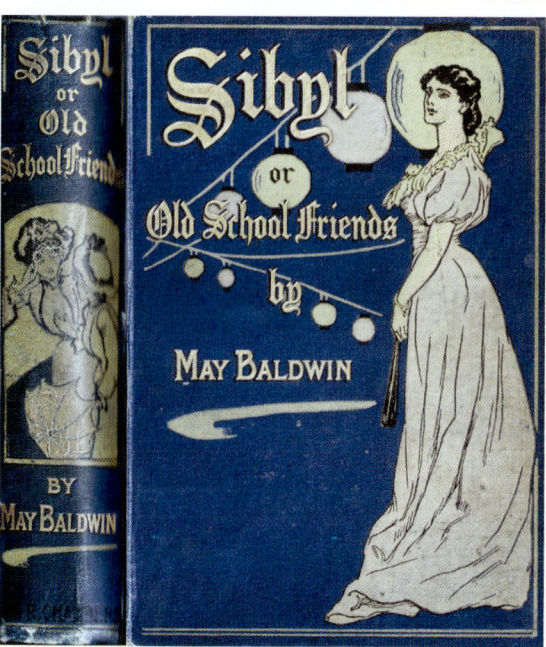

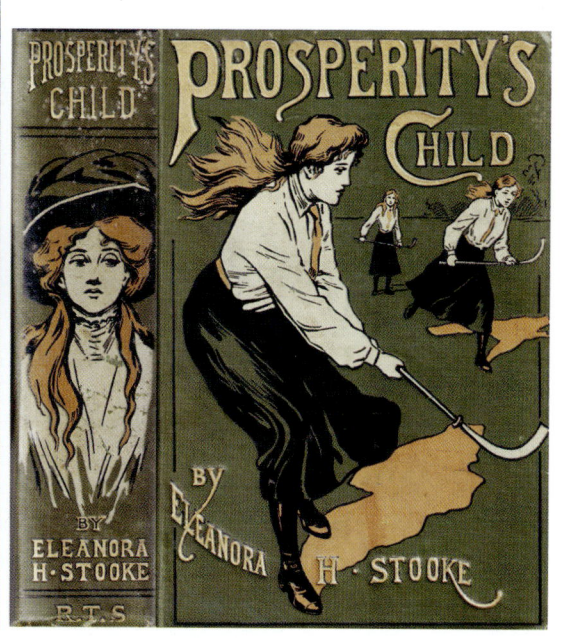

Early Decorated Boards
(from an era when dustwrappers rarely survived)

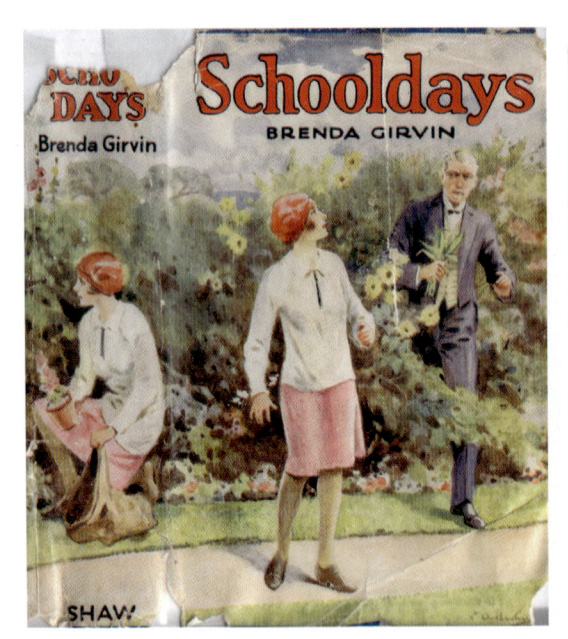

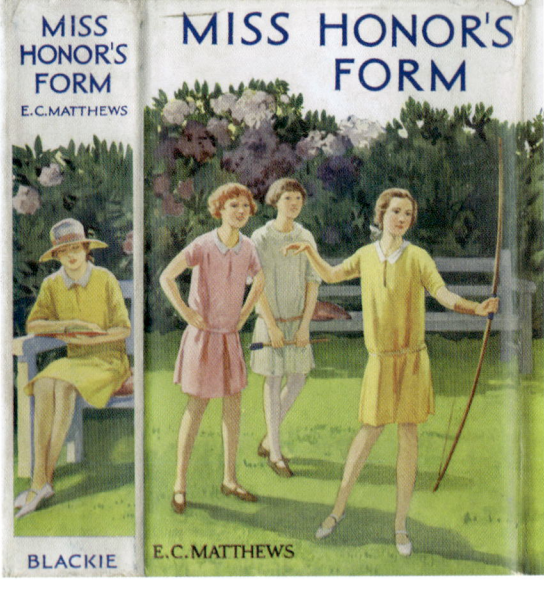

In the Garden

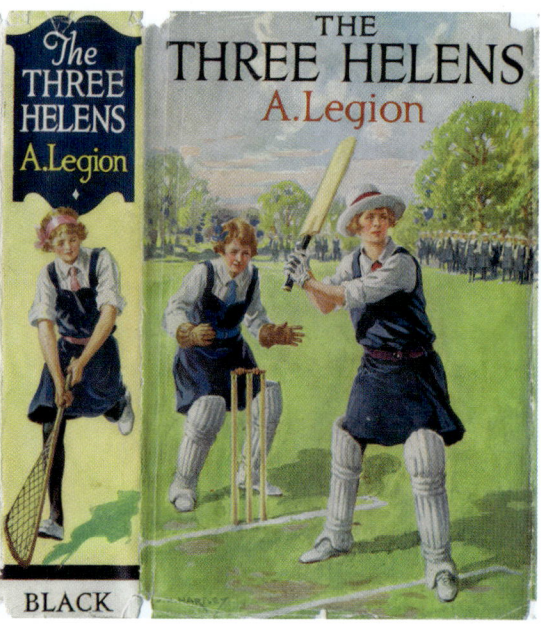

Leg before wicket?

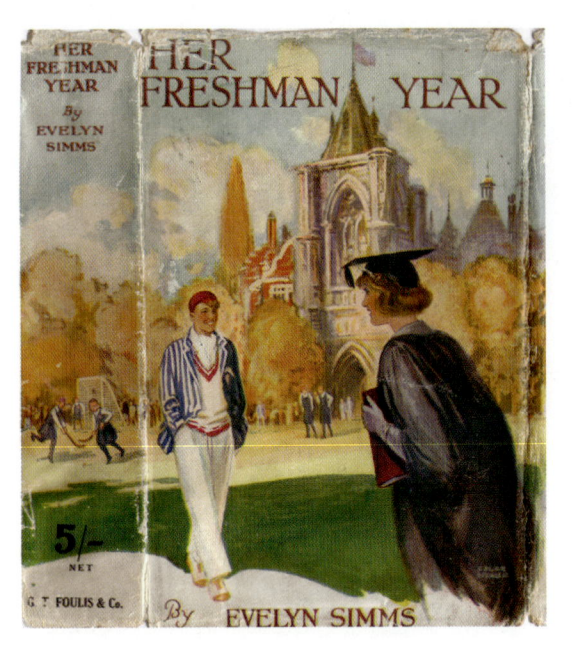

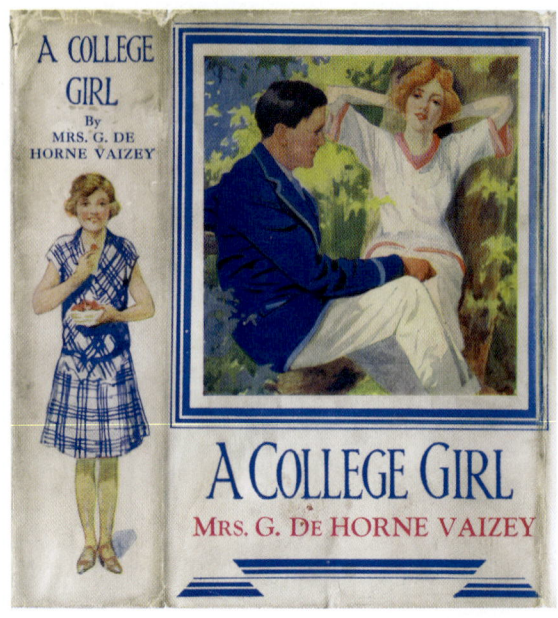

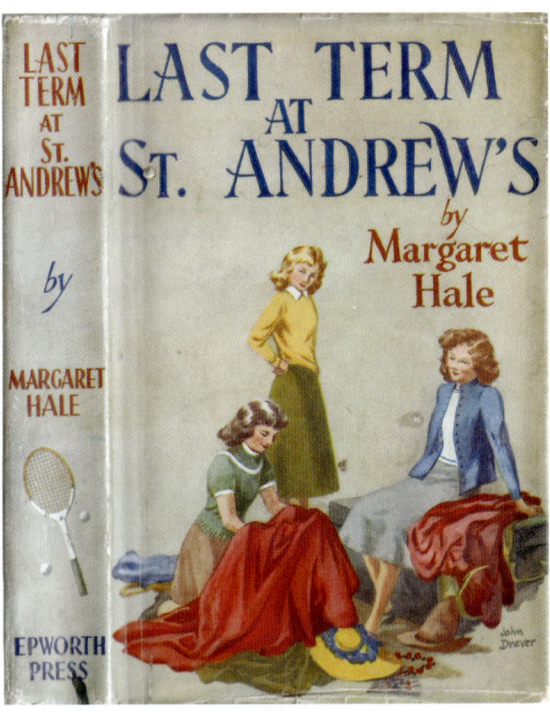

College Girls - or Almost

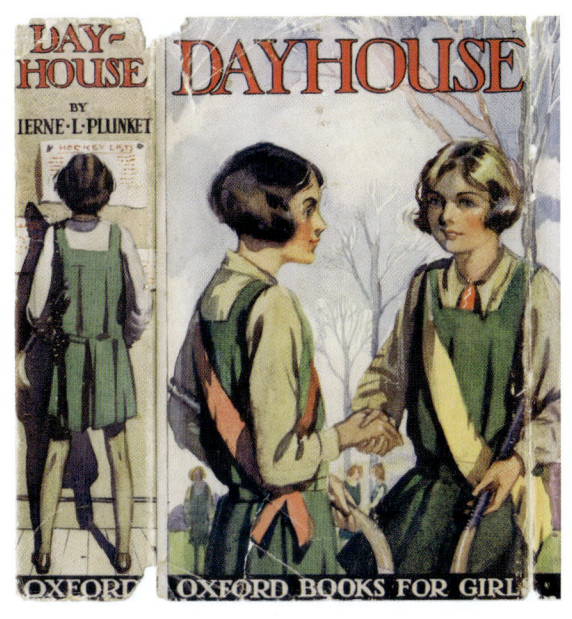

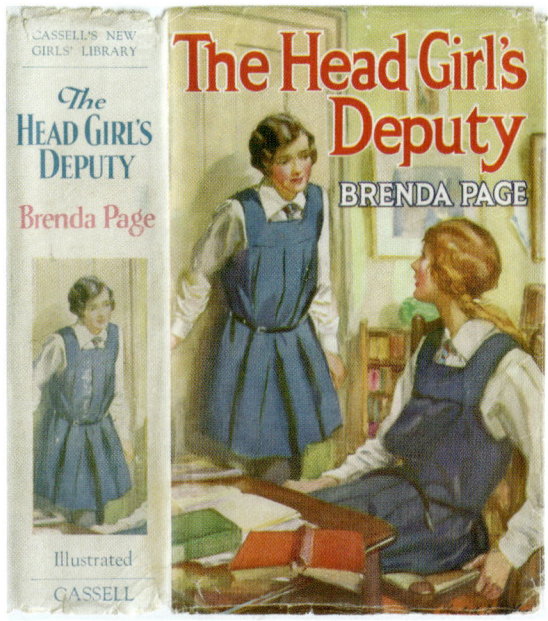

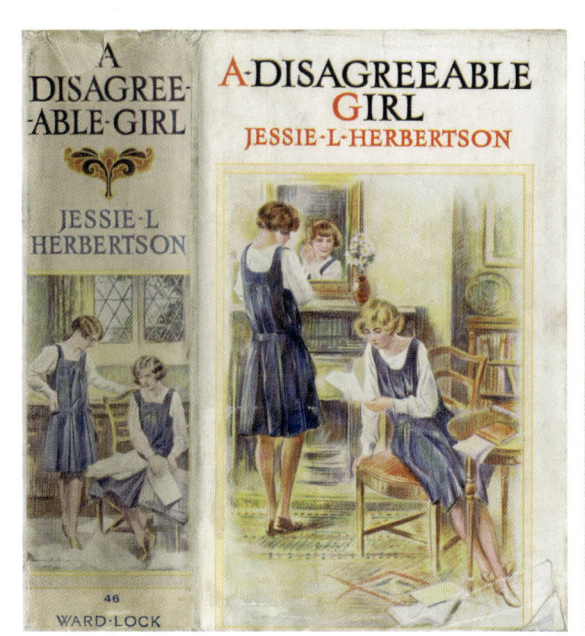

The School Tunic

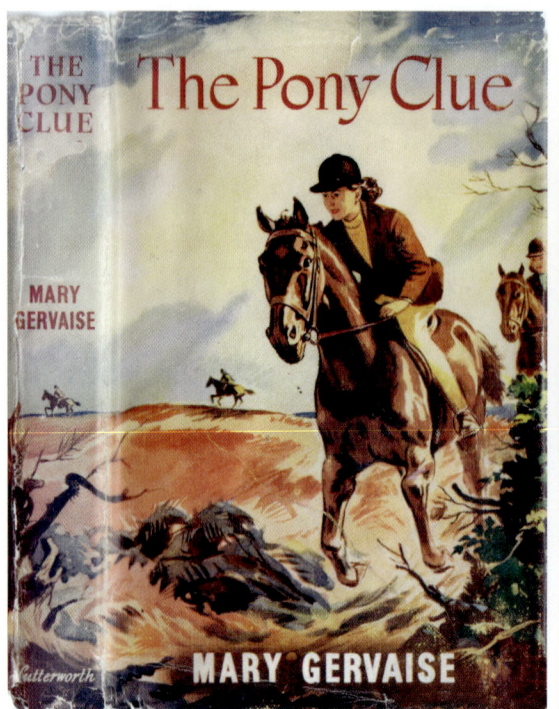

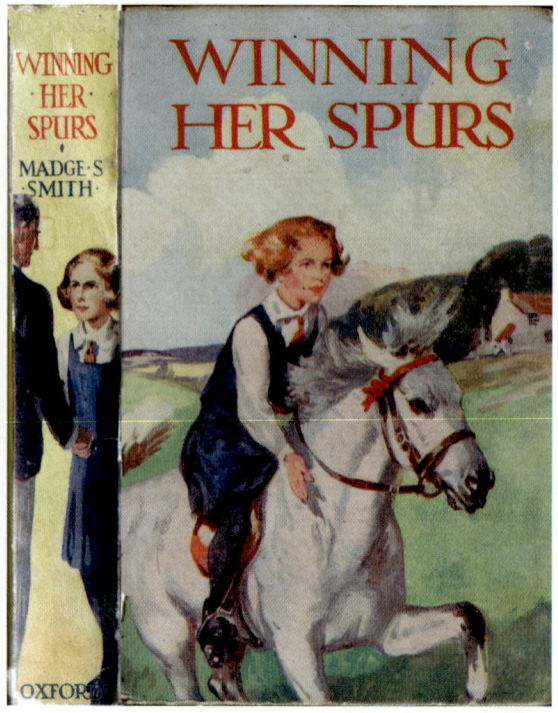

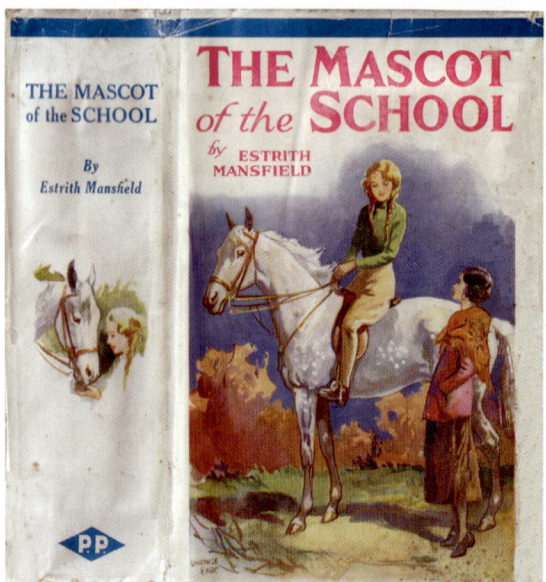

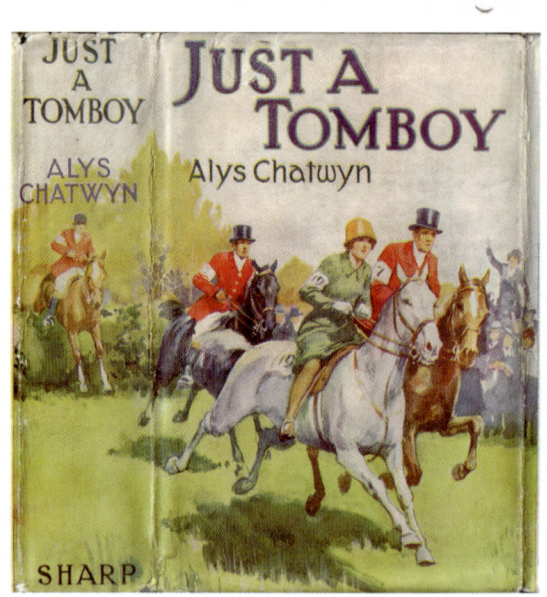

Heroines on Horseback

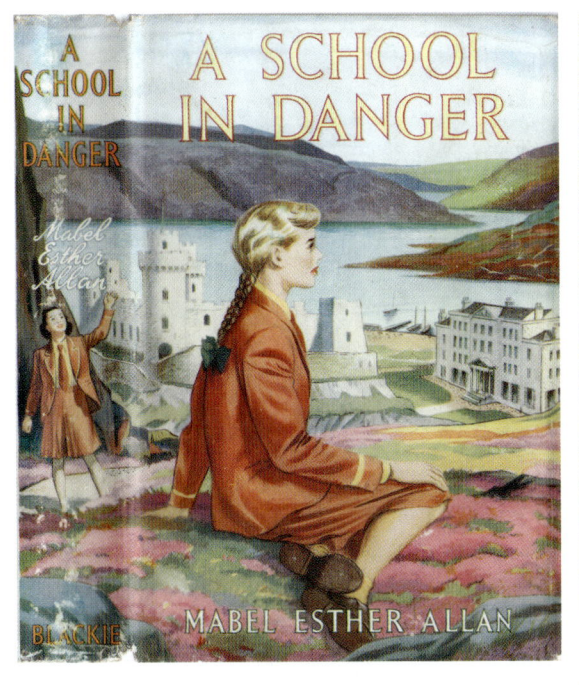

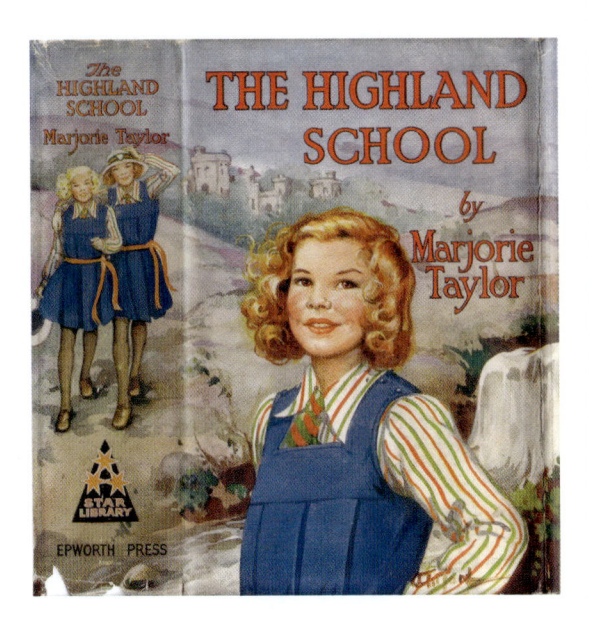

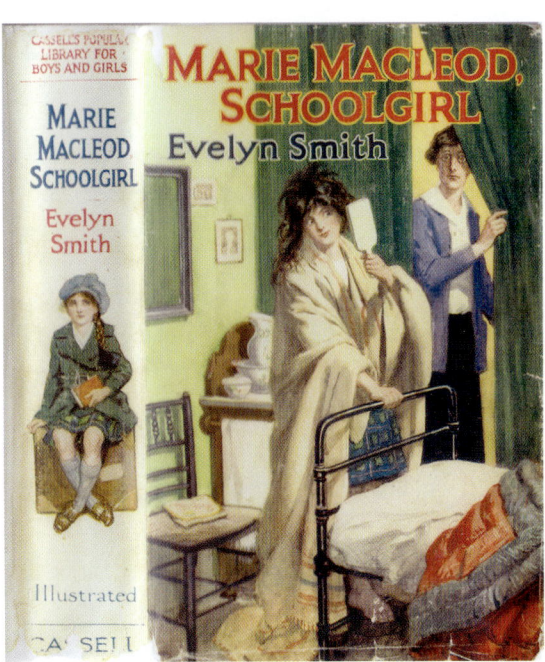

Schoolgirls in Scotland

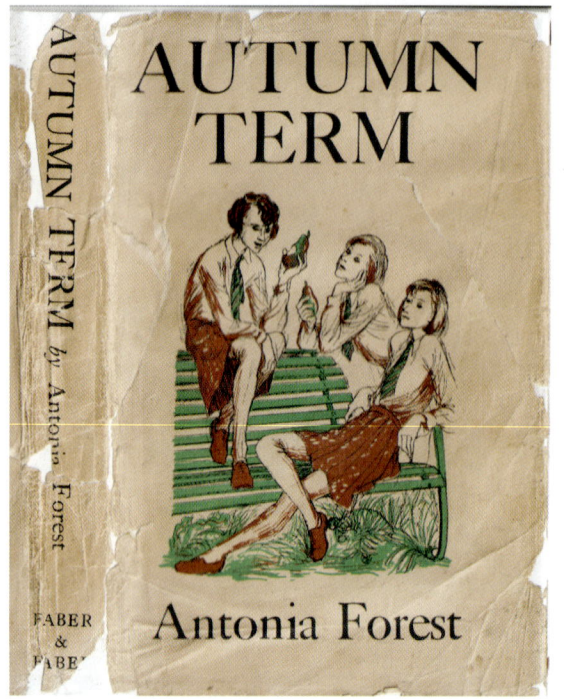

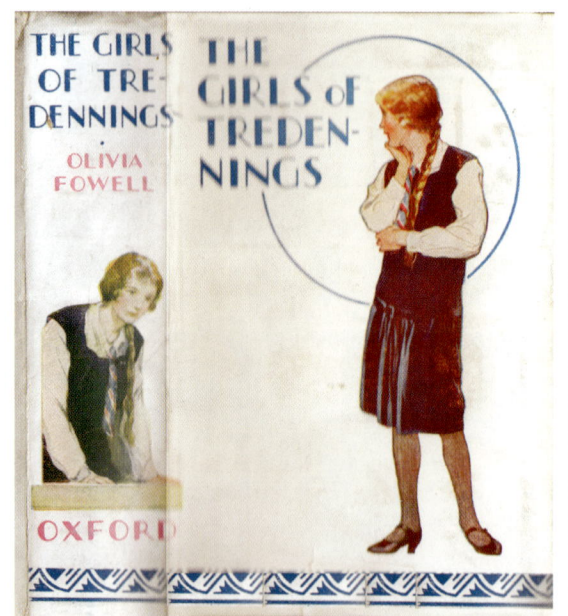

Favourite Fs - *Autumn Term* was Antonia Forest's own copy

C4 *Squibs at School*, Newnes ([1951]). Illus.
  The Wishing Well Adventure*, Newnes (1952)

Also an adult novel, *The Philanthropists* and numerous articles, stories and poems

C = Carols series
L = Lancasters series

Florence Bone
1876-1971

Florence Bone was born in Liverpool on 26 January 1875, the elder daughter of the Rev. Henry Bone, a Methodist minister, and his wife Lydia. She was educated at a Moravian school. She spent much of her life in Ripon, where she lived for at least 40 years before her death on 17 February 1971. She produced only three girls' school stories, each set in a different public school of between 150 and 200 pupils. Bone's plots are somewhat melodramatic, with burglars, lovable gypsies, and descendants of guillotined aristos and Bavarian princes, but thoroughly enjoyable: she writes well, and there is a streak of romantic Ruskinite socialism running through them, unusual for the genre. She was a supporter of women's suffrage and, despite appearances, defiantly unsnobbish: kind hearts are definitely worth more than coronets, though her heroines tend to end up with both. Her books are still worth reading today.

Margot's Secret, or The Fourth Form at Victoria College, Partridge ([1911]). Illus. S Spurrier
Curiosity Kate, Partridge ([1913]). Illus. Treyer Evans
Just like Fay, Nelson ([1928]). Illus. S Brier

Also many romantic and historical novels set in Yorkshire
See also *The Encyclopaedia of Boys' School Stories*, **FLORENCE E BONE**

Agnes Booth
(Agnes Clara Booth)
1888-1975

Agnes Booth was born in Willesden, London, the daughter of an excise officer, in September 1888, worked as an elementary school teacher, and from before 1949 lived in Sussex where she died in Goring-on-Sea on 6 July 1975.

The Secret of the Harvest Camp (High School form camping holiday), Faber (1948). Illus. Marjorie Owen
The Forest Mystery (mixed), Faber (1949). Illus. Reg Foster

M Cathcart Borer
(Mary Irene Cathcart Borer, sometime Myers)
1906-1994
Mary Cathcart Borer was the author of more than 50 books of fiction and non-fiction, including a history of girls' education, but this is her sole girls' school story. She was born in Stoke Newington, London, in 1906, married Oliver Humphrys Myers in 1935 and was divorced from him in 1939. She had a BSc from London University and a variety of jobs before the Second World War, when she became a script-writer for the British film industry. After a period as the story editor and a script-writer for the Rank Children's Film Foundation, she became a freelance writer and wrote scripts and plays for television, the theatre, radio and films. She lived in Hertfordshire, where she died in 1994.

The First Term at Northwood, Pitman (1948). Illus. 'W S'

Also many other books

Anne Bracken
These Australian series are not, strictly speaking, school stories, but have enough school involved, if very peripherally, to scrape in here. Bracken prefers adventures to school, and ensures that her heroines have plenty of them.

J1 *Jancy Wins Through* (part school: Australia), Jons Production ([1945]). Not illus.
T1 *The Twins Take Charge** (Australia), Jons Production ([1946]). Not illus.
T2 *The Twins to the Rescue* (school trip on houseboat: Australia), Jons Production ([1947]). Not illus.
J2 *Jancy Scores Again* (part school: Australia), Jons Production ([1947]). Illus.
J3 *Jancy in Pursuit** (Australia), Jons Production ([1950]). Not illus.
J4 *Jancy Stands Alone* (Australia), Jons Production ([195-]). Not illus.

J = Jancy series
T = Twins series

Also other young children's books

Violet Bradby
(Violet Alice Milford Bradby)
1871-1956
Violet Milford, born 26 December 1871, was one of the elder sisters of Humphrey Sumner Milford, publisher of the London branch of the Oxford University Press, which no doubt explains why all her children's books except the first (which was published by Blackie) were published by that

firm. She was a prolific writer, but only *A Summer Friendship*, set in a French convent orphanage, is remotely a school story. She married Henry Christopher Bradby, a poet and housemaster at Rugby School, in 1895; her only daughter (there were also three sons) was the poet Anne Ridler. She died on 21 May 1956.

A Summer Friendship, OUP 1925. Illus. M D Johnson (*see also* **CONVENT SCHOOL STORIES**)

A W Bradley
Won by Pluck, Pilgrim Press ([1925]). Illus. 'R J'

Norma Bradley
1   *The New Girl at Greylands*, Arthur J Stockwell ([1948]). Illus. M W Whittington
2   *Ghostly Guests at Greylands School*, Arthur J Stockwell ([1950]). Illus. M W Whittington

Mary Bramston
(Mary Eliza Bramston)
1841-1912
Mary Bramston was born in 1841, the elder daughter of the Rev. John Bramston of Witham, Essex, who in 1872 became Dean of Winchester. In 1868 Mary accompanied her brother John Trant Bramston to Winchester to assist him in his work as a housemaster at the College. Here she came in touch with the Anglican writer Charlotte Mary Yonge. Her brother's marriage in 1875 left Mary without a job. Although her family was now also in Winchester it contained her stepmother and grown-up half-sister Anna (1847-1931) and clearly Mary preferred to move on. In 1878 she went to Truro to run the boarding house at the newly founded Truro High School (*see* **MRS HENRY CLARKE**), a connection brought about by her friendship with the family of Edward White Benson, then newly Bishop of Truro and later Archbishop of Canterbury. Mary followed the Bensons to Croydon and became head of a boarding house for the Girls' High School (*see* **JOSEPHINE ELDER**). Some years after Benson's death in 1896, Mary Bramston retired to Winchester where she helped her half-sister and friend Amelie Leroy (the writer Esmé Stuart) with their work for Winchester High School (now St Swithun's; *see* **WINIFRED NORLING**). Amongst other interests, she studied theology, becoming in 1906 one of the first five women to gain the Anglican diploma of Student in Theology. She died in Winchester in 1912.

Bramston's contemporary fiction, both for adults and children, tends to deal with aspects of education and moral and spiritual development. Her interest in theology (she was a High Anglican, as one might expect from a friend of Charlotte Yonge) is very clear in her writing. She is particularly interesting from a school-story point of view in that she was possibly the first British writer to develop a series, beginning with *The Snowball Society*, about the same group of girls and women, which included a significant amount of school interest. The school focus is admittedly patchy in the three 'school stories'; where the thrust of each novel is the spiritual and moral growth of an individual, brought about by the careful guidance of an older woman (mother or teacher).
Source: unpublished work by Dr Julia Courtney

1   *The Snowball Society**, SPCK ([1877]). Illus.
2   *Home and School* (part school), SPCK ([1883]). Illus. Alfred Pearse
3   *Rosamond Ferrars**, SPCK (1875). Illus.
4   *Rosamond's Girls*, SPCK ([1905]). Illus. Mabel R Peacock
    Barbara's Behaviour (part school), SPCK ([1907]). Illus. Harold Piffard

Also adult novels, miscellaneous material for girls, verses and theological writings
See also **EARLY SCHOOL STORIES**

Esther Brann *see* **CONVENT SCHOOL STORIES**

Angela Brazil
1868-1947
Angela Brazil was born in Preston on 30 November 1868 (not, as in Gillian Freeman's biography, 1869), the youngest child of Clarence Brazil, a cotton mill manager, and Angelica McKinnel, who already had two sons and a daughter. The family lived in the north-west until Clarence's death in 1899, notably, between 1877 and 1886, in Manchester. Angela's first education took place at a small private school (The Turrets) in Wallasey, when the Brazils lived at Egremont on the Mersey. In Manchester she attended first the preparatory department of the High School and then Ellerslie, a more exclusive girls' school near Victoria Park, boarding in the school hostel after her family had moved to Bolton. From 1883 holidays were spent at Llanbedr in the Conwy valley in North Wales, first in a cottage and then in a larger house, which became the family base between 1899 and 1911. At some point, probably rather briefly, Angela acted as a governess; her experiences may be reflected in *Loyal to the School* (1920) but were not mentioned in her autobiographical volume *My Own Schooldays* (1925). In 1911 she moved to Coventry to keep house for her doctor brother, being joined after their mother's death in 1915 by her elder sister Amy. In the 1920s the Llanbedr house was given up and replaced by a cottage at Polperro, Cornwall; both places were used as the settings for several books. Before World War I Angela had travelled in Italy, France, Austria, Ireland, Egypt and the Holy Land with her mother and sister; after it Angela visited Italy again, Paris and Switzerland. All these experiences (except the Austrian trip) were used in her books.

After Angela left school, she and her sister studied at Heatherley's Art School in London, and sketching (primarily Amy's hobby) remained one of Angela's interests. She was a keen botanist, as again the books testify. She liked to think of herself as musical, although her hearers disagreed. In the 1920s she had a young pianist protegé, but apparently displayed no real understanding of his needs or of the world of professional music; even so, several of her characters (for instance, Mildred Lancaster in *The Girls of St Cyprian's*, Claudia Castleton in *The Head Girl at the Gables*

and Gwenda Carrington in *Schoolgirl Kitty*) embark on serious musical careers. Music and art are the only careers Brazil seems to have approved of for girls, writing being barely mentioned and even teaching taking very much a second place. Home life and duties tended to be portrayed as paramount, in a way which must have been old-fashioned even to her first readers.

With her brother and sister she took part in the cultural life of Coventry, including the Natural History and Scientific Society, and the City Guild (an antiquarian society), encouraging younger members. She extended hospitality to many young people and visited local private schools, but unlike many girls' writers seems not to have become involved in any girls' organisations. She was a regular church-goer at St Michael's (from 1918 Coventry Cathedral) until it was destroyed in the Blitz in 1940. She died on 12 March 1947, living to see victory in World War II but not the permanent disappearance of the safe, middle-class world which had sheltered both her and her fictional schoolgirls for so long.

Angela Brazil was essentially a product of late Victorian England. The daughter of a cotton manufacturer (not that she was prepared to admit it, with all the Victorian distaste for trade) and the sister of a solicitor and a doctor, she had the unquestioning acceptance of the class structure, the jingoistic patriotism and the ineffable optimism of an age and a class which had not yet had its self-confidence shaken. The cataclysm of 1914-18, which she deals with in her war-time books with as much detail as she thought appropriate for her young readers, does not seem to have made much personal impact: her brothers were too old and her only nephew (in any case an invalid) too young to be involved. When it came to the Depression, she was living in Coventry, which with its thriving motor and aircraft industries was far less affected than the north-west of her birth; not for Brazil the problems of the girl whose family has to retrench at the cost of her education. Nor, for all her love of nature and the countryside, did she have any real appreciation of the problems of rural communities.

Moreover, not only was her social position such as to boost her self-confidence and cushion her materially, but (as her biographer Gillian Freeman has observed) her family situation as the youngest of a close-knit family seems to have had the same effect on her character. All her life she was sheltered by her parents and older siblings; only at school did she move outside their protection. In her writing, she went her own way and was impervious (or claimed she was) to criticism. Girls liked her books, and that was enough.

The great question about her is: why were her books so popular? For popular they undoubtedly were. Adult readers may be aware of their repetitive plots, flowery style and extraordinary slang, and may see little merit in her works, yet she was so successful that her name has become synonymous with her chosen genre. She was certainly well served by her main publisher, Blackie, who kept her books in print well into the paperback era and ended by claiming that she had originated the girls' school story; but Blackie would not have kept the books going if they had not been selling. What was the secret of her success?

The answer seems to lie in the extent to which she retained the point of view of the pre-sexual adolescent schoolgirl. There is nothing in the books which could not have been written by a very able fourteen-year-old—no irony, subtlety, originality or variation in pace and style. When she included an account of a hockey match written by a real schoolgirl (*A Popular Schoolgirl*) there is no difference between that passage and the rest of the books, save that Angela, not having played games at Ellerslie, was somewhat unsound on their technical details and tended to skate over them.

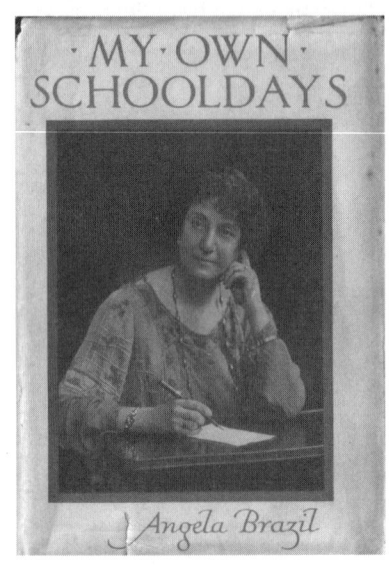

Combined with this identity of outlook, described by her in *My Own Schooldays* as having 'all my heart ... with the young folks,' was an immense appetite for the minutiae of school life and a facility in reproducing them. (This is particularly apparent in her short stories, which are short on plot if long on incident.) On top of this, and perhaps the most important ingredient in her success, she set the everyday world of school in romantic settings and introduced a lavish spice of adventure. Girls were able to identify with the heroines and recognise or aspire to their surroundings; more, they could entertain the delicious possibility that they too might discover the missing will, unmask a German spy or, at the very least, save the life of their best friend. It is interesting to note that almost all Brazil's heroines are excessively ordinary. The beneficiary of the last chapter's inevitable discovery is nearly always somebody else. Of course there are exceptions to the rule that the dénouement of the book is the finding of lost papers, but they are comparatively few. On the whole, there was no need, if you were a Brazil heroine, to be a Ruritanian princess or even especially gifted: all you had to do was to make the most of your opportunities and you too could play your part in a modern fairy-tale. If all else failed, you could always hope to find a rare plant on your nature ramble.

One factor which played remarkably little part in Brazil's success was the lure of the series. She preferred to use a new setting for each story, with a new set of characters and a similar plot. (This, of course, was part of their charm.) There are only three pairs of books among her 46 full-length school stories: *A Fortunate Term/Monitress Merle*, where the thrust of the second book is the modernisation of the school from the first; *At School with Rachel/St Catherine's College*, where Rachel changes schools and the plot contains Brazil's only Ruritanian escapade; *The Little Green School/Jean's Golden Term*, which uses the same school but different heroines. *Monitress Merle* also has a substantial character overlap with *The Head Girl at the Gables*; and *A Fortunate Term* has a slight connection with *The Girls of St Cyprian's*. Otherwise Brazil dressed her most constant plot (the discovery of missing papers or the clearing up of a mystery) in different guises for almost every book, diversifying so brilliantly that the basic similarity went unheeded. She seems to have disliked the idea of making the main plot of a school story depend on school routine: the winding-up of the mystery is always something external. But every kind of school patronised by middle-class girls (except convent schools and mixed schools) was used as a background, with the small private school predominating: as Brazil grew older, the schools tended to get smaller. Romantic settings in picturesque countryside also came to predominate (she set several stories abroad), although the earlier books included a fair number of High Schools and the occasional big public school, sometimes set in a large city.

Brazil was uninterested in the mechanics of running a school, and the only glimpse we get of staff conferring without pupils is the discussion at the beginning of *The Head Girl at the Gables* as to who shall fill the eponymous position. This is one of Brazil's more interesting books, dealing as it does with the combined themes of the problems of a slightly unexpected, slightly unpopular Head Girl and the discovery by all the leading characters (three girls and one boy) of unexpected talents. It is entirely typical of Brazil that it is the school problems which are lost sight of in the excitement of discovering hidden artistic gifts, and again typical that the book contains the obligatory discovery, though only of German spies, not a missing will. Untypically, the book is one of the very few to contain an embryonic romance; usually boys are absent or are kept firmly on the level of jolly chums.

Friendship, not love, was Brazil's great theme, and one which has been misinterpreted. No one who has had anything to do with small girls can doubt the importance of The Best Friend; until at least 1939 girls matured later, socially and physically, and this phase tended to be prolonged. Too much has been made of Brazil's use of names such as Lesbia and Regina (her taste in nomenclature was always exotic) and of the physical contact which takes place, at least in the earliest books. The—to us—extraordinary descriptions of girls sharing beds (for instance in *The Manor House School*, 1910) occur only in the early books and reflect customs which were even then going out of fashion.

It should be noted again that Brazil never stepped outside the charmed family circle. Her brothers and sister—doctor, solicitor and nurse—must have come into contact with the harsh outside world, but Angela apparently never even wanted to. Friends came inside the family circle; she did not leave it. Perhaps this was why, for instance, she so resented her eldest brother's wife: she was not just to be despised as of lower class, but also threatened the integrity of the home sanctuary. If at any time Angela dreamed of marriage herself, she certainly hid the dream efficiently. What she revealed of her dreams concerned friends and schools—and what she wrote about were friends and schools, enhanced beyond probability but not beyond recognition. They are a schoolgirl's dreams, and it is no wonder that schoolgirls adored them and certain headmistresses came to denounce them. It also explains why Brazil's popularity among adult enthusiasts is smaller than one might expect: in the end schoolgirls grow out of dreams and she supplied nothing else to take their place.

Further Reading
Clare, Hilary, 'Angela Brazil' in *The Oxford Dictionary of National Biography*, OUP (2004)
Foster, Shirley and Simons, Judy, *What Katy Read: Feminist Re-readings of 'Classic' Stories for Girls*, Macmillan (1995), chapter 9
Freeman, Gillian, *The Schoolgirl Ethic*, Allen Lane (1976)
Book and Magazine Collector 3, 74
Simons, Judy, in *Popular Children's Literature in Britain*, Briggs & Butt (eds), Ashgate, (2008)

    *A Terrible Tomboy**, Gay & Bird (1904). Illus. Author & Amy Brazil
    The Fortunes of Philippa, Blackie (1907 on title page but published in 1906). Illus. Arthur A Dixon
    The Third Class at Miss Kaye's, Blackie (1909). Illus. Arthur A Dixon
    The Nicest Girl in the School, Blackie (1910). Illus. Arthur A Dixon
    *Our School Record**, Dow & Lester ([1909])
    *Bosom Friends**, Nelson ([1910]). Illus. Jennie Wylie
    The Manor House School, Blackie (1911). Illus. Arthur A Dixon
    A Fourth Form Friendship, Blackie (1912). Illus. Frank E Wiles
    The New Girl at St Chad's, Blackie (1912). Illus. John Campbell
    A Pair of Schoolgirls, Blackie ([1912]). Illus. John Campbell
    The Leader of the Lower School, Blackie ([1914]). Illus. John Campbell
    The Youngest Girl in the Fifth, Blackie ([1914]). Illus. Stanley Davis
(M) *The Girls of St Cyprian's*, Blackie ([1914]). Illus. Stanley Davis
    The School by the Sea, Blackie ([1914]). Illus. (possibly Treyer Davis)
    For the Sake of the School, Blackie ([1915]). Illus. Stanley Davis
    The Jolliest Term on Record, Blackie (1915). Illus. Balliol Salmon
    The Luckiest Girl in the School, Blackie ([1916]). Illus. Balliol Salmon
    The Madcap of the School, Blackie ([1917]). Illus. Balliol Salmon
    *The Slap-Bang Boys**, Nelson ([1917])
    A Patriotic Schoolgirl, Blackie ([1918]). Illus. Balliol Salmon
    For the School Colours, Blackie ([1918]). Illus. Balliol Salmon
    *The Language of Flowers**, Oxford (1919)
    *The Treasure of the Woods**, Oxford (1919)

A Harum-Scarum Schoolgirl, Blackie ([1919]). Illus. John Campbell
(M) *The Head Girl at the Gables*, Blackie ([1919]). Illus. Balliol Salmon
*Two Little Scamps and a Puppy**, Nelson ([1919]). Illus. E Blampied
A Popular Schoolgirl, Blackie ([1920]). Illus. Balliol Salmon
*A Gift from the Sea**, Nelson ([1920])
The Princess of the School, Blackie ([1920]). Illus. Frank E Wiles
Loyal to the School, Blackie ([1921]). Illus. Treyer Evans
M1 *A Fortunate Term*, Blackie ([1921]). Illus. Treyer Evans
M2 *Monitress Merle*, Blackie ([1922]). Illus. Treyer Evans
S1 *The School in the South*, Blackie ([1922]). Illus. W Smithson Broadhead
Schoolgirl Kitty, Blackie ([1923]). Illus. W E Wightman
*The Khaki Boys etc.** (short stories), Nelson ([1923])
Captain Peggie, Blackie ([1924]). Illus. W E Wightman
*My Own Schooldays** (autobiography), Blackie ([1925]). Photograph
(S2) *Joan's Best Chum*, Blackie ([1926]). Illus. W E Wightman
Queen of the Dormitory etc. (short stories), Cassell (1926). Illus. P B Hickling
Ruth of St Ronan's, Blackie ([1927]). Illus. Frank Oldham
R1 *At School with Rachel*, Blackie ([1928]). Illus. W E Wightman
R2 *St Catherine's College*, Blackie ([1929]). Illus. Frank E Wiles
G1 *The Little Green School*, Blackie ([1931]). Illus. Frank E Wiles
Nesta's New School, Blackie ([1932]). Illus. W Spence (reissued as *Amanda's New School*, Armada, 1970)
G2 *Jean's Golden Term*, Blackie ([1934]). Illus. Frank E Wiles
The School at the Turrets, Blackie ([1935]). Illus. Francis E Hiley
An Exciting Term, Blackie ([1936]). Illus. Francis E Hiley
Jill's Jolliest School, Blackie (1937). Illus Francis E Hiley
The School on the Cliff, Blackie (1938). Illus. Francis E Hiley
The School on the Moor, Blackie (1939). Illus. H Coller
The New School at Scawdale, Blackie (1940). Illus. M Mackinlay
Five Jolly Schoolgirls, Blackie (1941). Illus. W Lindsay Cable
The Mystery of the Moated Grange, Blackie ([1942]). Illus. W Lindsay Cable
The Secret of the Border Castle, Blackie ([1943]). Illus. Charles Willis
The School in the Forest, Blackie ([1944]). Illus. J Dewar Mills
Three Terms at Uplands, Blackie ([1945]). Illus. D L Mays
The School on the Loch, Blackie ([1946]). Illus. W Lindsay Cable

G = Little Green School pair
M = Merle pair and connected works
R = Rachel pair
S = *School in the South* and connected work

Nancy Breary
(Anne Florence Breary)
1907-1988

Nancy Breary was born in Brixham, Devon on 7 March 1907, eldest daughter of Arthur Henry Breary, a manager for Barclay's Bank, and Edith Florence Robinson. Her sister Gertrude (always called Gretchen) was born in 1908, and her brother Gerald in 1913. The family moved to London while she was a baby, initially to Clapham Park, then to Streatham. In 1918 she was sent as a boarder to Kingsdown School in Dorking, a school of about 90 pupils on which most of her fictional schools would be based. On leaving school in 1924 she took a domestic science course, intending to become a dietitian, but instead became a mannequin in a court dressmaker's in Bond Street. She was also running the Breary household, as her mother was an invalid (she died in the early 1930s), and writing in her spare time, becoming a full-time writer after the publication of *Give a Form a Bad Name* in 1943. She shared a house with her father and Gretchen, whose income as an artist (the 'G E Breary' whose illustrations are to be found in many books and annuals of the period) was the mainstay of the family. In the 1950s the family moved to Canada for some years, but returned to Britain in 1955, settling first in Rye and finally in Winchelsea. Nancy Breary died of a stroke on 8 December 1988; there is a garden bench in her memory in Winchelsea churchyard.

Any girl going to boarding school for the first time would be unwise to base her expectations on Breary's books. Certainly there are many realistic aspects to the stories: the agonies of jealousy felt by Sally (*Two Thrilling Terms* et seq), Primrose (*Study Number Six*) or Lydia (*Hazel, Head Girl*) are treated with understanding, if not approval; and she depicts beautifully the anguish of being an outsider, whether through lack of money (*Rachel Changes Schools*), age (*The Amazing Friendship*) or personality (*So This is School!*). She is interested in the conflict between duty and pleasure; and Lyndsay's dilemma, in *The Impossible Prefect*, between her urge to write and her role as school prefect, is both probable and convincing. She tracks the corrosive power of falsehood, from the first small lie to the final web of deceit which traps Bridget (*This Time Next Term*) or Carole (*The Form that Liked to be First*). She tackles that stand-by of the school-story writer, the unconventional misfit who needs to become part of the school community, such as Gay (*Junior Captain*) or Philippa (*The Fourth was Fun for Philippa*).

Nevertheless, her school stories are not intended primarily as sensitive studies of flawed individuals. Nor do they attempt to depict much of the normal life of a boarding school. Games are there in the background, but only one match is described, in eight lines of dialogue (*A School Divided*); lessons exist, but mainly as a setting for funny things to happen; examinations are unheard of. There are plenty of plays, a variety of film stars, Drusilla Cathcart in the series which begins with *Two Thrilling Terms* being the most memorable, a fourteen-year-old concert pianist (*Dimity Drew's First Term*) and even a form opera; but there is little attempt to treat these with sober realism. The girls in these books spend most of their time pursuing form feuds, running secret societies, having midnight expeditions or hunting ghosts in the boot-room; they fall through roofs, get stranded on islands, and develop frantic plans to get themselves out of trouble. The books, in other words, are written for the most part to amuse.

Not everyone shares Nancy Breary's sense of humour; for those who do, no other writer can match her distinctive turn of phrase. Only extensive quotation will give the full flavour of the writing; here, a small sample must suffice. This is Tess attempting to burgle the sanatorium:

> It was dark in the san, and Tess was not very sure of the lay-out, but she admitted to herself … that such minor hindrances did not matter to a person with such an unusual detective flair as her own. Now for some data. Gentle breathing told her that Miss Logan was asleep; experience told her that the patient's fruit would be placed within reach of the bed, and a resounding crash told her that she had knocked over a small table laden with china. (*So This is School!*)

The balance of the final sentence, with its deadpan climax, is characteristic; so is the way in which a character's inanities are revealed through her own thought processes. Perhaps, though, it is Breary's irony which one relishes most; sometimes in the narrative, frequently in the plot, most often in the dialogue:

> 'A sonnet is a short poem composed of twelve iambic pentameter lines followed by a rhyming cutlet,' [Ruth] declaimed …
> 'Thank you, Ruth, for a most illuminating statement. I have, of course, come across cutlets in various guises, but I have not until now had the pleasure of meeting one that aspired to literary status.' (*The Lower Fourth Excels Itself*)

Breary is quite capable of self-parody. The plot of *Dimity Drew's First Term* is not original—there are other school stories where an unpopular teacher turns out to be a (pseudonymous) Famous Writer—but Breary's details are inspired:

> 'I have a question. Dimity Drew, in which of Thea Gretard's books did the Lower Fourth mistakenly hang the Head?'
> That was an easy one.
> 'In *Nobody Meant to be Nasty*.' (*Dimity Drew's First Term*)

The only writer who created titles exactly like that was, of course, Nancy Breary, her mockery here turning on herself.

Nancy Breary's books mingle serious ideas with ironic humour and slapstick comedy in about equal measure; her own witty, charming personality lies beneath them all. There are other writers of school stories (though not nearly enough) who make us laugh; but Breary's voice is unique.

Source: Gretchen Breary, Nancy's sister

Further Reading
Folly 7, 8, 14

    Give a Form a Bad Name, Newnes (1943). Not illus.
1   *Two Thrilling Terms*, Blackie ([1943]). Illus. J Dewar Mills
    No Peace for the Prefects, Newnes (1944). Not illus.
    A School Divided, Newnes (1944). Not illus.
    This Time Next Term, Blackie ([1945]). Illus. P B Hickling
2   *The Lower Fourth Excels Itself*, Newnes (1945). Not illus.
    The Snackboat Sails at Noon*, Newnes (1946). Illus. Alfred Sindall
    Junior Captain, Blackie ([1946]). Illus. D L Mays
    The Impossible Prefect, Blackie ([1947]). Illus. Leo Bates
3   *Juniors will be Juniors*, Newnes (1947). Not illus.
    It was Fun in the Fourth, Nelson ([1948]). Illus. Joan Martin May
    Rachel Changes Schools, Blackie ([1948]). Illus. D L Mays
    The Form that Liked to be First, Blackie ([1948]). Illus. W Spence
4   *Mainly About the Fourth*, Newnes (1949). Not illus.
    Five Sisters at Sedgewick, Blackie ([1950]). Illus. W Spence
    Dimity Drew's First Term, Newnes ([1951]). Illus.
    The Reluctant Schoolgirl, Blackie ([1951]). Illus. Louis Ward
    Hazel, Head Girl, Blackie ([1952]). Illus. W Spence
    At School with Petra, Blackie ([1953]). Illus. Newton Whittaker
    Fourth Form Detectives, Blackie ([1954]). Illus. Newton Whittaker
    The Rival Fourths, Blackie (1955). Illus. Frank Haseler
    Study Number Six, Blackie (1957). Illus. Betty Ladler
    The Mystery of the Motels*, Blackie (1958). Illus. Victor Bertoglio
    So This is School!, Blackie (1959). Illus. Drake Brookshaw
    The Amazing Friendship, Blackie (1960). Illus. Drake Brookshaw
    The Fourth was Fun for Philippa, Blackie (1961). Illus. Drake Brookshaw
    Too Many Girls*, Nelson (Canada) [c1962]. Illus. Gretchen E Breary

Elinor M Brent-Dyer
(Elinor Mary Brent-Dyer)
1894-1969

Elinor M Brent-Dyer published a hundred books of many different kinds, but unquestionably she is remembered today mainly for her Chalet School series. Born on 6 April 1894, the elder child of Charles Morris Brent Dyer and his wife, Eleanor (Nelly) Watson Rutherford, she grew up as Gladys Eleanor May Dyer[1] in the northern industrial town of South Shields. Her home was a modest red-brick terraced house with no garden or inside sanitation—very unlike the homes of most of her fictional heroines. Her family circumstances also differed greatly from theirs, for she was the child of a broken home, her father having walked out when she was three years old. There was further family tragedy when her brother Henzell, born only fourteen months after Elinor, died of cerebrospinal fever (the older term for meningitis) when he was only sixteen.

Elinor Brent-Dyer attended the Misses Stewart's School, a local private school of about 50 pupils, and on her eighteenth birthday started work as an unqualified teacher. In 1915 she gained a place at the City of Leeds Training College, graduating in 1917 and moving back to South Shields to teach. From September 1921 to July 1923 she was on the staff of the well-known St Helen's School in Northwood, Middlesex, moving to Moreton House School in Dunstable, Bedfordshire, in September 1924, and then to Western House in Fareham, Hampshire in September 1925, where she taught for two years. She was extremely versatile: at different times she taught English, History, Latin, and class-singing; she also coached hockey and ran folk-dancing groups and a Guide company. She wrote plays and pageants for her pupils and colleagues, and edited the school magazine at Moreton House. In 1927, she left teaching temporarily to follow a course at the Newcastle Conservatoire of Music, and continued to play the piano and to sing with local choirs.

Her estranged father had died in 1911, and two years later her mother remarried: Elinor apparently disliked Septimus Ainsley, but continued to live with her mother and stepfather between teaching posts. In 1933 the family moved to Hereford, where, after five years working as a private governess, she set up her own school for girls, the Margaret Roper School, which she ran from 1938 to 1948. By the time it closed, she was able to live off the royalties from her books. She lived for over 30 years in Hereford; but in 1964 she moved to Redhill in Surrey, sharing a house with **PHYLLIS MATTHEWMAN** and the latter's husband, where she died, in her sleep, of heart failure on 20 September 1969.

From an early age Brent-Dyer showed ability as a writer: even before she left school some of her stories had appeared in magazines and local newspapers. She also wrote numerous poems and two plays, which were produced at a small repertory theatre in South Shields. Her first published book, *Gerry Goes to School*, which appeared in 1922, was a conventional school story: at eleven years old (or twelve—even in her first book, Brent-Dyer's talent for inconsistencies is apparent), the eponymous protagonist, brought up by elderly great-aunts, finds it hard to cope when plunged into a Charlotte-Yonge-sized family and a modern High School. The sequel, *A Head Girl's Difficulties*, was published the following year: Brent-Dyer kept St

Peter's High School as the location but set the book three years after *Gerry*, and focused on one of the minor characters from the previous book, Rosamund Atherton, the Head Girl of the title.

Even in these early works, Brent-Dyer's characteristic approaches are clear. She is influenced by school stories that she has read, so there is plenty of rivalry, both between contemporaries and between seniors and juniors; there are troubled relationships which lead eventually to reconciliation, and ardent friendships; and of course there are dramatic incidents, ranging from a bolting horse to a near drowning. However, there's far more concentration on the real life of school—lessons, homework and ordinary duties for the girls—than in most school stories of any period, and she is extremely unusual in presenting interaction between staff—even other teacher-writers such as **WINIFRED DARCH** and **EVELYN SMITH** rarely followed Brent-Dyer into the staffroom.

She was to write another five books in the same series, none of them school stories, later to be known collectively as the La Rochelle series. The third of the sequence, *The Maids of La Rochelle*, published in 1924, was the first to be set on Guernsey, and the book's convincing topographical details clearly demonstrated that a capacity for capturing the atmosphere of places was among Elinor Brent-Dyer's gifts: it's probable that Elinor had holidayed on the island in the summer of 1923. Infinitely more important, though, was the summer holiday of the previous year. In 1922, she and her St Helen's colleague Lilian Kirkby had spent eight weeks in the Tyrolean village of Pertisau on the Achensee, and Brent-Dyer was enchanted by the loveliness of the region and the charm of the inhabitants. Pertisau is now known to innumerable readers as Briesau on the Tiern See (which with typical inconsistency becomes in later books the Tiernsee), the location of Madge Bettany's gallant experiment in school-keeping. *The School at the Châlet* [2] was published by Chambers in October 1925, and while no one could have predicted that the series would eventually run to 59 titles (in hardback), plus three annuals and a recipe book, the first book sold well enough for Brent-Dyer to write an immediate sequel.

There are indications in the La Rochelle books that Brent-Dyer was sympathetic to the Catholicism of the Guernsey people, and *The School at the Châlet* showed her appreciation of the peasants' 'simple faith'. We don't know how much she was influenced by her Guernsey and Austrian holidays—together with a possible, though unproven, attendance at the Oberammergau Passion Play in the summer of 1930—but on 12 December 1930 she was received into the Catholic Church at St Bede's Church in South Shields. The two non-series books from this period, *The School by the River* (1930) and the historical novel *The Little Marie-José* (1932) were issued by the Catholic publishers Burns & Oates, though neither book is particularly proselytising. Financial reasons may have discouraged Brent-Dyer from offering further titles to Burns & Oates: both had small initial print runs, and *The School by the River* only one further impression, while *The Little Marie-José* had none at all.

Until 1948, when her own school closed, Brent-Dyer's published output averaged between one and two books a year; but at this point it increased dramatically, the record period being between 1948 and 1958, when 38 books were published, sixteen of them within two years. Her final published total of a hundred books includes, in addition to the Chalet School series and stories set at other schools, many different genres: family tales such as the La Rochelle books; historical novels, *Elizabeth the Gallant* (1935) and *The Little Missus* (1942), as well as *The Little Marie-José*; five connected thriller/adventure stories collectively known as the Fardingales series (1950-55); three novellas written for the evangelical publisher Oliphants between 1954 and 1956; several books with 'doggy' themes (she had a great love of animals, especially cats and dogs), including a career novel (*Kennelmaid Nan*, 1954); four Geographical Readers, commissioned by Chambers and published in 1951; a Girl Guide school story in *Judy, the Guide* (1928); and even a recipe book: *The Chalet Girls' Cook Book* (1953). During 1930, she contributed a serial story to the local newspaper, the *Shields Daily Gazette*; this full-length romantic novel, *Jean of Storms,* was rediscovered only in 1995 and subsequently published by Bettany Press in book form. She also contributed a number of short stories to annuals.

Of all Brent-Dyer's juvenile novels, the Chalet School books have had the most staying power. The books form the longest-running series of girls' school stories ever known, sustained well after the author's death by HarperCollins, who began publishing a paperback edition of the entire series in 1967, an enterprise which took almost 30 years to complete. Until the end of the 20th century many of the titles were kept in print, with annual sales of around 100,000 copies. Girls Gone By Publishers obtained the copyright to the estate in 2005, and have gradually been bringing out all the Chalets and many other Brent-Dyer titles. The abiding popularity of the series is also confirmed by the existence of several Chalet School fan clubs. The first was started by Chambers in 1959 and ran during the ten years preceding Elinor Brent-Dyer's death, when its membership numbered 4,000 fans. Chambers issued a newsletter roughly twice a year, with competitions, news about forthcoming and reprinted titles, and messages from Brent-Dyer herself. Proud members received a membership card and a pretty enamel edelweiss badge. There followed a twenty-year gap, but today this club has two flourishing successors, Friends of the Chalet School and the New Chalet Club; both have an enthusiastic worldwide membership, including fans of all ages, some of whom have written sequels and fill-in stories (*see* author's bibliography). Since the growth of the internet there are also many websites run by Chalet School devotees, some of which feature 'fanfic'.

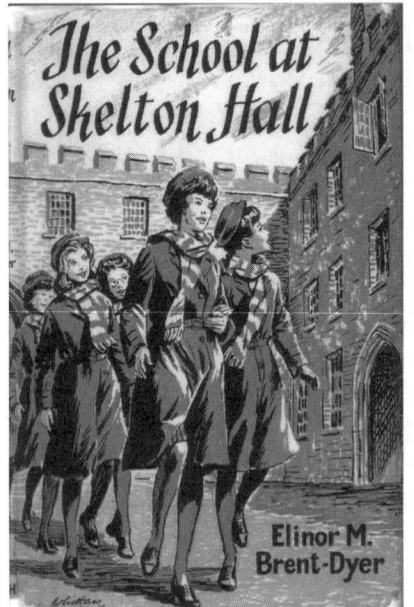

What, then, are the books about? It's hard to summarise a series written over 45 years and covering 27 years of fictional time, but the task must be attempted. *The School at the Châlet* introduces the 24-year-old twins Madge and Dick Bettany, and their 'delicate' twelve-year-old sister Josephine (always known as Joey or Jo). They are more or less penniless orphans: Dick can't stay in Taverton, as he has a job in India, and despairs of supporting Madge and Joey. Inspired by a holiday in the Austrian Tyrol (at that time, extraordinarily cheap for British tourists), Madge decides to open a school there, in partnership with a French governess friend, Mlle La Pâttre, with Joey, local girl Grizel Cochrane, and Mlle La Pâttre's niece Simone as the first pupils. The school is an immense success, and the next thirteen books see it grow, reform a number of difficult girls, and take over a rival school in the area. Early in the series, Madge marries Jem Russell, a doctor who has set up a sanatorium for tubercular patients in the mountains, but the school continues with Jo still a central character; even after her schooldays she returns to the school to help with teaching, and becomes a successful writer, very like her creator.

At this point, real life impinged dramatically on Brent-Dyer's fictional creation. She was one of the few contemporary children's writers who not only recognised the Nazi threat, but described at the time what was happening in Germany and Austria, with its persecution of Jews and expansionist foreign policy. *The Chalet School in Exile* (1940) shows the impact of this on the school: it has to close, and the main characters flee for their lives. The school eventually re-opens in Guernsey—a natural choice for Brent-Dyer, of course, and one that allowed the La Rochelle characters to make a reappearance, but rather unfortunate, given the German occupation which followed shortly after she'd made that decision. Jo Bettany marries (a doctor, naturally) during the action of this book, becoming Jo Maynard, and in almost no time, the mother of triplets (another eight children would follow). In the following book (*The Chalet School Goes to It*, 1941)

the school re-opens in 'Armiford' (a renamed Hereford, where Brent-Dyer was living), remaining there for the five books covering the war-time years and introducing another pupil who would become central to Chalet School life, Mary-Lou Trelawney. In 1949, in *The Chalet School and the Island*, Brent-Dyer (presumably tiring of the limited opportunities for adventures in the Marches) moved the school to St Briavel's, a fictional island off the Welsh coast. The lure of the Alps, however, never really disappeared, and though post-war Austria, so near the Soviet bloc, was out of the question, Switzerland beckoned. *The Chalet School in the Oberland* (1952) established a finishing branch, the unglamorously named St Mildred's, and the greater part of the main school followed two years later in *The Chalet School and Barbara*. And there it remained for the rest of the series, with Jo's triplets gradually taking a central part in the action; the final book, *Prefects of the Chalet School* (posthumously published in 1970) depicts their last term, with the oldest triplet, Len, Head Girl.

This précis does make the Chalet School's history sound somewhat implausible. Nor is this the only reason that critics disparage Brent-Dyer's writing. Leaving aside those who simply dismiss all girls' school stories as rubbish, it should be acknowledged that Brent-Dyer was not concerned with 'fine writing': she would never have appeared on a Carnegie Medal shortlist, and her books, particularly in the Chalet series, are full of clichés, from Miss Annersley's glasses-free eyes to Rufus's magnificent head. She was a picker-up of unconsidered trifles, and her books are full of tropes she's lifted from other authors, from major themes (the Alpine sanatorium and its school connection seems to have come from **ELSIE J OXENHAM**'s Swiss series) to minor but memorable events such as the sheets-and-pillowcase parties (in *Jo Returns*, re-used in *Adrienne*), which are taken from **MRS GEORGE DE HORNE VAIZEY**'s *Pixie O'Shaughnessy*. The books can feel rather snobbish by today's standards, and the anachronisms can be irritating (the Chalet girls are still putting up their hair as a mark of maturity in the 1960s). So notorious are her inconsistencies that fans gleefully submit 'EBDisms' to the club journals, and have long ago stopped trying to sort out the real surname of 'Matey', the relative ages of Peggy Bettany and Natalie Mensch, or why Biddy O'Ryan temporarily becomes Biddy O'Hara. And there is general agreement that the second half of the series, when the school has moved to Switzerland, is inferior to the first half, with the last dozen or so books mostly repeating plots and motifs already used. The Chalet series is indeed formulaic: as long ago as 1961, with another fourteen books still to come, Margery Fisher described it as 'a clear case of fossilization' (*Intent upon Reading*, 1961), and even the most ardent fans could hardly disagree.

And yet, with all these admitted flaws, the books have continued to appeal to countless readers for nearly a century. What is their secret?

Some of the attraction may lie in the exotic locations, with their beauty and concomitant dangers, which offer plenty of room for adventure and gallant rescues. The Chalet School itself has aspects that are rare, or even unique, among school stories, such as the trilingual regime, alternating between English, French and German (impractical but a wonderful idea). The multinational nature of the pupils, particularly in the earlier books, is very engaging: plenty of school stories have a single American, French or Australian girl, but they're generally presented as rather peculiar: at the Chalet School, with occasional exceptions for plot purposes, they are generally quite normal—just part of the community. Brent-Dyer incorporated her own teaching experience into the books, not only by including many of the plays and pantomimes she'd written for the Margaret Roper School, but by creating believable events, problems and relationships, and by making the staff almost as important as the pupils; we frequently eavesdrop on staff-room conversations. Even lessons in Brent-Dyer's hands become considerably more interesting than the lessons most of us recall from our own schooldays. Over the years the school becomes almost a character in its own right, personified in Jo, Mary-Lou and Len, able to straighten out difficult or troubled pupils and turn them into 'real Chalet girls'. The nurturing, all-female community in which hostility is eventually conquered by friendship is a mainstay of many girls' school stories; Brent-Dyer established this very early on, and better than many of her contemporaries.

There is, though, one extra ingredient in the mix, a most necessary one: what Sue Sims—in an essay in *The Chalet School Revisited* (1994) called 'The Series Factor'—the addictive nature of a long-running series. The success of soap operas such as *Coronation Street* and lengthy drama series such as *Downton Abbey* or *Game of Thrones* is partly due to exciting plots, but even more to our need to know not just What Happens Next (that would be true of any book, play or film) but What Happens to the Characters. The Series Factor allowed Brent-Dyer to create an entire world, and to people it with characters who we follow through the series and experience as friends. They may leave school, but they don't leave the series: we see them marry, have children (chiefly girls who attend the school in their turn), drop into the school as visitors, or perhaps return as teachers. Once the reader has mastered the Chalet world and its inhabitants, each further book slots into a pre-existent space. As Victor Watson pointed out, quoting a Year 6 pupil: 'When you begin a new novel ... it is like going into a room full of strangers, but reading the latest book in a series which you already know is *like going into a room full of friends* [italics in original]' (Watson, *Reading Series Fiction*, 2000). Margery Fisher (op.cit.) notes that 'many of the later volumes are filled up with the reminiscences of Old Girls'. Her comment is intended as a reproach, but she misses the point—long-time readers relish the familiarity, and newer ones are motivated to explore further.

Furthermore, Brent-Dyer's habit of interlacing her books, while not quite up to Oxenham levels, means that attractive characters can pop up in series where in theory they have no right to be. Gerry Challoner, the heroine of Brent-Dyer's first book, turns out to be studying the piano in Florence with the same master as Grizel after the latter leaves school; the La Rochelle personnel take full advantage of the Chalet School's exile to Guernsey; and in a slightly Escher-like move, Brent-Dyer makes Jo Bettany/Maynard, now a famous author, write the stories we know as *The Lost Staircase* and *Chudleigh Hold* whose protagonists now attend the Chalet School. (For a full analysis of these connections, see Chapter 7, 'The Series Factor', in *The Chalet School Revisited*.)

For all these reasons, Elinor Brent-Dyer is probably the most popular author among fans of the girls' school story, the standard by which all others are judged. Her Chalet School books, at their best, can hold their own among the most distinguished examples of the genre; and the series as a whole, for all her faults, represents an achievement unsurpassed in the history of the girls' school story.

---

[1] She seems to have adopted the double-barrelled 'Brent-Dyer' for her first book, *Gerry Goes to School*, in 1922, when she also changed the spelling of her Christian name to 'Elinor'. She retained the simple 'Dyer' in private and professional life until 1926.

[2] The circumflex on *Châlet* was only used for the first two books in the series: *Princess* and subsequent books have *Chalet* throughout. Compare *Tyrol*, the normal spelling in the first few titles, which was eventually updated to *Tirol*, though the spellings varied between and even within books until the early 1950s.

Helen McClelland and Sue Sims

Further Reading
Auchmuty, Rosemary, *A World of Girls*, Women's Press (1992), 2nd ed. Bettany Press (2004)
Auchmuty, Rosemary and Gosling, Juliet, eds, *The Chalet School Revisited*, Bettany Press (1994)
McCallum, Alison, *The Chalet School Encyclopaedia* vols. 1-4, Girls Gone By (2013-16)
McClelland, Helen, *Behind the Chalet School*, New Horizon (1981); 2nd ed. Bettany Press (1996)
McClelland, Helen, *The Chalet School Companion*, HarperCollins (1994); 2nd ed. Bettany Press (2004)

McClelland, Helen, *Elinor Brent-Dyer's Chalet School*, HarperCollins (1989)
McClelland, Helen, 'Elinor Mary Brent-Dyer' in *The Oxford Dictionary of National Biography*, OUP (2004)
Book and Magazine Collector 10, 48, 86, 122
Folly passim
Friends of the Chalet School magazine (August 1989 –). Ann Mackie-Hunter and Clarissa Cridland, The Vicarage, Church St, Coleford, Radstock, Somerset BA3 5NG
New Chalet Club Journal (Autumn 1995 –). Membership Secretary, New Chalet Club, 5 Pinetree Gardens, Whitley Bay, Tyne & Wear, NE25 8XU

For the Chalet School series (CS), three numberings are given: reading order; official hardback/GGBP numbering; Armada paperback numbering.

	h/b	p/b	
LR1			*Gerry Goes to School*, Chambers (1922). Illus. Gordon Browne
LR2			*A Head Girl's Difficulties*, Chambers (1923). Illus. Nina K Brisley
LR3			*The Maids of La Rochelle**, Chambers (1924). Illus. Nina K Brisley
CS1	1	1	*The School at the Châlet*, Chambers (1925). Illus. Nina K Brisley
CS2	2	2	*Jo of the Châlet School*, Chambers (1926). Illus. Nina K Brisley
CS3	3	3	*The Princess of the Chalet School*, Chambers (1927). Illus. Nina K Brisley
LR4			*Seven Scamps**, Chambers (1927). Illus. Percy Tarrant
J1			*A Thrilling Term at Janeways*, Thomas Nelson & Sons (1927). Illus. Florence Mary Anderson
CS4	4	4	*The Head Girl of the Chalet School*, Chambers (1928). Illus. Nina K Brisley
			The New Housemistress, Thomas Nelson & Sons (1928). Illus. Florence Mary Anderson
			Judy the Guide, Thomas Nelson & Sons (1928). Illus. Lilian A Govey
CS5	5	5	*The Rivals of the Chalet School*, Chambers (1929). Illus. Nina K Brisley
LR5			*Heather Leaves School**, Chambers (1929). Illus. Percy Tarrant
			The School by the River, Burns, Oates & Washbourne (1930). Not illus. Some connection with the Chalet School series
CS6	6	6	*Eustacia Goes to the Chalet School*, Chambers (1930). Illus. Nina K Brisley
CS7	7	7	*The Chalet School and Jo*, Chambers (1931). Illus. Nina K Brisley
			The Feud in the Fifth Remove, Girl's Own Paper Office (1932). Illus. Ellis Silas
			The Little Marie-José *, Burns, Oates & Washbourne (1932). Not illus.
LRS6			*Janie of La Rochelle**, Chambers (1932). Illus. Percy Tarrant
CS8	8	8	*The Chalet Girls in Camp*, Chambers (1932). Illus. Nina K Brisley
CS9	9	9	*The Exploits of the Chalet Girls*, Chambers (1933). Illus. Nina K Brisley

			Carnation of the Upper Fourth, Girl's Own Paper Office (1934). Illus. 'Sutcliffe'
CS10	10	10	*The Chalet School and the Lintons*, Chambers (1934). Illus. Nina K Brisley
		11	2nd half: *A Rebel at the Chalet School*
			*Elizabeth the Gallant**, Thornton Butterworth (1935). Not illus. Some connection with *Caroline the Second*.
CS11	11	12	*The New House at the Chalet School*, Chambers (1935). Illus. Nina K Brisley
CS12	12	13	*Jo Returns to the Chalet School*, Chambers (1936). Illus. Nina K Brisley
			Monica Turns Up Trumps, Girl's Own Paper Office (1936). Illus. not credited
J2			*Caroline the Second*, Girl's Own Paper Office (1937). Illus. not credited
			They Both Liked Dogs, Girl's Own Paper Office (1938). Illus. not credited
CS13	13	14	*The New Chalet School*, Chambers (1938). Illus. Nina K Brisley
		15	2nd half: *A United Chalet School*
CS14	14	16	*The Chalet School in Exile*, Chambers (1940). Illus. Nina K Brisley
CS15	15		*The Chalet School Goes to It*, Chambers (1941). Illus. Nina K Brisley
		17	Retitled: *The Chalet School at War*
CS16	16	18	*The Highland Twins at the Chalet School*, Chambers (1942). Illus. Nina K Brisley
			*The Little Missus**, Chambers (1942). Illus. Mackay
CS17	17		*Lavender Laughs in the Chalet School*, Chambers (1943). Illus. Nina K Brisley
		19	Retitled: *Lavender Leigh at the Chalet School*
CS18	18		*Gay from China at the Chalet School*, Chambers (1944). Illus. Nina K Brisley
		20	Retitled: *Gay Lambert at the Chalet School*
CS19	19	21	*Jo to the Rescue**, Chambers (1945). Illus. Nina K Brisley
			*The Lost Staircase**, Chambers (1946). Illus. Nina K Brisley
CS			*The Chalet Book for Girls*, Chambers (1947). Illus. not credited. Part reissued as *The Mystery at the Chalet School*, Armada (1994)
L1			*Lorna at Wynyards*, Lutterworth Press (1947). Illus. 'Victor Bertolglio'
L2			*Stepsisters for Lorna*, C & J Temple (1948). Illus. John Bruce
CS			*Second Chalet Book for Girls*, Chambers (1948). Illus. not credited
CS			*Third Chalet Book for Girls*, Chambers (1949). Illus. not credited
CS22	20	24	*Three Go to the Chalet School*, Chambers (1949). Not illus.
CS23	21	25	*The Chalet School and the Island*, Chambers (1950). Not illus.
CS24	22	26	*Peggy of the Chalet School*, Chambers (1950). Illus. Nina K Brisley
F1			*Fardingales**, Latimer House (1950). Illus. 'Louis Ward'
CS25	23	27	*Carola Storms the Chalet School*, Chambers (1951). Not illus.

CS21		23	*The Chalet School and Rosalie* (paperback), Chambers (1951). Not illus.
			Verena Visits New Zealand*, Chambers (1951). Illus. not credited
			Bess on her Own in Canada*, Chambers (1951). Illus. Mackay
			Quintette in Queensland*, Chambers (1951). Illus. Mackay
			Sharlie's Kenya Diary*, Chambers (1951). Illus. not credited
CS26	24	28	*The Wrong Chalet School*, Chambers (1952). Illus. Nina K Brisley
CS27	25	29	*Shocks for the Chalet School*, Chambers (1952). Illus. Nina K Brisley
CS28	26	30	*The Chalet School in the Oberland*, Chambers (1952). Illus. Nina K Brisley
CS			*The Chalet Girls' Cook Book**, Chambers (1953). Illus. not credited
CS29	27	31	*Bride Leads the Chalet School*, Chambers (1953). Illus. Nina K Brisley
CS30	28	32	*Changes for the Chalet School*, Chambers (1953). Illus. 'Louis Ward'
LR7			*Janie Steps In**, Chambers (1953). Not illus.
F2			*The 'Susannah' Adventure**, Chambers (1953). Illus. Nina K Brisley
CH1			*Chudleigh Hold**, Chambers (1954). Illus. not credited
CH2/F3			*Condor Crags Adventure**, Chambers (1954). Illus. not credited
			Nesta Steps Out, Oliphants (1954). Illus. not credited
			Kennelmaid Nan*, Lutterworth Press (1954). Illus. 'Alice Bush'
CS31	29	33	*Joey Goes to the Oberland**, Chambers (1954). Illus. 'KHS' (?)
CS32	30	34	*The Chalet School and Barbara*, Chambers (1954). Illus. 'D Brook'
CS20	31	22	*Tom Tackles the Chalet School*, Chambers (1955). Illus. 'D Brook'
CS33	32	35	*The Chalet School Does it Again*, Chambers (1955). Illus. 'D Brook'
CS34	33	36	*A Chalet Girl from Kenya*, Chambers (1955). Illus. 'D Brook'
CH3			*Top Secret**, Chambers (1955). Illus. 'D Brook'
			Beechy of the Harbour School, Oliphants (1955). Illus. Wardill
			Leader in Spite of Herself, Oliphants (1956). Not illus.
CS35	34	37	*Mary-Lou of the Chalet School*, Chambers (1956). Illus. 'D Brook'
CS36	35	38	*A Genius at the Chalet School*, Chambers (1956). Illus. 'D Brook'
		39	2nd half plus extra chapter: *Chalet School Fête*
CS37	36	40	*A Problem for the Chalet School*, Chambers (1956). Illus. 'D Brook'
CS38	37	41	*The New Mistress at the Chalet School*, Chambers (1957). Illus. 'D Brook'
CS39	38	42	*Excitements for the Chalet School*, Chambers (1957). Illus. 'D Brook'
CS40	39	43	*The Coming of Age of the Chalet School*, Chambers (1958). Illus. 'D Brook'
CS41	40	44	*The Chalet School and Richenda*, Chambers (1958). Illus. 'D Brook'
CS42	41	45	*Trials for the Chalet School*, Chambers (1959). Illus. 'D Brook'
CS43	42	46	*Theodora and the Chalet School*, Chambers (1959). Illus. 'D Brook'
CS44	43	47	*Joey and Co. in Tirol*, Chambers (1960). Illus. 'D Brook'
CS45	44		*Ruey Richardson, Chaletian*, Chambers (1960). Illus. 'D Brook'
		48	Retitled: *Ruey Richardson at the Chalet School*
CS46	45	49	*A Leader in the Chalet School*, Chambers (1961). Illus. 'D Brook'
CS47	46	50	*The Chalet School Wins the Trick*, Chambers (1961). Illus. 'D Brook'
CS48	47	51	*A Future Chalet School Girl*, Chambers (1962). Illus. [Dorothy Brook]

CS49	48	52	*The Feud in the Chalet School*, Chambers (1962). Illus. 'D Brook'
S1			*The School at Skelton Hall*, Max Parrish (1962). Not illus.
S2			*The Trouble at Skelton Hall*, Max Parrish (1963). Not illus.
CS50	49	53	*The Chalet School Triplets*, Chambers (1963). Illus. 'D Brook'
CS51	50	54	*The Chalet School Reunion*, Chambers (1963). Illus. Dorothy Brook (credited on dustwrapper)
CS52	51	55	*Jane and the Chalet School*, Chambers (1964). Illus. 'D Brook'
CS53	52	56	*Redheads at the Chalet School*, Chambers (1964). Illus. 'D B' [Dorothy Brook]
CS54	53	57	*Adrienne and the Chalet School*, Chambers (1965). Illus. 'D Brook'
CS55	54	58	*Summer Term at the Chalet School*, Chambers (1965). Illus. 'D Brook'
CS56	55	59	*Challenge for the Chalet School*, Chambers (1966). Illus. 'D Brook'
CS57	56	60	*Two Sams at the Chalet School*, Chambers (1967). Illus. 'D Brook'
CS58	57	61	*Althea Joins the Chalet School*, Chambers (1969). Illus. 'D Brook'
CS59	58	62	*Prefects of the Chalet School*, Chambers (1970). Illus. 'D Brook'
			Jean of Storms*, Bettany Press (1997). Illus. photographs
CS various			*The Chalet Club Newsletters* (1959-69), Friends of the Chalet School (1997)
			Elinor M Brent-Dyer's Short Stories, Girls Gone By Publishers (2004) (includes EBD articles from school magazines)
			Elinor M Brent-Dyer: Collected Verse, ed. Joy Wotton, NCC (2006)

CH = Chudleigh Hold series
CS = Chalet School series
F = Fardingales series
J = Janeways pair
L = Lorna pair
LR = La Rochelle series
S = Skelton Hall pair

Brent-Dyer continuations

One development of recent years has been the appearance of Brent-Dyer sequels and fill-ins, of varying quality and popularity but all testifying to the enduring appeal of the Chalet School.

To indicate where they slot into the series (following the original order of publication listed in the second column above), they have been marked thus:
CS 3+ After, for example, book 3 of the series
(CS 14) During the action of, for example, book 14 of the series
CS -1 Precedes the series
CS +1 Follows the series

Inevitably, different authors have contributed different versions of the same time-slots.

Allan, Carol	*Gillian of the Chalet School*, FOCS (2001), CS 13+
Barber, Helen	*A Chalet School Headmistress*, Girls Gone By (2004), CS 18+
Barber, Helen	*The Bettanys of Taverton High*, Girls Gone By (2008), CS -1
Barber, Helen	*Chalet School World* (short stories), Girls Gone By (2013), Various
Barber, Helen	*The Bettanys on the Home Front*, Girls Gone By (2015), CS -1
Barber, Helen	*Last Term at Taverton High*, Girls Gone By (2018), (CS 1)
Barber, Helen	*The Bettany Twins and the Chalet School*, Girls Gone By (2020), CS 19+
Berry, Jane	*Guides of the Chalet School*, Girls Gone By (2009), CS 2+
Bruce, Katherine	*Peace Comes to the Chalet School*, Girls Gone By (2005), CS 19+
Bruce, Katherine	*The Müller Twins at the Chalet School*, Girls Gone By (2012), CS 12+
Bruce, Katherine	*Juniors of the Chalet School*, Girls Gone By (2016), CS 3+
Bruce, Katherine	*The Chalet School and Cornelia*, Girls Gone By (2019), (CS 4)
Bruce, Katherine	*The Chalet School in Guernsey*, Girls Gone By (2020), CS 14+
Fitzpatrick, Adrianne	*Champion of the Chalet School*, Girls Gone By (2014), CS 19+
Fitzpatrick, Adrianne	*The Chalet School Annexe*, Girls Gone By (2018), (CS 9)
Fletcher, Amy	*Sisters at the Chalet School*, Girls Gone By (2017), CS 21+
Fletcher, Amy	*A Refuge for the Chalet School*, Girls Gone By (2019), (CS 14)
German, Caroline	*The Chalet School and Robin*, Girls Gone By (2003), CS 15+
German, Caroline	*Juliet of the Chalet School*, Girls Gone By (2006), CS 2+
German, Caroline	*Deira joins the Chalet School*, Girls Gone By (2010), CS 3+
Green, Lesley	*Hilda Annersley—Headmistress*, Matador (2005), CS 18+
Hardman, Josephine M	*Nicola Goes to the Oberland*, Blurb (2010), CS 33+
Jolly, Ruth (ed.)	*The Chalet School Christmas Story Book*, Girls Gone By (2007), Various
McClelland, Helen	*Visitors for the Chalet School*, Bettany Press (1995), CS 3+
McClelland, Helen	*Joey and Patricia: A Reunion in Guernsey* (short story), NCC (2000), (CS 14)
Priyadarshini, Narendra	*Two Chalet Girls in India*, Bettany Press (2006), CS 13+
Paisley, Heather	*New Beginnings at the Chalet School*, FOCS (1997), CS +1
Roberts, Jackie	*Cornelia of the Chalet School*, Yersinia Press (2009), CS 22+
Roberts, Jackie	*Surprises for the Chalet School*, Yersinia Press (2014), (CS 24)
Roberts, Jackie	*Joey & Co in Canada*, Yersinia Press (2016), CS 25+
Townsend, Lisa	*A Difficult Term for the Chalet School*, Girls Gone By (2011), CS 22+
Williams, Merryn	*The Chalet Girls Grow Up*, Plas Gwyn Books (1997), CS +1
Willimott, Pat	*The Chalet School Librarian*, Matador (2005), CS +1

Hilda Bridges
(Hilda Maggie Bridges)
1881-1971
She was born in Hobart, Tasmania, on 19 October 1881 and died there on 11 September 1971; for much of her life she lived with her younger brother, the novelist Roy Bridges.

Further Reading
Australian DNB under Roy Bridges

Connie of the Fourth Form (Australia), Whitcombe & Tombs ([1930]). Illus. The book is a school reader, no 542 of the Whitcombe's Story Book series.

Also other children's books and a boys' school story

Emma Frances Brooke
This author's only school story is a heavily religious boarding-school tale. Only the first part is set at school, where one of the girls is accused of theft; the rest of the book follows the lives of the three girls first introduced to us, and shows how the heroine eventually clears her name.

Reaping the Whirlwind (part school), RTS ([1885]). Illus. W Wymper

Also adult novels, and books as 'E Fairfax Byrne'

Monica Brooke
The Girl Who Hated School, Wells Gardner (1950). Not illus.

Dorita Fairlie Bruce
(Dorothy Morris Fairlie Bruce)
1885-1970
Dorita Fairlie Bruce (Dorothy Morris Fairlie Bruce) was born in Palos, Spain, on 20 May 1885. She was the daughter of a Scottish civil engineer, who soon moved back to Britain. Her early childhood was spent in Blanefield on the Campsie Hills in Stirling until the family finally settled in Ealing, West London, in about 1895. Her school at Clarence House in Roehampton, south-west London, would later serve as the model for the Jane Willard Foundation in the Dimsie books. Not until 1949, after the war and the death of her father, was she free to move back to Scotland, to Upper Skelmorlie in North Ayrshire, where she died on 21 September 1970.

When her first novel, *The Senior Prefect* (reissued in 1925 as *Dimsie Goes to School*) appeared in 1921, she had already been publishing poems and short stories in various magazines and annuals for fifteen years. Her first school short story, 'The Rounders Match', appeared in 1909. Like many other unmarried middle-class women of earlier generations she divided her time between family duties and voluntary work. During most of her writing career she looked after her parents and helped bring up her brother's three children. She was also deeply involved with the Girls' Guildry, an organisation rather like the Girl Guides, which plays a great part in many of her school stories. In the 1930s she was President of the Guildry's West London Centre, and these duties are one reason why her literary output never became as enormous as those of **ELINOR M BRENT-DYER** or **ELSIE J OXENHAM**.

Dorita Fairlie Bruce is most famous for the Dimsie books, seven of them set in a boarding school, the Jane Willard Foundation, on the Kent coast, and two about Dimsie's adult life on 'Loch Shee' in Argyll, Scotland. Her second series, generally known as the Nancy books, is more complex; it is partly set in Maudsley Grammar School, a day school in southern England (starting with *That Boarding-School Girl,* 1925), and partly at St Bride's, a boarding school on a small island off the west coast of Scotland. The first St Bride's book, *The Girls of St Bride's* (1923), actually takes place before Nancy's arrival in the school. Neither of these two series appeared in strictly chronological order. Many of her short stories are connected with the Dimsie and Nancy books; the earliest Jane Willard story, 'The Jane-Willard Election', appeared in 1911.

The third principal series of school stories, the six Springdale books (starting with *The New House-Captain,* 1928), are wholly set in Scotland, in the little seaside town of 'Redchurch' (Largs in Ayrshire). The Toby books, *The School on the Moor* (1931) and *The School in the Woods* (1940), return to England, but the three very late Sally books (1956-61) are set in another part of Scotland. Both the Nancy and Toby books have 'adult' sequels set during the war, *Nancy Calls the Tune* (1944) and *Toby at Tibbs Cross* (1942). *Dimsie Carries On* (1942) deals with characters from both the Dimsie and Springdale series, grown up in war-time.

Many of her school stories are set in southern England, but Bruce is above all a Scottish writer, and her particular landscape is the Firth of Clyde area around Largs, from Skelmorlie in the north, where she spent the last twenty-one years of her life, to West Kilbride in the south, the home of her maternal grandparents. The St Bride's stories are set on the Cumbrae Islands just opposite Largs. About half of her short stories are set in Scotland, many of them historical, and several in the Campsie Hills of her childhood. All her books and stories from Scotland abound with local traditions, national history, and prehistoric monuments. The nine, more adult, Colmskirk novels follow a group of interrelated families, living in the neighbourhood of Largs, here called 'Colmskirk', from the 16th century in *The King's Curate* (1930) to *The Bartle Bequest* (1955), which re-introduces Primula Mary Beton from the Springdale books.

Though Dorita Fairlie Bruce wrote no perennial series of school stories like Elinor Brent-Dyer's Chalet School books, it was the Dimsie books that popularised the concept of a series of stories set at the same school. Each of her principal series of school stories follows one group of girls—the Anti-Soppists in the Dimsie books, the Blue Dorm Gang at Springdale— through their whole school career from juniors to prefects while new groups of younger girls take over the roles of the juniors from the first books. She was perhaps the most skilful exponent of the traditional girls' school story of the 20s and 30s, with plots deftly exploring the narrative potential of the schoolgirl community, in particular relationships between girls of different age groups and conflicts between friendship and rivalry. Even the elements of mystery and adventure are wholly integrated into the plots. Charming dogs and cats are often important characters. Bruce's juniors, though often mischievous, have typically more common sense and innocence than the seniors; but at the same time, the seniors with their conflicts and dilemmas are portrayed with great sympathy.

Many of Dorita Fairlie Bruce's school stories were reprinted several times up to the 60s, but never in modern paperbacks like Elinor Brent-Dyer's Chalet School series. The new editions published by John Goodchild in the 80s were unfortunately radically modernised. The Dimsie books, however, experienced a period of popularity in Scandinavia in the early 1950s when the first four were translated into Swedish, and all but the last into Norwegian.

Eva M Löfgren

Further Reading

Book and Magazine Collector 14
Folly 6, 15, 54, 56, 58
Serendipity: The Magazine of the Dorita Fairlie Bruce Society (1994—2007).
Auchmuty, Rosemary, *A World of Girls*, The Women's Press (1992)
Cadogan, Mary, *Chin Up, Chest Out, Jemima!: A Celebration of the Schoolgirls' Story*, Bonnington (1989)
Cadogan, Mary and Craig, Patricia, *You're a Brick, Angela!: A New Look at Girls' Fiction from 1839 to 1975*, Gollancz (1976)
Löfgren, Eva Margareta, *Schoolmates of the Long-Ago: Motifs and Archetypes in Dorita Fairlie Bruce's Boarding School Stories*, Symposion Graduale (1993) Stockholm/Stebag

D1   *The Senior Prefect (Dimsie Goes to School*, 1925), OUP (1921). Illus. Wal Paget. Some early editions say 1920, but we think 1921 is correct
D2   *Dimsie Moves Up*, OUP (1921). Illus. Wal Paget
D3   *Dimsie Moves Up Again*, OUP (1922). Illus. Gertrude Demain Hammond

D4	*Dimsie among the Prefects*, OUP (1923). Illus. Gertrude Demain Hammond
N1	*The Girls of St Bride's*, OUP (1923). Illus. Henry Coller
D7	*Dimsie Grows Up**, OUP (1924). Illus. Henry Coller
D5	*Dimsie, Head Girl*, OUP (1925). Illus. Mary Strange Reeve
N3	*That Boarding-School Girl*, OUP (1925). Illus. 'R H Brock'
N4	*The New Girl and Nancy*, OUP (1926). Illus. Mary Strange Reeve
D8	*Dimsie Goes Back*, OUP (1927). Illus. Mary Strange Reeve
S1	*The New House-Captain*, OUP (1928). Illus. Mary Strange Reeve
S2	*The Best House in the School*, OUP (1930). Illus. Mary Strange Reeve
C1	*The King's Curate**, John Murray (1930). Not illus.
T1	*The School on the Moor*, OUP (1931). Illus. Mary Strange Reeve
N6	*The Best Bat in the School*, OUP (1931). Illus. 'D Stone'
S3 (D)	*Captain of Springdale*, OUP (1932). Illus. Henry Coller
C2	*Mistress Mariner**, John Murray (1932). Not illus.
N2	*Nancy at St Bride's*, OUP (1933). Illus. M D Johnston
S4	*The New House at Springdale*, OUP (1934). Illus. M D Johnston
N7	*Nancy in the Sixth*, OUP (1935). Illus. M D Johnston
S5	*Prefects at Springdale*, OUP (1936). Illus. M D Johnston
D6	*Dimsie Intervenes*, OUP (1936). Illus. M D Johnston
N5	*Nancy to the Rescue*, OUP ([1937]). Illus. 'G B'
N8	*Nancy Returns to St Bride's*, OUP (1938). Illus. M D Johnston
S6	*Captain Anne*, OUP (1939). Illus. M D Johnston
T2	*The School in the Woods*, OUP (1940). Illus. G M Anson
D9 (S)	*Dimsie Carries On**, OUP ([1941]). Illus. W Bryce Hamilton
T3 (N)	*Toby at Tibbs Cross**, OUP (1942). Illus. Margaret Horder
N9	*Nancy Calls the Tune**, OUP (1944). Illus. Margaret Horder
C3	*A Laverock Lilting**, OUP (1945). Illus. Margaret Horder
C5	*Wild Goose Quest**, Lutterworth Press (1945). Not illus.
C6	*The Serendipity Shop**, OUP (1947). Illus. Margaret Horder
C7	*Triffeny**, OUP (1950). Illus. Margaret Horder
C4	*The Bees on Drumwhinnie**, OUP (1952). Illus. Margaret Horder
C8	*The Debatable Mound**, OUP (1953). Illus. Patricia M Lambe
C9	*The Bartle Bequest**, OUP (1955). Illus. Sylvia Green
Sa1	*Sally Scatterbrain*, Blackie (1956). Illus. Betty Ladler
Sa2	*Sally Again*, Blackie (1959). Illus. Betty Ladler
Sa3	*Sally's Summer Term*, Blackie (1961). Illus. Joan Thompson
D+	*Dimsie Takes Charge* (annual stories), Goodchild (1985); reissued as *Dimsie and the Jane Willard Foundation*, Girls Gone By (2011)

C = Colmskirk series
D = Dimsie series
N = Nancy/St Bride's series
S = Springdale series
Sa = Sally series
T = Toby series

Emily M Bryant
(Emily Mary Bryant Grant)
1868-1949

Emily Bryant was the youngest of the seven children of Joseph Bryant, draper, of Alford, Lincolnshire; her mother died when she was a year old and until her father remarried the household was supervised by her mother's sister. They appear to have been Wesleyan Methodists. In the 1891 census Emily is described as a school teacher; by 1901, boarding in Enfield, she is 'authoress'. She married John Henry Grant, a bank clerk, in 1904, but seems to have had no children; she died in Crawley, Sussex, on 5 September 1949. Her writing career seems only to have lasted for a couple of years.

Norma, Digby, Long & Co, ([1897]). Illus. 'W G R Browne'
1 *Dolly and Syb*, Charles H Kelly ([1897]). Illus. 'C G Hards'
2 *Dolly and Syb at Boarding School*, Charles H Kelly (1898). Illus.

See also *The Encyclopaedia of Boys' School Stories*, **EMILY M BRYANT**

Marjorie Buckingham
'They Shall be Mine' Oliphants (1954). Illus.

Anna Jane Buckland *see* **EARLY SCHOOL STORIES**

Harriette E Burch
(Harriette Emma Burch)
1845-1894

Harriette Burch, eldest daughter of George Burch, a fairly prosperous cotton dyer and draper, was born in Westminster but moved around the country with her family until they finally (in the later 1850s) settled in Chesham, Herts; she died on 20 December 1894. Her younger sister Florence Edith (1857-1918) was also an author, of much the same sort of books as Harriette, but with no school stories. Both her brothers seem to have attended Chesham School, and it seems probable that the sisters were also reasonably well educated. The family, and presumably Harriette, was Congregational.

Her one school story, published anonymously, is a standard falsely accused story, this time over an art prize.

Tempted; or, The Old Lady's Prize, RTS ([1888]). Illus. 'J F W'

Also other moral books
See also *The Encyclopaedia of Boys' School Stories*, **HARRIETTE E BURCH**

E M R Burgess
(Esther Margaret Rooke Archibald Burgess)
1895-1977

Esther Margaret Rooke Archibald was born on 14 March 1895 in Ventnor, Isle of Wight. She taught at Clifton High School for Girls, founding a Guide company there which she ran from 1918 to 1921, moving on to Tunbridge Wells and Hamilton Kings, where she ran a company from 1921 to 1926 (possibly at a school called Hamilton House, which **MARGARET MASTERMAN** attended). She married Gordon Llewelyn Burgess, a civil servant. She moved to North London in 1926, lived in Kensington in the 1930s and was District Commissioner for Upper Holloway from 1930 and Tufnell Park from 1930 to 1935. She captained a Haywards Heath Guide company in 1936, and again 1938-41; she is also recorded as running a Cadet company in the area (undated). She captained a company at Cuckfield 1937-8. She was also District Commissioner for the Haywards Heath area 1937-41, and rose to Division Commissioner for Mid-Sussex 1940-46. She died near Uckfield on 8 July 1977.

Her three school stories all, understandably, feature Guides, but are otherwise very varied. Her first book, *Hilary Follows Up*, is a competent story in the classic tradition of a new girl having to live up to her talented older sisters; the other two are rather episodic, and published by Stockwell, a vanity publisher: the lack of editing is unfortunately clear.

Source: Girlguiding UK Headquarters

Hilary Follows Up, Blackie ([1939]). Illus. Inez Topham
Cherry Becomes International, Arthur H Stockwell (1946). Illus. M W Whittingham
Ready for Anything, Arthur H Stockwell ([1948]). Illus. M W Whittingham

Frances Hodgson Burnett
1849-1924

Frances Eliza Hodgson was born in 1849, the daughter of an ironmonger who died when she was three. She was raised in Manchester, and educated in a small private school until she was fifteen, when the ironmonger's (which had been continued by her mother) failed, and the family emigrated to the USA, where Mrs Hodgson's brother had a grocer's store in Knoxville, Tennessee. Here Frances began to write, trying to add to the family income; her mother died in 1870, and Frances became responsible for her siblings. She married Dr Swan Burnett in 1872, and had two sons, Lionel and Vivian, but the marriage gradually crumbled, and in 1898 she filed for divorce and married a young actor, Stephen Townsend, an equally unsuccessful husband. Meanwhile she had become extremely well known in England and America for her adult novels and children's books, and was able to afford a manor house in England and a newly built house on Long Island, where she died in 1924.

The publishing history of *A Little Princess* is somewhat complex. It first saw the light of day in 1888 as *Sara Crewe; or, What Happened at Miss Minchin's*, published with the short story *Editha's Burglar*. Much of the story was identical to the later version, but it was shorter, and the focus was more clearly on Sara's fall and rise; not so much was made of the long days of her attic existence. In 1902 Burnett dramatised *Sara Crewe* as *A Little Princess*, and very quickly rewrote the original novel to include some of the characters introduced into the play: Becky, the little servant, Lottie, the spoilt little girl and Melchisedec the rat. It is this version which has survived to the present day, though Heinemann produced a facsimile of the first edition in 1969 which may be of interest to collectors.

A Little Princess is a school story only in the sense that it is set at a girls' school. It does not belong to the type of book only just beginning at this period, in which the school is desirable and can mould a non-conformist pupil to its own image: this follows the parallel tradition of the unpleasant school run by a despot—the tradition which one recognises in many adult books, notably *Jane Eyre*. Miss Minchin, who is obsequiously reverent in her treatment of rich Sara and spitefully brutal to the impoverished Sara, is an ogress, a feminised and de-clericalised Mr Brocklehurst; the schoolgirls, particularly in *Sara Crewe*, hardly exist as personalities, apart from poor, stupid, loving Ermengarde, and (in the revision) Lottie. Like all Burnett's major children's books, this is a version of the Cinderella story, and its mythic quality, culminating in the superb climax where Sara awakes in an earthly paradise and Miss Minchin is utterly routed, is possibly what has ensured its survival to the present day when far better school stories have disappeared from public memory.

Further Reading
Book and Magazine Collector 118
Thwaite, Ann *Waiting for the Party: The Life of Frances Hodgson Burnett*, Secker & Warburg (1974)

Sara Crewe; or, What Happened at Miss Minchin's, Warne (1888). Illus. 'Birch' Rewritten as *A Little Princess*, Warne ([1905])

Many other adult novels and children's books

A E Burns
A E Burns' only school story is an unusual one in that it is set in an English Roman Catholic convent school. The girls play a trick on a snobbish cohort by pretending that a new girl is a Grand Duchess—the book is amusing and well-written, and the Catholic ambience is never stressed, just taken for granted.

The Grand Duchess Benedicta, Longmans (1915). Illus. T Baines

Marguerite L Butler
(Marguerite Lucy Butler)
1879-1951?

Marguerite Butler is assumed to have been born in Hastings in 1879, one of the daughters of a (private) schoolmaster and entomologist and his Madras-born wife; the family subsequently moved to Islington, London, and later to Crouch End. She graduated from the University of London with a third class BA degree in English in 1902, following private study, having matriculated as an Intermediate Student in 1895. She was not living with her family in 1911, having perhaps departed to India, from which she returned, aged 65 and described as a missionary, in 1944. She may well be the Marguerite L Butler who died in Maidstone, Kent, in 1951. Her one book, *Tulsi*, is interesting in that it is a girls' school story about an Indian girl at an Indian boarding school. The author (who is described on the title page as being 'of Bangalore, South India') was presumably a missionary, quite possibly a teacher at an English-run High School like the one described in the book (which is never given a name or locality). Tulsi is a Hindu girl from a high-caste family whose father wants more for her than a childhood marriage: when he becomes a Christian, he determines, much against his family's will, to send her to the school where she herself becomes a Christian. The book is clearly derived from the writer's experiences: she shows a knowledge and understanding of Indian culture which is rarely patronising. Nor does she soften the harsher outlines of life: a small English friend of Tulsi and two of her sisters die during the course of the book (which covers several years), and it is made very clear that life is not easy for many Indians. Nevertheless, despite its darker side, this is quite a charming book.

Tulsi, London Missionary Society (1934). Illus.

Joan Butler-Joyce
(Joan Marguerite Butler Joyce)
1904-2001

Joan Butler was born on 24 September 1904 in East Dulwich, the only daughter of Frank Butler (clerk in the General Post Office) and his wife Margaret Cotterell; she had two elder brothers. The family moved to Sydenham, where she went to school. While working as a clerk in the Bank of England she met and married (in 1930) Frederick Joyce. Unusually for the period, she continued to work after her marriage, and in 1939 was evacuated with other staff from the Bank of England to Whitchurch, Hants, where her son was born. Her books were written during her early married life; regrettably, war-time motherhood seems to have brought her writing career to an end. After the war the Joyces returned to south-west London, where Joan died in 2001.

Joan Butler-Joyce's two school stories, significantly, were published by Harrap, who tended to eschew 'standard' school stories and school titles. *Hot Water* opens in a deceptively normal manner with a couple of madcap schoolgirls, plenty of cricket, and a worried older sister; but with the arrival of Leah Weinburg half-way through (possibly the only realistic and sympathetically presented Jewish girl in school fiction until **ANTONIA FOREST**'s Miranda West), irony creeps in until, by the start of *No Responsiblity*, we are enjoying all the conventions of school and, simultaneously, their subversion. Leah, who may well have been initially intended for light relief, steals every scene she is in, and ends up as the protagonist whose thoughts we are most frequently allowed to follow: and since she cannot take school completely seriously, we also find ourselves questioning some of the clichés. These books are most certainly worth tracking down.

Biographical information from her son

1   *Hot Water*, Harrap (1935). Illus.
2   *She Went to London**, Harrap (1938). Illus. Helen McKie
3   *No Responsibility*, Harrap (1940). Illus. Gordon Robinson

Also an adult novel: *Catherine-Wheel*, Hodder & Stoughton (1939)

"*These girls have something to tell us, Reverend Mother,*" said Sister.

An illustration from *The Secret of Storm Abbey* by Ann Castleton

C

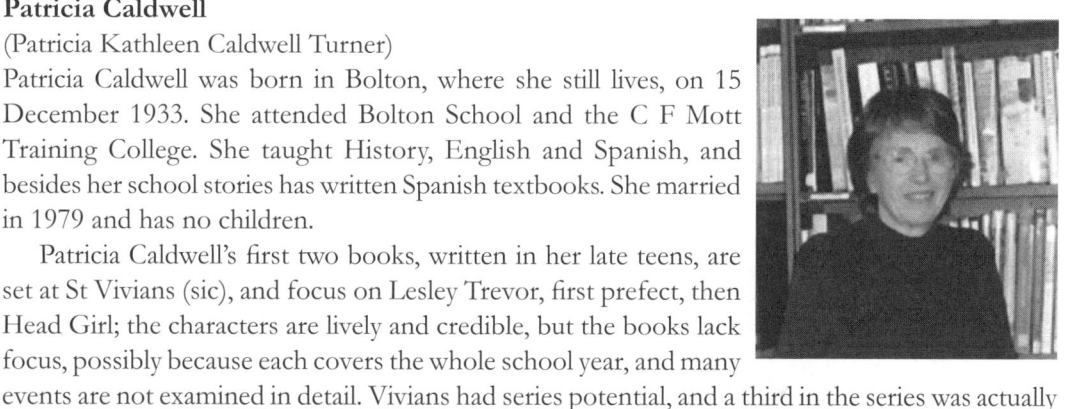

Patricia Caldwell
(Patricia Kathleen Caldwell Turner)
Patricia Caldwell was born in Bolton, where she still lives, on 15 December 1933. She attended Bolton School and the C F Mott Training College. She taught History, English and Spanish, and besides her school stories has written Spanish textbooks. She married in 1979 and has no children.

Patricia Caldwell's first two books, written in her late teens, are set at St Vivians (sic), and focus on Lesley Trevor, first prefect, then Head Girl; the characters are lively and credible, but the books lack focus, possibly because each covers the whole school year, and many events are not examined in detail. Vivians had series potential, and a third in the series was actually written, but not published by Chambers, which in the late 1950s withdrew from publishing any school stories apart from the best-selling **BRENT-DYER**. However, that title and three further sequels were later privately published during the 1990s and early 2000s. All six titles, plus a final seventh book in the series, have now been published by Girls Gone By.

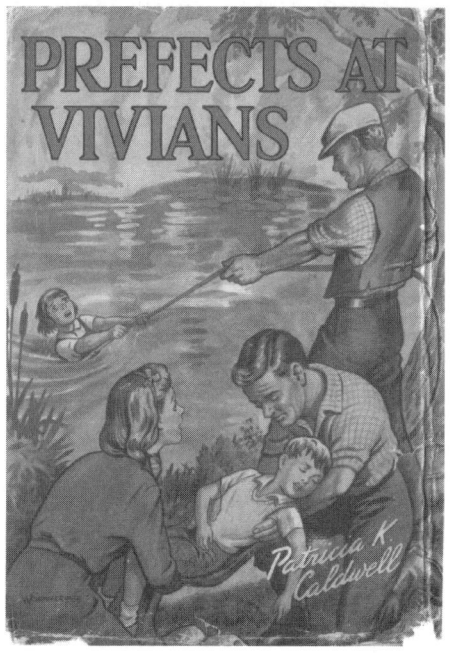

1. *Prefects at Vivians* (sic), Chambers (1956). Illus.
2. *Head Girl of Vivians*, Chambers (1957). Illus.
3. *Strangers at Vivians*, privately printed (1996). Not illus.
4. *Left Until Called For at Vivians*, privately printed (2003). Not illus.
5. *A Last Year at Vivians*, privately printed (2006). Not illus.
6. *¡Viva Vivians!* privately printed (2006). Not illus.
7. *Winter at Vivians,* Girls Gone By (2016). Not illus.

Margaret Locherbie Cameron *see* **MARGARET LOCHERBIE-CAMERON**

Harriette R Campbell
Patsy's Brother, Harper & Bros (1926). Illus.

Doris Canham *see* **DOREEN IRELAND**

Peggie Cannam *see* **PONY SCHOOL STORIES**

Joanna Cannan *see* **PONY SCHOOL STORIES**

Annie Carey
1825-1879
It now seems certain that this author is to be identified with Annie, daughter of Eustace Carey, a Baptist missionary, who was born in Philadelphia, USA when her parents were en route to England from India. Her father's health obliged him to give up the Indian mission field and the family remained in England. In 1851 Annie was in London with her stepmother and was 'at the Ladies' school of design', but in 1861 and 1871 she is found visiting at Burton House, a 'ladies' boarding school' in Burton, Westmorland. The school seems smaller than her fictional portrait—perhaps half the number of pupils—but has about the same number of staff. In 1871 Carey was described as 'authoress' in the census (as is Jane M Hooper, 53, also visiting, accompanied by her sixteen-year-old daughter), which suggests that she was not formally attached to the school, but possibly boarded there on a permanent basis. She certainly appears to have died there in the summer of 1879.

We are told in a preface that this is a posthumous book, published by Miss Carey's brother and a friend; and the school could easily be real. Set in a romantic old house in Westmorland, the school is 50 strong, with five resident staff and a visiting French teacher; there are five 'head monitors', elected by the girls. We are given a detailed account of the school day, with a compulsory fifteen minutes of gymnastics every day, and the new girl is allowed to pursue photography. There is no real plot, and the book focuses on school in general, not on a single girl. One wonders whether this was Annie Carey's own school.

School-girls; or, Life at Montagu Hall, Cassell, Pepper, Galpin & Co. ([1881]). Not illus.

Frances Carpenter
(Pseudonym of Horace Eli Boyten)
1901-1986
H E Boyten, journalist and author, also wrote as Enid and Hilda Boyten in various publications of the Amalgamated Press; *A Rebel Schoolgirl* appears, however, to be his only full-length girls' school story. He is much more famous as the co-author of *The Silent Three*, a picture story which

appeared in the comic and annual *School Friend* between 1950 and 1963.

A Rebel Schoolgirl, Blackie ([1938]). Illus. F G Moorsom

Other children's books

Judith Carr
(Pseudonym of Eveleen Leonora Hannah Fairbank)
1891-1986

Eveleen Leonora Hannah was born in North Shields, Tyneside, on 25 March 1891, the daughter of William Hannah, a sea captain, and his wife Elizabeth Morley, née Emerson. She married Henry Carl Fairbank in 1920, a marine engineer, from whom she was later divorced; they had three children. (Her daughter Helen, educated at Brighton College, was a code-breaker at Bletchley Park in Hut 6.) The family spent some time in Romania in the 1920s and 30s. Following her divorce she settled in Edinburgh, working as a governess; this was also the period when she wrote her school stories. She also used the pseudonym Elisabeth Morley, derived from her mother's Christian names. She returned to England and died on 22 October 1986.

Judith Carr's school stories (none of them connected) are lively and down-to-earth: thrilling rescues are markedly absent, and melodrama in any form is resolutely eschewed. The only heroine who doesn't know who she really is still isn't certain by the end of *Gipsy at Greywalls*. However, the books are unmemorable (save for their alliterative titles), despite a number of odd, eccentric characters. This may be because Carr, though full of ideas, is incapable of structuring a book. Her stories consist of a succession of incidents illustrating a theme—generally a conflict between individuals (as in *Scholarship Sue* or *Madcap Melody*) or groups within a form (*Penelope's Prefects* or *The Jays of St John's*). The ups and downs of such conflicts are reasonably true to life: but they lack the pattern which needs to be imposed to make them into art.

Carr has an ear for realistic dialogue, but this can work against her: so much of the story is recounted in this way that there is little sense of narrative drive, and we rarely know what is going on in a character's mind. Nor is there any distinction between modes of speech, apart from the Irish girls—Honor in *The Templeton Twins* or the eponymous Melody—and the various foreigners. This is the more surprising in that Carr has a jackdaw mind, and loves to provide the full text of essays, limericks, musical composition (*The Templeton Twins* and *The New Girls at Netherby* both print rather elementary piano pieces) and even, in *Penelope's Prefects*, a knitting pattern for a child's woolly ball! Unfortunately she also has a habit of jumping over events which the reader would really like to have in detail: she will spend pages leading up to examinations, half-term holidays or rows with the Head, and then end the chapter, beginning the next hours or days later.

The three books written under her 'Elisabeth Morley' pseudonym all feature heroines with vivid personalities and quick tempers who have settled down and become more balanced by the end. Stephanie (*Girls in Green*), the spoilt, red-headed tennis prodigy, is perhaps the most memorable, though the reader probably feels more affection for Jess 'of the Juniors' (one of two Jessica Manvilles at school and seven Jessica Manvilles in total, all named after a Duchess great-aunt). Jess's energy is used creatively, to try and capture the first place in class; Judy cares mainly about doing down the class's new mistress.

Judith Carr/Elisabeth Morley strikes one as a potentially good writer *manqué*; a tough editor might have done wonders with her.

The Templeton Twins, Blackie ([1947]). Illus. D L Mays
Scholarship Sue, Blackie ([1948]). Illus. MacGillivray
The Jays of St John's, Blackie ([1948]). Illus. Eric Winter
Screen Fashions* ['edited & devised by J Carr etc'], Dewynters (1948)
Penelope's Prefects, Blackie ([1950]). Illus. W Spence
The New Girls of Netherby, Blackie ([1951]). Illus. Louis Ward
Madcap Melody, Warne (1953). Illus. W Spence
Gipsy at Greywalls, Blackie (1955). Illus. Joanna Curzon

As Elisabeth Morley
Jess of the Juniors, Epworth Press (1947). Illus.
Girls in Green, Epworth Press (1949). Illus. Betty S Ladler
Judy's Triumph, Spring (195–). Illus.

Wallace Carr
Mascot for a Month, John Crowther ([1946]). Illus. 'L R'

Several other children's books; 'Wallace Carr' may be a pseudonym.

Ann Castleton

Ann Castleton's books often concern unhappy girls who, by discovering their true identity, also find happiness. Her first book, *The Secret of Storm Abbey*, is reasonably school-centred, concerning a Rajah's daughter who comes to this convent school (one of the few Catholic convent schools in the English school-story tradition) and is, naturally, kidnapped and rescued. There is an interesting study of racial prejudice here in Joan's attitude towards Dilkusha—prejudice roundly condemned by Castleton. After *Storm Abbey*, she only uses one plot: girls brought up in ignorance of their true identity by adoptive parents and discovering their real mothers (or someone very similar) in the final chapter. The eponymous Bracken Rodney, whose 'secret' is her gypsy upbringing, finds that the school matron is her mother (they have, of course, shared a mysterious sympathy throughout); Jenifer (sic: there are three Jenifers and one Jennifer in these five books) finds *her* true mother living in a cottage in the nearby woods; the family found by Gen turn out to be her aunt and cousin—Castleton having quite cleverly misdirected the reader to believe that her aunt would turn out to be her mother. Admittedly in *That Holiday at School* Hermie is incontestably an orphan; but she nevertheless manages to get herself and her small invalid brother adopted by great friends of her parents who just happen to run over her in their car.

Castleton, in fact, seems a somewhat obsessive writer, and not only regarding plots. She has a habit of taking an object—a sketch-book, a sheet, a letter—and trying to make its loss central to the plot, rather in the style of **BRENDA GIRVIN**. Unfortunately, she is incapable of interesting us in the fate of these objects, though spending an inordinate amount of time on them. We do care to an extent about most of her heroines, who are well delineated, although prone to bouts of self-pity which would disqualify them from starring in more traditional school stories. In fact, apart from *The Secret of Storm Abbey*, school is nothing more than a background. It is noticeable that *That Holiday at School*, which is, as its title indicates, not a school story, is indistinguishable in mood, setting and plot from the other three 'finding a family' books. Castleton was not really interested, it seems, in schools; why she was so enthusiastic about orphans finding true love is probably a task for the psychoanalyst rather than the literary critic.

The Secret of Storm Abbey, Hollis & Carter (1946). Illus. S van Abbé
Bracken had a Secret, Blackie ([1947]). Illus. G R Day
The Witch's Wood, Blackie ([1948]). Illus. F Stockmay
Gen Finds a Family, Hollis & Carter ([1949]). Illus. Andrew Wilson
That Holiday at School*, Hollis & Carter (1949). Illus. S van Abbé

Harriet Castor *see* **BALLET AND STAGE SCHOOL STORIES**

Nancy Catty
1873-1959
Nancy Margaret Catty was a lecturer in the University of London, possibly in the Education Department; she had a BA in English and a teaching qualification, and appears to have been a school teacher before moving on to university level.

This slender book concerns a little girl's first term at infant school, and is presumably intended as an introduction for five-year-olds in the same position. Its illustrations, by Joyce Lankester Brisley, are as charming as one would expect; but it is only included here for the sake of readers who, seeing the title on sales lists, might be deceived (as I was) as to its true nature!

Jane's First Term, Harrap (1936). Illus. Joyce Lankester Brisley

E M Channon
(Ethel Mary Bredin Channon)
1875-1941
Ethel Mary Bredin, daughter of the Rev. Edwin Bredin, was born in Ireland on 17 October 1875. After her father's death when she was four, she and her mother settled in St Leonards, Sussex, where they had relatives, and Ethel attended the Ladies' College; she had a final school year at Cheltenham Ladies' College. On 3 August 1904 she married the Rev. Francis Granville Channon, a Cambridge mathematician who was about to exchange a fellowship at Corpus Christi College for a post at Eton, where he was to spend the rest of his working life; here their six children were born, and here Ethel wrote for pleasure and to supplement the family income. In 1932 they retired to Bucknell, Shropshire, where Ethel died on 6 June 1941.

Although Channon seems to have published nothing before her marriage, after it she wrote prolifically and in a variety of genres, her books for young people tending to reflect the stages of her own children. Her novels are ingenious and perceptive and underlaid by a delicious sense of irony, but they tend to be marred by over-melodramatic climaxes. Her children's books are charming and her books for girls notable for the same restrained sense of humour as her novels. School stories represent only a fraction of her output and among their scant half-dozen only one, *The Honour of the House*, is outstanding. *A Fifth-Form Martyr*, of the same calibre, is, despite its title, only minimally a school story: it is a time-slip which takes a modern schoolgirl, the same age as her youngest daughter, back to 1890, when Ethel was a schoolgirl. The periods are contrasted beautifully in atmosphere as well as in physical details and the book deserves to be better known. (*See also* **HISTORICAL AND FANTASY STORIES**.)

Of her minor school stories, the first, *That Awful Term*, is very much a prentice piece, and *A Countess at School* a routine, if well-done, exposé of snobbery. *Expelled from St Madern's* and *Her Second Chance* are related in that the villain of the first book, who schemes

to wreck the school in revenge for her cousin's expulsion, appears in the second as a reformed character come back to teach who now saves the school from misfortune. (This is the school story where the new girl turns out to be the wife of a jewel thief.) Both are amusing and have well-drawn characters, but are somewhat sensational.

But *The Honour of the House* is a masterpiece. The basic theme is the regeneration of house pride (and consequently achievement) by a new girl who is appalled by the situation into which she comes, rather late, after typhoid. Closely entwined with this—because it is their attitude which she manages to change—is the Kibble family, four sisters (two elder ones have left) who consistently drag Norman House down and contribute largely to its depression. The Kibbles are plain ('plate-like' is the adjective applied to their faces), lumpen and apparently stupid, Fatima, Paulina's form-mate, being the worst of the lot. It is only gradually that we come to realise the person behind the lump, and her connection with the major sub-plot, the teasing disasters which befall the odious, snobbish and wealthy Annabel Clay (all deliciously funny both to her contemporaries and to us). The climax of the book, concerning Paulina's explorer father (hitherto presumed dead) is almost irrelevant besides the importance of the changing relationship between Paulina and Fatima which the discovery highlights. We are pleased for Paulina—one of the few fictional schoolgirls to have convincing feelings about her parents—but more excited by Fatima's placid winning of the Tollington Verse Prize. (How wise of Channon merely to report the winning, not to attempt to write the poem for her!) *The Honour of the House*, for all its non-school dénouement, is a true, and very fine, school story.

Source: Mrs Judith Waite, E M Channon's youngest daughter

The bibliography below lists all E M Channon's girls' books, but not her books for adults and younger children. A complete bibliography may be found in *Folly* 14.

    That Awful Term, GOP ([1924]). Illus.
    The Cotton-Wool Girl*, Sheldon (1924)
    The Perfect Miss Coverdale*, Nisbet ([1925])
    The Honour of a Guide*, Nisbet (1926). Illus. G W Goss
    The Surprising Holidays*, Sheldon ([1926])
    The Handsome Hardcastles (part school), Nisbet ([1927])
1   *Expelled from St Madern's*, Nisbet ([1928]). Not illus.
2   *Her Second Chance*, Nisbet ([1930]). Illus.
    The Honour of the House, Nisbet ([1931]). Illus.
    A Countess at School, Sheldon Press ([1931]). Illus. D Osborne
    Rose Leaves School*, Ernest Benn (1933)
    A Fifth-Form Martyr, Sheldon Press ([1935]). Illus. 'Ogle'
    The Cinderella Girl*, Nelson ([1937])

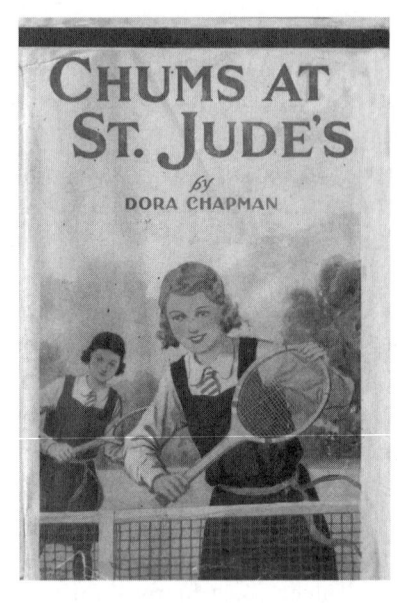

Dora Chapman
(Dora Barr Chapman Francis)
1893-1941

Dora Barr Chapman was born in Nottingham on 5 August 1893, the youngest of the four surviving children of Henry Chapman, at the time of her birth a grocer but previously a commission agent, later a 'house furnisher' and then a poultry farmer. She was educated privately, and during World War I worked as a canteen inspector. In 1925, she married James Harold Francis, another grocer, later a commercial traveller; at this point she was living in Truro, where she died. She had one daughter.

We have no proof of any teaching experience, but there is clear internal evidence that she knew boarding school from the inside, as pupil, staff or both. All her books are set in public schools of between 200 and 350 pupils, generally focusing on girls of around fifteen, and the picture of schoolgirl life is credible and convincing. *That Rebellious Schoolgirl* has all the hallmarks of being based on the writer's memories of her own schooldays or observation of pupils; and apart from the numerous part-lessons given verbatim (normally geography) throughout the corpus, *Beryl the Rebel* reproduces two essays, one with a footnote which reads 'Part of an actual essay written by a schoolgirl on this subject'.

Chapman aims for realism of content in her books: secret passages, kidnappings and mysterious Chinamen are conspicuous by their absence, and the only time that a girl is suspected of being a princess, she turns out to be a gamekeeper's daughter (*That Eventful Term*). She limits herself to five rescues in nine books, and avoids situations that most school-story writers take for granted: all but one of the protagonists have a full set of parents, and (apart from Jill and Jack in *Chums at St Jude's*) have no money difficulties. Even when she uses a stereotyped plot, it is developed credibly: bottom-of-the-league Croft House (*Jennifer of Croft House*) doesn't win the cup despite the charismatic Jennifer being installed as Captain; it only moves up one place and is third at the end of the year—but one can believe that it will continue to improve.

However, Chapman provides plenty of drama, mostly derived from the personalities of her protagonists, many of whom are rebellious and undisciplined girls, though with some reason for their misbehaviour: Betty (*Betty Plays Up*) resents the departure of a beloved teacher and 'plays up' Miss Dunkley, her successor; Beryl (*Beryl the Rebel*) hates the new School Council, and stirs up trouble for herself and others; Rita (*That Eventful Term*) loathes the idea of school and tries to be expelled. Others, such as the eponymous Unruly Trio, do not rebel: but they do set rules at naught when they have a noble objective (such as distempering their study at midnight).

Nevertheless, although there is a fair amount of sub-Brazilesque madcappery, there is no narrative approbation of rebellion; we sympathise with the rebels, but can see that they are acting foolishly. These tumultuous pupils all settle down, often well before the end of the book, having been talked into responsible behaviour by the Head; they are all presented as magnetic and attractive girls, good at games and with enormous leadership potential. Marjory (*That Rebellious Schoolgirl*) has actually become Head Girl in the sequel, *That Detestable New Girl*. Chapman's attitude to these rebels may be summed up by the words of one of her characters: 'Elsie … (is) much too righteously smug … I hate the type; they never seem to want to be anything other than good. I'd much rather have a girl that gets into trouble. Marjory and Olive have both been through the mill, and that's why they are always so humane' (*That Detestable New Girl*).

Interestingly, her last school story was written under her married name: *The Knights of Study Thirteen* introduces Guides, but is otherwise undistinguished. In general, Chapman cannot be placed in the front rank of school-story authors; her writing is a little flat, and she is unwilling or unable to explore the psychology of her protagonists, preferring dialogue to narrative, and not really communicating the individuality of the characters through that dialogue. But her books are pleasant to read, even if they do not linger in the memory.

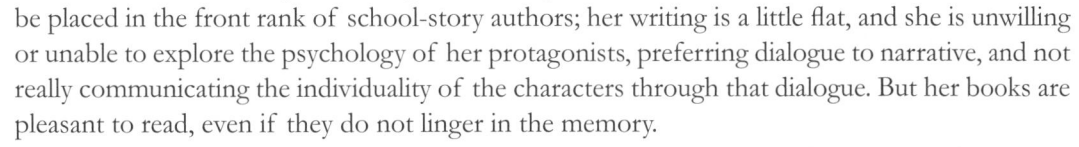

1   *That Rebellious Schoolgirl*, Partridge ([1924]). Illus. 'HLB'
    Betty Plays Up!, Partridge (1925). Illus. Joyce L Brisley
    An Eventful Term, Partridge ([1927]). Illus. 'J F'
    That Unruly Trio, Partridge ([1928]). Illus. S Moorsom
2   *That Detestable New Girl*, Newnes ([1931]). Illus.
    Treacle of St Mike's, Newnes ([1933]). Illus.
    Jennifer of Croft House, Newnes ([1934]). Illus.
    Chums at St Jude's, Pilgrim Press ([1935]). Illus. 'Vernon Soper'
    Beryl the Rebel, Newnes ([1935]). Illus.

As Dora B Francis

The Knights of Study 13, Pilgrim Press ([1935]). Illus. 'M Murray'

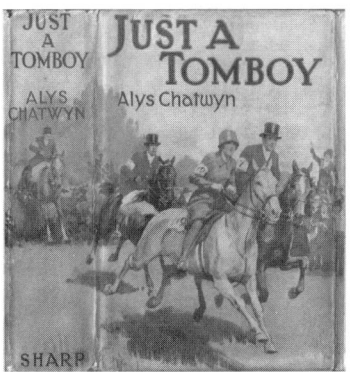

Alys Chatwyn
(Pseudonym of Ernest Protheroe)
For a bibliography and critique, *see* **ERNEST PROTHEROE**.
See also *The Encyclopaedia of Boys' School Stories*, **ERNEST PROTHEROE**

Christine Chaundler
1887-1972

Christine Chaundler was born on 5 September 1887 in Biggleswade, Bedfordshire, the eldest daughter and surviving child of Henry Chaundler, a solicitor (1858-1933) and Constance Julia Thompson (1862-1938). The couple had, in total, six sons and four daughters, of whom three sons and a daughter died in childhood. Christine attended Queen Anne's School, Caversham, until she was sixteen, and then (for reasons we do not know) St Winifred's School in Llanfairfechan, North Wales. She wrote from childhood, and spent all her very long working life in writing and publishing. The first earnings from her pen came in 1912, when she won 10s 6d in a Prize Poem competition run by *Girls' Realm*; and from then on she made a steady and growing income from her writing—children's stories, girls' and boys' stories and books, columns for periodicals such as *The Quiver* and even a couple of 'Cinematograph Film Scenarios'.

She had a brief spell in the Land Army, but for most of the First World War worked for the publishing firm of Cassell's, where she was on the editorial team of the periodical *Little Folks*. Although that magazine serialised several of her earlier girls' school stories, she sold the copyrights for the books to other publishers, particularly James Nisbet, whose firm she joined in 1919 as Juvenile Book Editor. Her books were so successful that she was able to leave Nisbet's in 1922 when she was making enough income from her writing to do without the regular salary. Throughout the 1920s and 30s she continued to make an excellent living from her children's books and stories. She had moved with her mother to Haslemere in Surrey after the war, and during the 20s had a house built in Fittleworth on the Sussex Downs, where she lived until her death.

After World War II, the market for the traditional girls' and boys' stories was not so large, and Chaundler made much of her income from book reviews, broadcast fees (many of her short stories were read on the BBC's *Children's Hour*) and reading for publishers. She became slightly reclusive as she grew older, but chaired the local Writers' Circle and grew interested in spiritualism. She died on 15 December 1972.

With Chaundler's very first book, we are in the world of the large (200-400) public girls' school, and, apart from the occasional foray into High Schools (with a very similar atmosphere), we never leave it—there are no ladies' seminaries. We have the full hierarchy of Head Girls, Games Captains, prefects and houses. Games are important (although Chaundler rarely shows us matches for their own sake) and girls are less inclined towards passionate and exclusive friendships—at least in the earlier, more influential books. We also have a marked change in the ethical atmosphere. Chaundler rejects the older pattern, where the reader watched the fall from grace of a girl increasingly succumbing to temptation. There is no specifically Christian message, not even desperate prayers as the tide comes in. Ethics consist almost entirely of following the code of honour: one doesn't lie, sneak, swank, or complain. Her heroines are generally hard-working without being too 'clever', sociable, impulsive and honourable to a fault. As sub-editor of *Little Folks*, Chaundler helped to establish the standards followed by girls' school stories for the next 25 years.

Initially, Chaundler's main interest is the girl who does not fit in. The 'outsider' theme may be positive, involving a girl too good for her school or form-mates who brings about reformation, like Jacqueline (*The Right St John's*) and Penelope (*Reforming the Fourth*). Sometimes we are shown a more negative image of the rebellious individual or form, as in *Jan of the Fourth*, *A Fourth Form Rebel*, or *The Feud with the Sixth*. More frequently, the protagonists are outsiders because their community ostracizes them: *Philippa's Family*, *Just Gerry*, *A Credit to the House* and *Sally Sticks it Out* are good examples of this situation, and there are many others. *Pat's Third Term* in particular is such a painful and authentic record of the emotional cruelty which girls can inflict that one wonders whether Chaundler experienced this herself. We know that she moved from Queen Anne's, Caversham, to St Winifred's at the age of sixteen; did she leave because she was miserable, or did she find herself an outsider at her new school?

Sally, the scholarship girl whose adventures may well have been the basis for Denise Deegan's successful play *Daisy Pulls it Off*, epitomises not just the outsider making good, but also the classic shape of a Chaundler novel, in which the heroines, despite all their efforts, find their situation deteriorating until a final twist of events brings reconciliation. Sally, the most unfortunate of all Chaundler's heroines, being appallingly (and totally unfairly) persecuted and misjudged, is also given the most wonderful ovation at the final concert, in a sequence nicely calculated to leave the reader in floods of happy tears. The gallant rescues and sudden revelations which bring about these reversals of fortune are, rationally considered, ridiculous; Chaundler makes them believable by making her heroines so real and so sympathetic that one desperately wants the eucatastrophe. It is wish fulfilment to the highest degree, but it works beautifully.

Chaundler also succeeds in laughing at some school-story traditions while simultaneously using them herself. 'What a splendid opportunity it would be for the heroines of those rotten, old-fashioned school stories I used to get out of the Sunday-School library at home,' says Jacqueline in *The Right St John's*, contemplating how she can refuse to use the cribs employed by the rest of her form; but she manages it. And Cara, unable to deny smoking because it would incriminate her protégée Jean who is on the verge of expulsion, thinks: 'I shall just have to console myself, as best I can, with the knowledge of what a first-class story-book ass of a misused heroine I am! And I've always despised those misunderstood heroines in story-books so!' (*Captain Cara*). *The Story-Book School* is centred entirely on a form uniting to convince new girl Mary that St Margaret's is just like the schools in books. Some of the 'adventures' with which the form 'stuff' Mary are things which Chaundler has previously used herself, such as holding up a burglar with a toy revolver (cf *Jan of the Fourth*). In this book, the midnight feast is cold and dull; the great rescue (from a canal lock) is wet, cold, and severely punished by authority. The irony here is patent.

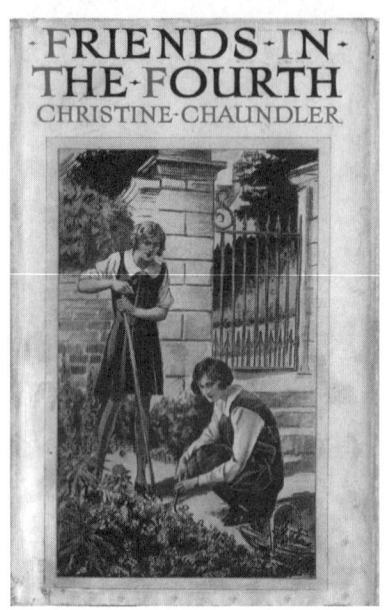

Irony, in fact, is one of Chaundler's great strengths, particularly in her plots. *A Credit to the House* exemplifies this type of dramatic irony: Daisy is sent to Coventry (led by Jill) for refusing to confess her crime, losing order marks for her house. But her 'crime' consists of secretly mending Jill's torn clothes so that the latter can play in the House hockey finals. We see a similar plot device in *The New Girl in Four A*, where the hapless June, constantly losing marks in her form's effort for the shield, actually wins it for them by sticking to her self-imposed task of keeping the form-room tidy (as does Nicola Marlow in *Autumn Term*, see **ANTONIA FOREST**). A slightly different use of irony occurs in those books which turn on the motif of good intentions going dreadfully wrong: *The Reputation of the Upper Fourth*, *The Fourth Form Detectives* and the two *Evangeline* books (which, like *Bunty of the Blackbirds* and *A Credit to the House*, have lovable duffers as their protagonists) are all examples of this: one might also include under this heading *The Chivalrous Fifth*, probably her most popular book, judging by the number of reprints. Here the irony depends on two simultaneous and contrasting visions. The discerning reader instantly places new girl Jane Smith by her cool self-assurance, her language ('the Mater ... wrote to Miss Graham and bullied her into taking me') and the subjects in which she is 'miles ahead'—French, dancing and general knowledge. Meanwhile, Jane's classmates believe that she is the working-class daughter of an old-clothes dealer, and decide to be Terribly Kind to her. All is, of course, revealed at the end (Jane's mother is actually a Marchioness who runs an excessively smart antiques business), but it would not work so well had we not realised from the beginning that Jane is amusing herself by playing up to her form's belief.

It is impossible in this space to mention all Chaundler's other school stories, though some are excellent, such as *The Junior Prefect*, with its study of a diffident girl very different from the standard heroine, or *Meggy Makes her Mark*, which tackles snobbishness head-on by using a working-class girl who does *not* turn out to be a stolen heiress. Some of her later books do not, perhaps, come up to the standard of those written during the 1920s, and her account books show that she gradually found it more difficult to sell girls' stories (despite her introduction of Guides in the last few); but she must be considered one of the major girls' school-story writers of the last century.

The following bibliography gives Chaundler's girls' fiction and children's stories published separately in hardback. It does not list her boys' school stories (see *The Encyclopaedia of Boys' School Stories*, **PETER MARTIN**), the series of Everyman books which she compiled for Mowbrays or short stories in annuals (which run into hundreds).

In each case, the list below gives the date of first publication in book form. It ignores previous serialisations in periodicals unless the title of the serial differed from the later hardback version, in which case both are given.

Further Reading
Folly 21, 22

    *The Magic Kiss**, Cassell (1916)
    *Little Squirrel Tickletail**, Cassell (1917). Illus. Harry Rountree
    *Ronald's Burglar**, Nelson (1919). Illus. Helen Stratton
    Pat's Third Term, Hodder and OUP (1920). Illus. Harold Earnshaw
C1 *The Reputation of the Upper Fourth*, Nisbet ([1920]). Illus. 'Coller'
    Just Gerry, Nisbet ([1920]). Illus. 'Coller'
    The Right St John's, OUP ([1920]). Illus. 'Savile Lumley'
    *The Thirteenth Orphan**, Nisbet ([1920]). Illus. Honor Appleton
    *The Binky Book** (2 volumes), Nisbet ([1920]). Illus. Will Owen
    The Fourth Form Detectives (*Little Folks* serial titled *The Amateur 'Tecs*), Nisbet ([1921]). Illus. 'G W Goss'
    *Snuffles for Short**, Nisbet ([1921]). Illus. Honor Appleton
    A Fourth Form Rebel (*British Girls' Annual* serial titled *The Rebel of the Fourth*), Nisbet ([1922]). Illus. 'G W Goss'
    The Reformation of Dormitory Five, Nisbet (1922). Illus.
    Jan of the Fourth, Nisbet ([1923]). Illus. 'G W Goss'
C2 *Captain Cara*, Nisbet ([1923]). Illus.
    *Tomboy Toby** (semi-school story), Partridge ([1924]). Illus. 'H L Bacon'
    Jill the Outsider, Cassell (1924). Illus. Elizabeth Earnshaw
    Judy the Tramp (part school), Nisbet ([1924]). Illus. 'G W Goss'
    Winning her Colours, Nisbet ([1924]). Illus. 'G W Goss'
    Sally Sticks It Out, Partridge ([1924]). Illus.
    *Dickie's Day**, Nelson ([1924])
    *Princess Carroty-Top and Timothy**, Warne (1924)
    Bunty of the Blackbirds, Nisbet ([1925]). Illus. 'G W Goss'
    An Unofficial Schoolgirl (semi-school story), Nisbet ([1925]). Illus. 'G W Goss'
    *The Adopting of Mickie**, RTS ([1925]). Illus. T Peddie
    Twenty-Six Christine Chaundler Stories for Girls, RTS ([1926]). Not illus.
    A Credit to her House, Ward Lock ([1926]). Illus. 'J Dewar Mills'
E1 *The Exploits of Evangeline*, Nisbet ([1926]). Illus.
    The Chivalrous Fifth, Nelson ([1927]). Illus. Anne Rochester

Reforming the Fourth, Ward Lock ([1927]). Illus. J Dewar Mills
Philippa's Family, Nisbet ([1927]). Illus.
Meggy Makes her Mark, Nisbet ([1928]). Illus.
The Games Captain, Ward Lock (1928). Illus.
Friends in the Fourth, Ward Lock (1929). Illus. 'J Dewar Mills'
The Madcap of the School (two novella-length school stories), Nelson ([1930]). Illus. 'J M Anderson'?
A Disgrace to the Fourth, Nelson ([1930]). Illus. M D Swales
The Technical Fifth, Ward Lock (1930). Illus. 'Sutcliffe'
The New Girl in Four A, Nisbet ([1930]). Illus.
Two in Form Four, Cassell (1931). Illus. 'P B Hickling'
The Junior Prefect, Ward Lock (1931). Illus. 'J Dewar Mills'
The Story-Book School, OUP (1931). Illus. 'Margaret Horder'
Jill of the Guides, Nisbet ([1932]). Illus.
The Feud with the Sixth, Nisbet ([1932]). Illus.
Cinderella Ann*, Ward Lock (1932)

E2   *Five B and Evangeline* (*Schoolgirl* serial titled *Some Further Exploits of Evangeline*), Newnes ([1932]). Illus.
The Amateur Patrol, Nisbet ([1933]). Illus. 'Jean Stuart'
The Children's Author: A Writer's Guide to the Juvenile Market*, Pitman (1934). Not illus.
The Lonely Garden: & Ronald's Burglar*, Nelson ([1934])
Tales of Nicky-Nob* (4 volumes), Chambers (1937)
The Children's Story Hour*, Evans (1938). Illus. Alfred E Kerr
The Odd Ones*, Country Life (1941). Illus. Harry Rountree
Winkie Wee and the Silver Sixpence*, Museum Press (1947)
Winkie Wee's Spring-Cleaning*, Museum Press (1947)
Prize for Gardening*, Nelson (1948). Illus. L M Dufty
More Stories for the Children's Hour*, Hale (1949). Illus. Cyril Foster

C = Cara pair
E = Evangeline pair

Anne Chesney

The only copy located of this author's sole school story has an Australian publisher, but the book seems to be English. One hopes that no Australian fourth-former would hit the English mistress over the head with a weighted shoe in order to steal an examination paper so that she could coach her favourite sixth-former surreptitiously.

Leslie Wins Through, The Shakespeare Head (Sydney, Australia; 1947). Not illus.

Alice M Chesterton
(Alice Mary Chesterton)
1874-1952

The author was born in Tonbridge, Kent, and died in St Leonards, Sussex. By 1911 she had left the parental home and had set up house with a friend and the friend's sister, describing herself as 'authoress'.

Whittenbury College is, as suggested by its title, a college story—set in a college 'for training in domestic affairs', designed for middle-class girls. *Christal's Adventures* is not quite a sequel, as the eponymous heroine does not appear in *Whittenbury College*.

Whittenbury College: A School Story for Girls, Nelson ([1915]).
　　Illus. Ethel Everett
Christal's Adventure: The Story of a 'Whittenbury College' Student*, Nelson ([1919]). Illus.

Also other books for children and young adults

Catherine Christian
(Mamie Mühlenkamp)
1901-1985

Catherine Mary Christian was born on 22 June 1901 in Chelsea, London, as Mamie Mühlenkamp, the daughter (and only child) of Christian John Mühlenkamp and his wife Catherine Harriett Ellett. Her father was a businessman of German origin, but the family had been domiciled in England for some time before Mamie's birth. As a child she travelled extensively abroad with her father, but that period of her life came to an end with the First World War. It is thought that it was at this time that the family changed its name to avoid the opprobrium of being labelled German—in fact, Mamie's grandfather, who had property near the Kentish coast, was accused of signalling to the enemy.

Mamie and her parents had by now moved to Croydon, where she attended Croydon High School. She was a violinist but failed to reach professional standards. During the 1920s she ran various Guide companies and seems to have lived at home. In the 1930s she was involved with what would now be called a form of alternative medicine—it involved therapy by use of coloured lights—but this ended with the outbreak of the Second World War. In December 1938 Mamie Mühlenkamp became officially Catherine Mary Christian, a name she was already using for her writing. Between 1939 and 1945, she edited *The Guide*, the official journal of the Guide movement, while her great friend Margaret ('Peg') Tennyson, with whom she was now sharing a flat in Battersea, edited *The Guider*. Peg also wrote Guide stories as Carol Forrest. Their flat was a casualty of the Blitz and for a time they lived in a gypsy caravan at Blacklands Farm, West Hoathly, Sussex, which was, and still is, a Guiding Centre. In 1942 they moved to Woldringham, Surrey, where again Catherine was involved with a local Guide company. At the end of the war the friends were first involved with the Guide International Service and then moved down to south Devon, where Catherine was for a time Curator of the Salcombe National Trust Museum. Eventually they moved to Hawson Court, near Buckfastleigh, where they ran a small-holding and assisted another friend, the former Polish Chief Guide, with a home for war orphans.

At this period Catherine found herself unable to write, but after Peg's death (1972) she took up her pen again, producing an Arthurian work. She died of lung cancer on 12 November 1985. By her desire her ashes were scattered on Dartmoor, below Cave-Penney Cross.

Catherine Christian's main interest was always Guiding, and her two or three school stories (the Marigolds who make good are part of a day-school company, but there is very little action set in school) have a very strong Guide focus. She takes the common theme of girls 'finding themselves' and applies it in a variety of ways: Mary Ellen in *A Schoolgirl from Hollywood*, who has been a schoolgirl film star and a very superficial Guide, finds out what Guiding is all about at the spartan Whitehaven School; Guiding makes a community out of the desolate orphans at Emery's End; and the Marigolds, from a slack school, learn what hard work really means.

Christian's writing is wryly humorous, and rarely idealises Guides—no patrol leaders saving countless lives here! Guiding, though, and its quasi-religious ability to change lives, is given a somewhat mystical aura; though this is never as strong as in the books she wrote as Patience Gilmour, these school stories are probably not for convinced anti-Guides.

The Marigolds Make Good (part school), Blackie ([1937]). Illus. R H Brock
A Schoolgirl from Hollywood, Blackie ([1939]). Illus. E Baker
The School at Emery's End, Pearson (1944). Not illus.

Also many Guiding stories, children's books and adult novels including historical and Arthurian books. She also wrote a series of four Ranger books under the pseudonym 'Patience Gilmour'.
See also **GUIDE SCHOOL STORIES**

Mrs Henry Clarke MA
(Amy Key Clarke)
1853-1908
Amy Key was born on 17 August 1850 in Plymouth, the second daughter of Joseph Henry Key, manager of the Devon and Courtenay Clay Company, and his first wife Elizabeth née Barnes, both of Cornish descent. Elizabeth had one other daughter and two sons; after her death, Joseph married her sister, a union which also produced two sons and two daughters. Amy was educated initially in Newton Abbot, where the family had moved in 1857, then at a small boarding school at Whitchurch. She became a governess in 1869, in which year her first published work (a short story in the magazine *Good Words*) appeared; she continued her writing, which was undertaken to

boost the family income, until her death.

In 1873, she was appointed to the staff of Plymouth High School, on condition that she passed the Cambridge 'Women's Examination', in which she subsequently took a first. She was released from her post for a year to take up a scholarship to read Mathematics at Newnham College from 1875-6. She refused a further scholarship to read for the Moral Sciences Tripos, feeling that she had to contribute to the family finances. She taught at Plymouth High School from 1876 to 1880, when she was appointed as the first Headmistress of Truro High School (see **MARY BRAMSTON**).

During her headship, she gained an external MA degree (first class) from London University (1888); her studies clearly led to more than academic qualifications, as on 10 January 1889 she married Henry Clarke, a lecturer and tutor at London University, by whom she had three sons and a daughter. Although she did some lecturing at Westfield College, most of her time was taken up with her family and her writing. In 1898, she had an operation for breast cancer; the family moved, first to Acton, then to Herne Bay, and finally back to London where her children attended St Paul's Boys' and Girls' Schools. The cancer recurred, and she died on 4 March 1908, leaving a number of books for posthumous publication.

Mrs Henry Clarke's books are interesting for their early portrayals of High Schools, which all her heroines attend. As one might expect, she is a supporter of academic education for girls, although Cecily (*The Ravensworth Scholarship*) is shown to have acquired a far better classical education from her brother's private tutor than her contemporary Ruth has gained from the High School she attends. Like many of the early headmistresses, she was very concerned that education should not defeminise its students, and her books contain a fair amount of propaganda for traditional ideas of femininity. Indeed, *A High School Girl* and *A Clever Daughter* (neither of which are school stories despite their promising titles) both contrast intellectual eminence with home-making skills; not only are the latter approved to the detriment of the former, but in *A High School Girl*, the despised Bab actually takes a higher place in the Matriculation exam than Nan, the representative of advanced thought and castigator of 'the domestic chains we women have wrought for ourselves'.

Mrs Clarke's school stories, like those of **MAY BALDWIN** or **RAYMOND JACBERNS**, may be viewed as a bridge between the sentimental tales set in small private schools which characterise the late Victorian period, and the stories of larger High Schools and public schools, with their emphasis on games, and discouragement of outward emotion which dominate after the First World War. Her girls are vividly drawn, use colloquial speech, and are concerned to achieve academic honours in a society which has until recently denied these to them; but her agonies (typical of many writers of the period) lest such aspirations should corrupt girls may make her books less appealing to modern readers.

Source: *The Story of Truro High School*, by her daughter, A K Clarke: Truro, 1979

The majority of Mrs Henry Clarke's many books are adult romances, often historical and set in Cornwall; the list below only includes the books which are either school stories or have school and educational interest.

The Ravensworth Scholarship: A High School story for Girls, Blackie ([1894]). Illus. John H Bacon
*A High School Girl or: The Secret of the Old Bureau**, RTS ([1895]). Illus. M A Boole
*A Clever Daughter**, SSU ([1896]). Illus. Ida Lovering
Nan's Schooldays, RTS ([1906]). Illus. Dorothy Travers-Pope
*Dorothy's Discovery**, SSU (1909). Illus. John Jellicoe

Margaret Bruce Clarke
The Little Heiress (part school), Nelson ([1904]). Illus. P B Hickling

Renee Clarke
A Turbulent Term, Gerald Swan (1948). Illus.

Marjorie Cleves
(Ivy Marjorie Doreen Cleves)
1904-1994
Marjorie Cleves was born in Cardiff on 26 September 1904 and seems to have been a Ranger there in the 1920s. She died in 1994, but few other details of her life are known; her father was a journalist, and in 1939 she was working in that profession in Cardiff. Alternatively, she may have been a teacher, as several of her books feature a pretty young mistress to whom the girls are devoted. Her books are run-of-the mill school stories; her characters are in general somewhat shadowy and unreal, and her plots unoriginal, tending towards stock situations: identical twins substitute for each other, new girls have Dark Secrets, and ghosts (invariably of the non-supernatural variety) abound. Like many of her contemporaries, she is easily seduced by thriller elements: her first school story features a 'mysterious stranger in a red fez', and in *A School Goes to Scotland*, the dénouement reveals a young man kidnapped five years previously and kept in captivity by a wicked uncle in a secret room in the school buildings. The books in which she has controlled these urges are considerably more readable; *Holly House School* demonstrates a modicum of psychological insight.

A Term at Crossways, etc (novella in compilation), Epworth Press (1939). Illus. (various)
Chums at Pinewood, Warne (1943). Illus.
A School Goes to Scotland, Hutchinson ([1944]). Illus.

Christmas at the Priory* (holiday at school), Lutterworth Press (1946). Illus.
Holly House School, Epworth Press (1947). Illus. 'E T'
Houseboat Holiday*, Lutterworth Press (1948)
The School in the Dell, Warne ([1948]). Illus.
The Secret of Cheswood, Brockhampton (1949). Illus. Greta Jones
The Lilac Grange Ghost* (holiday at school), Epworth Press (1949). Illus. Berry M Ladler
The Merryfield Mystery, Hutchinson (1960). Not illus.

Susan Clifford
The Mugwump, Wells, Gardner, Darton ([1930]). Illus. Gordon Robinson

Rita Coatts
(Marguerite Harcourt Burrage Coatts)
1883-1955

Rita Coatts came of a writing family: her father was Edwin Harcourt Burrage (1839-1916; see *The Encyclopaedia of Boys' School Stories*, **EDWIN HARCOURT BURRAGE**), a journalist and prolific writer for boys; Athol Harcourt Burrage (1899-1951; see *Boys' School Stories*, **A H BURRAGE**), also a boys' writer, was her brother; Alfred McLelland Burrage (see *Boys' School Stories*, **A M BURRAGE**), notable for his ghost stories and one part school story (*Poor Dear Esmé*), was a cousin. It was no wonder that she too turned her hand to popular fiction.

She was born on 2 February 1883, at Chipstead, Surrey, the second of the eleven children of Edwin Harcourt Burrage and his wife Alice Louisa Reynolds. Although two younger sisters followed her, both died in infancy, as did one of her brothers, with the result that she grew up as the only girl among seven brothers. Of these, only Athol followed the family tradition full time, but Douglas (1890-1965) became a circus clown and wrote two books about his experiences.

Rita (as she was always known) was educated at Gore House, Redhill (the family had moved to Redhill in her infancy), and then at an Ursuline convent in Brussels. On her 24th birthday she married William Bentley Coatts, an insurance agent, and their son James Harcourt Coatts was born in 1909. At some point they moved to Canada, but when, following an unsatisfactory university career, James was sent back to England, Rita followed him and thereafter lived apart from her husband; they were eventually divorced. She settled at Greatstone, New Romney, on the Kentish coast, and at this point began to write her books for girls—we may reasonably assume that this was because she needed to supplement her income. She was totally professional in her attitude to writing, working within set hours and demanding quiet while she did so, and her books, however unrealistic and far-fetched, are technically competent. They do, however, suggest that she did not care for school mistresses much. Hers have names like Crackers, Fule and Croker, and any who are young, attractive and sympathetic, instead of ancient, domineering or downright sinister, are soon whisked away into marriage.

Rita Coatts was a prolific writer, and certain elements are predictable. Chief amongst these is the heroine who comes late to school, dreading its restrictions: until now she has been 'running wild on the veldt', left alone with servants, or helping in her father's detective agency. She is usually rich, with easy access to guns, motorbikes and aeroplanes—and she needs them. Although the school, even in post-war books, resembles a Victorian reformatory, with high glass-strewn walls, solitary confinements and grim wardresses, she will escape, often by bribing servants (butlers abound) after vowing to investigate, on her very first day, the local deserted mansion or gang of art thieves. Her (fairly beautiful) friends romantically adore her (supremely beautiful) looks and recklessly spirited integrity, but after some mild verbal sparring a small, ugly, pale or pimply rival becomes her deadly enemy (literally—there are threats to kill).

Throughout the books, dialogue is stilted and plots are far-fetched, but one has to admire the author's energy and enthusiasm. She plainly aims to 'break bounds' herself by ranging beyond the 'milk and water' story conventions dismissed in *Schoolgirl Pluck*. 'School affairs mean so much to you sheltered girls—to me they mean *nothing*,' cries one of her heroines. *Bookworm, the Mystery Solver* and *Facing it Out* are perhaps the best of the bunch, though both are too long.

In addition to her writing, Rita Coatts started a caravan site on her Greatstone property, which her son helped to run. Photographs show her as a short, well-turned-out lady, rather formidable but with a twinkle in her eye—and, nearly always, a dog by her side. She died on 22 March 1955.

Kate Tyler and Hilary Clare

Source: Mrs Cynthia Coatts, Rita Coatts's daughter-in-law

I1   *The Taming of Patricia*, Wells Gardner ([1934]). Illus. 'Frederick Spurgin'
Bookworm, the Mystery Solver, Nelson (1936). Illus. E E Brier
Facing It Out, Juvenile Productions (1937). Illus. 'C P Shilton'
Ghosts at Stark Hall, Wells Gardner (1938). Illus. W Lindsay Cable
I2   *School on an Island*, Wells Gardner (1938). Illus. 'KMW'
Flying Escape, Richard Lesley ([1947]). Illus.
S1   *Lots of Pluck*, Chambers (1948). Illus.
Schoolgirl Pluck, Sampson Low ([1947]). Illus.
The Wrong School!, Wells Gardner (1949). Illus. W Lindsay Cable
S2   *Born Lucky*, Chambers (1949). Not illus.
S3   *No Stopping Her*, Chambers (1950). Not illus.
Breaking Bounds, Rylee Rewards (1951). Illus.
S4   *Under Sara's Wing*, Chambers (1951). Not illus.
Robin—the Rebel!, Rylee Rewards ([1953]). Illus. 'T Watts'

I= Island pair
S = Sara series

Also about fifteen children's thrillers

Christabel Coleridge *see* **ADULT SCHOOL FICTION**

P Catherine Coles
(Phoebe Catherine Coles)
1917-2003

P Catherine Coles was the daughter of the composer Cecil Coles (killed 1918), and was educated at St Paul's Girls' School. She was primarily a writer of evangelistic children's books: she was one of the Victory Press stable of authors, and her books (which, going by the presentation labels, were mainly given as prizes by Nonconformist Sunday schools) are all intended to bring children to conversion and help them lead a Christian life. She died in Glasgow in 2003.

Coles' most popular books (judging from reprintings) are her Glendorran series, which focus on Wendy, the daughter of missionaries. *Wendy of Glendorran* moves at a breathless pace, covering three or four years in 151 pages, and following Wendy from rebellious fourth-former to the end of her career as School Captain, loved and esteemed by all. At the start of the book, she is finding it difficult to 'give light to others', but by page 41, 'things never seem to ruffle her', and she eventually converts most of her unpleasant schoolmates ('Thanks, Wendy … I'm going to be saved tonight'). *At the King's Command* brings Wendy back to Glendorran as a teacher (temporarily, she thinks, before becoming a missionary in India), whisks her briefly through engagement and marriage to the Christian scion of a noble family (an ex-missionary in India), and ends with her almost converting her mother-in-law. This triumph, however, is reserved for Wendy's eldest son, Paul, whose artless prattle forces Lady Cobleigh 'humbly down on her knees' at the beginning of *The Cardinals of Cobleigh Hall*, which follows the fortunes of Wendy's family and friends, and the children's hospital she establishes in the Manor. *Goodbye, Glendorran* begins with the dramatic arrival of a long-lost cousin who is the legal heir to Cobleigh Manor. However, one could hardly expect Coles to confine herself to a single plot thread, and we soon forget the Cardinals' exile as Elspeth, Wendy's daughter, goes to school at Glendorran, scampers through seven years of school life in 90-odd pages, and finally confirms the book's title.

Coles' other girls' school stories are all 55-60 page board-covered books, designed for the cheaper end of the Sunday school prize market, and all using the standard conversion theme.

1. *Wendy of Glendorran*, Victory Press (1951). Not illus.
   Penelope's Secret, Victory Press (1953). Not illus.
2. *At the King's Command*, Victory Press (1953). Not illus.
   The Trio from Dormitory Five, Victory Press (1957). Not illus.
3. *The Cardinals of Cobleigh Manor**, Victory Press (1958). Not illus.
   The Affairs of the Third Form, Victory Press (1959). Not illus.
4. *Goodbye, Glendorran*, Victory Press (1961). Not illus.

Also over 20 other children's evangelistic stories between 1949 and 1976, including eight using the pseudonym **'PETER FRASER'** (see *The Encyclopaedia of Boys' School Stories*)

Joyce Colmer
(Evelyn Joyce Elliott Colmer, later Howard)
1889-1955

Joyce Colmer is assumed to be the journalist of that name who started her working life as a school teacher and auditor for the Ministry of Pensions before turning to journalism, working for *The Lady*, *Weldon's Ladies' Journal* and then, from 1924 to 1937, editing *Nursing Mirror*. In 1925 she helped to found, and for a time edited, *Nursery World*. She was born and lived in London, married Graham Colmer in 1913 (divorced 1919) and Geoffrey Howard, a judge, in 1930; she had one daughter, Rosemary. She died on 20 December 1955.

Rosemary to the Rescue is interesting mainly in the way in which it combines a standard school-story plot (ongoing thefts by an unknown pupil) with even greater anti-Semitism than is normal at this period in the girls' school story: not only has the villain, Schwarzstein (fat, oily and swarthy, and 'evil, utterly, totally evil'), driven at least one poor chap to suicide by his money-lending and blackmailing techniques, but his daughter Rachel is the unseen hand behind the thefts at school and drives one girl to attempted suicide. (She is, naturally, rescued by Rosemary.) All this, combined with a love affair between the heroine's uncle and one of the mistresses at St Wilfrid's, makes for mind-boggling stuff.

Rosemary to the Rescue, Jarrolds (1925). Illus.

Margaret S Comrie
Her Next-Door Neighbour, Shaw [1900]. Illus.

Also about eighteen other adult and children's books

Alice Corkran
Alice Corkran's two semi-school stories both use the 19th-century falsely accused convention. *Meg's Friend* follows its eponymous protagonist from her orphaned, slum childhood to her reconciliation with her noble grandfather, via the 'school for ladies' at which she is an outcast; *Margery Merton's Girlhood* centres on the heroine's art training at a Parisian convent, and is interesting for the sympathy and understanding with which the nuns and their faith are treated, though Miss Corkran was clearly not a Catholic: one wonders whether she or a close acquaintance had had similar experiences.

Margery Merton's Girlhood (art school/convent), Blackie ([1887]). Illus. Gordon Browne
Meg's Friend, Blackie ([1888]). Illus. Gordon Browne

Around 20 other books, including children's and adult fiction and non-fiction

Heather Cornish
Dumps Takes Charge, Venturebooks, Bath (1948). Not illus.

Theodora Cornish
One Term: A Tale of Manor House School, Wells Gardner, Darton (1910). Illus. Paul Hardy

Grace Couch *see under* **DEIRDRE O'BRIEN**

Gwendoline Courtney
1911-1996

Gwendoline Courtney was born on 23 September 1911 near Southampton, the younger daughter of Edwin Courtney, an antiques dealer, and Joanna née Potter. Although there seem to have been no professional writers among her forebears, Arthur Mee was a distant cousin, and among her first cousins was Phyllis Norris, who wrote eight girls' books. The family moved to Wallasey in the Wirral when Gwendoline was young; there she attended Oldershaw High School. She failed to matriculate because of ill health, and may have trained as a secretary; she seems to have worked for some time in her father's office. During World War II, she worked in Lord Goodman's office, and prided herself on being the only civilian to work on Operation Overlord. After the death of her parents (her father in the 1930s and her mother about fifteen years later) she and her sister (neither of whom married) lived together until the latter's death in 1995. They moved a great deal, partly because an ear injury from a bomb blast made all noise difficult for Gwendoline to bear. Between 1940, when they left Wallasey, and her death (from a stroke) in March 1996, they lived in Salisbury, Tisbury, Wilton, near Salisbury (in a house called Denehurst), East Knoyle, Cornwall, and Stour Row, a small village not far from Shaftesbury in Dorset.

Gwendoline Courtney's school stories are not numerous, nor, looked at objectively, particularly outstanding, but she attracts a considerable number of collectors. She is at her best when depicting girls having to pick their way through a hostile or difficult situation. Initially, her war-time heroines track down German spies—at school in *The Denehurst Secret Service*, and on holiday in *Well Done, Denehurst!*—but in the former, the spy plot is almost an irrelevance for much of the book, which focuses on the sisters' battle to reconcile the warring houses to which they have been assigned.

The eponymous heroine of the charming (if somewhat anachronistic) *A Coronet for Cathie* must battle against snobbery, in a situation redolent of **ELSIE J OXENHAM**'s *Girls of the Hamlet Club*; and the Loring sisters fight against prejudice, as well as a gang of robbers (*The Wild Lorings at School*) and a schoolgirl thief (*The Wild Lorings, Detectives*).

Courtney, who lived with her sister for much of her life, seems to find security in writing about girls in pairs or groups; even Cathie, an only child, has her two girl cousins accompanying her to school, and the only really solitary heroine, Rosalind (*At School with the Stanhopes*), is befriended by the lively Stanhope family—all five of them! She is also very happy to introduce boys and young men into her stories; *The Denehurst Secret Service*, in fact, relishes the discomfiture of the unpleasant pacifist, Miss Marshall, when faced with gallant cousin Deryk, a secret service agent who actually has permission to come into the sacred school grounds; and Elspeth and Maud Loring's brother, Nick, is conveniently awarded a rugger accident which necessitates a term at home, only a secret passage away from St Margaret's.

Courtney's books are well written and gently humorous, and we are willing to suspend our disbelief at the sensational goings-on at some of her establishments for the sake of the attractive characters she creates.

Sources: Phyllis Norris; Thelma Dawkins (Gwendoline Courtney's friend and legatee)

    Torley Grange*, Nelson ([1935])
    The Grenville Garrison*, Nelson (New Era series), ([1940])
D1 *The Denehurst Secret Service*, OUP (1940). Illus. Margaret Horder
D2 *Well Done, Denehurst!**, OUP (1941). Illus. Margaret Horder
    Sally's Family*, OUP (1946). Illus. Jennetta Vise
    Stepmother* OUP (1948); retitled *Elizabeth of the Garret Theatre*, Children's Press ([1965]). Illus. T R Freeman
    A Coronet for Cathie (part school), Nelson (1950). Illus. Edith Brier
    Long Barrow*, OUP (1950). Illus. Richard Kennedy
    At School with the Stanhopes, Nelson (1951). Illus. Valerie Sweet
    The Girls of Friar's Rise*, Nelson (1952). Illus. Edith Brier
    The Chiltons*, Nelson (1953). Illus. Spence/F Stocks May
L1 *The Wild Lorings at School*, Hutchinson ([1954]). Not illus.
L2 *The Wild Lorings, Detectives,* Hutchinson (1956). Not illus.

D = Denehurst pair
L = Loring pair

Also *Mermaid House,* published as a serial in the *Salisbury Journal* during 1953 and published in book form by Girls Gone By (2011)

Frances Cowen
(Frances Gertrude Cowen Munthe, later Minto-Cowen)
1901-1992
Frances Cowen was born in Oxford, the daughter of an elementary school headmaster. Her birth date is sometimes given as 1915 by her, but she was in fact born on 27 December 1901. She was educated at Oxford High School, but by 1937 she had moved to St Peter Port, Guernsey; she later returned to Oxford, and by 1970 was living in Wimbledon, south-west London. She married Heinrich Gesle Munthe with whom she had one daughter, lived in Wimbledon and became a prolific writer of thrillers for both adults and children. *The Milhurst*

Mystery seems to be her only excursion into school stories. Not that she travels very far: set at a day school, the book's plot turns on a series of thefts, eventually proved to be the work of 'Ginger Sharpe … one of the keenest one-man burglars on [the police's] book', plus his trained monkey.

Her later life history is not known, but she died in Cornwall in 1992 as 'Minto-Cowen'.

The Milhurst Mystery, Blackie ([1933]). Illus. E Brier

Around 50 other books, divided fairly evenly between children's mystery thrillers and adult thriller-romances

E E Cowper
(Edith Elise Cadogan Cooper, later Cowper)
1859-1933

Edith Elise Cadogan, born 1859, was the second daughter of the Rev. Edward Cadogan, incumbent of Walton, Warwickshire, and later (1873-90) of Wicken, Northamptonshire. At 17, she married Frank Cooper, a gentleman of independent means who later made his name as a yachtsman and writer on sailing. He changed his name by deed poll to Cowper in 1885, alleging that this was the original family spelling. They lived initially at Kivernall House, Hordle, Hampshire, where they ran a small prep school; later they built Lisle Court, Wootton, Isle of Wight, another school, but left there around 1891. Their marriage broke up because of Frank's cruelty and infidelity, although they may never have actually divorced. In 1901 Edith was living in London, describing herself as 'authoress', with her four daughters. There were also four sons, of whom one died in infancy; the eldest, Frank, became an artist and RA; Lionel, the second, was killed in a shipboard accident in the Yukon in 1906 and Gerald, the youngest, was a much-travelled ne'er-do-well. Cowper appears to have visited Canada: several of her books were set there. As a granddaughter was domiciled in Toronto in 1953 it may be that one (or more) of her daughters or sons settled there. By the early 1920s, however, Cowper had settled at Milford-on-Sea, Hampshire, where she died on 18 November 1933.

E E Cowper's published works run to some 70 volumes, the first two in 1881 and 1883, the remainder between 1899 and 1933, with 1919 the only year without at least one title. Apart from one early work for 'little girls', most of her books were aimed at the young teenage girl, with holiday and adventure stories prevailing, very much in the **BESSIE MARCHANT** tradition of girls making their adventurous ways through life without the encumbrance of adults. Sailing is a feature of many of her books, suggesting that she had shared her husband's pastime. There were also a few historical stories, and in the 1920s a series of tales of the Canadian wilderness, some apparently aimed at boys rather than girls—no doubt the androgynous form of name she used for her writing assisted this. Her comparatively few school (or school-related) stories date from the same period. Only two can in fact be classified as 'school stories', but *The Mystery Term* is the first of a series of four which follow Crystal and her friends through several holidays. The first book is really as much an adventure story as the rest, with all the paraphernalia of secret passages, 'ghosts' and villains (if somewhat low-key ones); but Cowper's characterisation is better than that of many comparable writers. *That Troublesome Term* is the only story which focuses on a purely school situation. There is something almost Dickensian about her villainess, Amalia Veron, whose golden hair and 'light blue eyes that were ... like a kitten's' hide a vicious and self-seeking soul. The book also contains what is probably the only silver fox farm in any British school story, though as in the same period Cowper wrote two other stories involving fox farms it may be that she had real, and recent, experience of one.

It is clear that E E Cowper was a professional writer who was willing to experiment with new varieties of story and to keep up to date with current trends—which in the 1920s included school stories. Her writing is always competent, her character-drawing good, and her plots not entirely improbable—in fact, her greatest failing is a desire to make her stories too plausible, for too often the expected climax proves not quite up to expectation through being too commonplace. Her school stories are not her best work—she was in her sixties by the time she wrote them—but even so are not wholly without merit.

Further Reading
Folly 60

1   *The Mystery Term*, Blackie ([1923]). Illus. R H Brock
    That Troublesome Term, Cassell (1926). Illus. Elizabeth Earnshaw
2   *The Holiday School**, Cassell (1927). Illus. Norman Sutcliffe
3   *The Fifth Form Adventurers**, Cassell (1929). Illus. P B Hickling
4   *The Invincible Fifth**, Collins ([1930]). Illus. 'THP'

Also many other Guide and adventure stories for girls

Pamela Cox *see under* **ENID BLYTON**

Jane Cranston
First-Term Rebel, Ward Lock (1955). Illus.

Isabel Crawford

Isabel Crawford's books fall into pairs: her stories of Phoebe Mornay, later Moore, at Malcombe House are really a single book divided into two. *Willowmeads* and *Lola's Exploration* are set at the same school, but have no characters in common save the headmistress, and the latter book is more an adventure than a school story. These are gentle stories which exploit the finding-relatives theme: Phoebe, who has 'a lower middle-class accent' and does not know which knives and forks to use, turns out to be an heiress in a small way and the cousin of a famous author. However, Crawford is capable of stinging humour at times, as the conversation between Megan and Virginia may show:

> Much ruffled, Meg drew back. 'You're dreadfully unkind, and rude as well.'
> 'Self-defence. Must live.'
> 'I wanted to help you.'
> 'Good. Then disappear.' (*Willowmeads*)

P1   *Phoebe's First Term*, Shaw (1928). Illus.
P2   *Phoebe and Company*, Shaw ([1931]). Illus.
W1   *Willowmeads*, Shaw ([1932]). Illus.
W2   *Lola's Exploration*, Shaw ([1933]). Illus.

P = Phoebe pair
W = Willowmeads sequence

Mrs J P Creed *see* LOUISE MACK

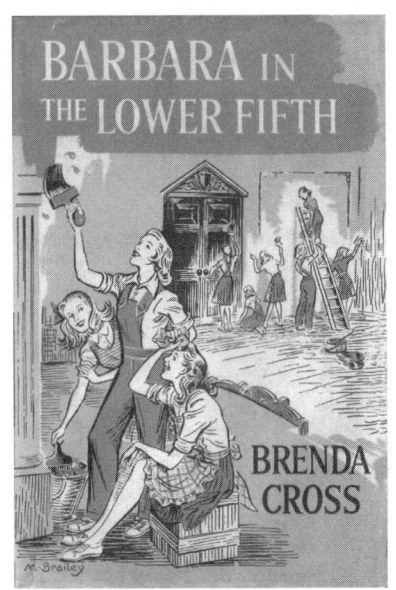

Brenda Cross
(Brenda Stenning Cross later Hughes later Colloms)
1919-2014

This author's books may remind the reader slightly of some of **NANCY BREARY**'s books in that the heroine, Barbara, is the daughter of a film star. Initially rebellious, she settles down and learns to love her school; her glamour is felt more by Barbara than by her form-mates. Cross clearly adores acting in any shape or form, no doubt a reflection of her work first as a film critic, then for Metro-Goldwyn-Mayer and later as a journalist for *Picturegoer* magazine; eventually she worked at Wood Tutorial College, Camden, and for the Working Men's College, Camden Town.

She was born in Tottenham in 1919, married three times (with sons by her first husband, John Cross), and died on 23 December 2014. From 1966 to 2005 she lived in Primrose Hill with her third husband, Albert Lionel Colloms, an American civil rights lawyer.

1   *Barbara's Worst Term*, Heinemann (1950). Illus. Monica Brailey
2   *Barbara in the Lower Fifth*, Heinemann (1953). Illus. Monica Brailey

E Philpot Crowther
(Ethel Clara Philpot Crowther)
1871-1956
Ethel Crowther, born 3 July 1871, was the second daughter and third child of Edwin Jonathan Crowther and his wife Annie Theophila Philpot. Her father, a stationer and bookseller in Godalming, Surrey, died when she was fourteen, but the family appears to have had enough to live on without Ethel undertaking regular employment. Her brother became an electrical engineer and her sister qualified as a doctor in Edinburgh (at a date when this was extremely rare for a woman) and went out to China as a medical missionary. Little is known of Ethel's adult life, but she was baptised (in St Paul's Clapham) in 1890 (less than a year after her sister), which suggests a definite Christian commitment, and her executrix (following her death in east London on 11 June 1956) was Edith Marjorie Chavasse, of the notable clerical family, which again suggests that she moved in church circles.

Her only school story, just 64 pages long, reflects her evangelical commitment: it describes how bad-tempered, passionate Olive, who longs to be a princess, becomes one of the 'King's daughters' when her trainee-clergyman brother talks to her, and is changed at school, helping everyone and putting up with false accusations.

Princess Olive, Nelson, (1898). Illus.

Miss Pember stood still, taking it all in

The frontispiece from *Her Second Chance* by E M Channon

"AS IN A DREAM SHE WATCHED THE THICK ROPE DESCENDING. THERE WAS A NOOSE AT THE END OF IT."

Frontispiece from *The Rebellion of the Upper Fifth* by Dorothy Dennison

D

Celia Damon
Author in the 1930s of books for young children; the name may well be a pseudonym as no details have been found. *See* **MARJORY DAMON**

Marjory Damon
No one of this name has been found at the right date, so it seems possible that 'Marjory Damon' is a pseudonym for a joint production by **MARJORY ROYCE** and **CELIA DAMON**. *The Slow Girl at St Jane's* is a substituting twin story, so similar to **BRENDA GIRVIN'S** *The Mysterious Twins* that it is hard not to suspect a certain degree of plagiarism. However, the writing is lively and the characters well-differentiated, and it is worth reading for its own sake.

The Slow Girl at St Jane's, OUP (1929). Illus. 'GB'

See also **MARJORY ROYCE** *and* **CELIA DAMON**

Winifred Darch
1884-1960
Winifred Darch was born in Brighton on 7 February 1884, the elder daughter of William Darch and Florence, née James; a brother, Oswald (five years younger), and sister, Kitty (ten years younger), followed her. William, educated at Haileybury and Jesus College, Cambridge, was a schoolmaster who went into a solicitor's office when his Brighton preparatory school failed. The family moved to Essex, and Winifred was educated at Leytonstone High School; finances prevented her from attending university, and she may have taken a post as unqualified Junior Mistress in a small boarding school of the type described so feelingly in *Jean of the Fifth*. In 1905-6 she was a student in the teacher training department of Cheltenham Ladies' College.

In 1906 she was appointed to the staff of the recently opened High School for Girls at Loughton (now Roding Valley High School) to teach English, French, Greek History and Scripture. Loughton was very much the centre of her life for the next thirty years: she edited the hand-written school magazine until 1922, produced (and often wrote) the annual school play, organised the Shakespeare Reading Group, ran the Cadet patrol of the school Guide company, accompanied school trips to the Continent, and acted as housemistress from 1923. In 1936, she took early retirement, caused by her parents' ill health and the retirement of Miss Hall, the Headmistress who had appointed her and supported her throughout her career. The family had a house called Honeyden built in the village of Ashington in Sussex; here Winifred lived until her death on 8 October 1960.

Any reader of Winifred Darch's books will have noted, from the brief biographical outline above, the resemblance between her experiences and her plots, based on the routine of day-school life. Her schools normally resemble Loughton, High Schools taking girls from all classes of society, from Heather (*Heather at the High School*), whose mother takes in washing to pay for her uniform, to the aristocratic Lyle sisters, who tend to play truant in order to go hunting (*The Upper Fifth in Command*). The plots are often drawn from Darch's activities: *Margaret Plays the Game* centres on a school production of Scott's *The Talisman*; Darch adapted that book for Loughton, and produced it twice. Judith, arriving at the one-term-old Uffington High School (*The New School and Hilary*) directs *As You Like It*; Darch, arriving at the two-terms-old Loughton High School, directed *As You Like It*. *The Upper Fifth in Command* concerns the time spent by the Upper Fifth and the Fourth at 'Birch Lodge', a house acquired by Farncombe High School as temporary accommodation, just as 'Braeside' was used as temporary accommodation for the Upper Fifth and the Fourth for a year, with Winifred Darch as mistress in charge. There are many more examples one could quote.

But there is far more in these books than a simple transmutation of experience into fiction. Darch's plots are almost always beautifully crafted, with each episode integrated into the whole. The accounts of school trips which one finds in five of her books are never tacked on (as one sees in some of the later Chalet School books); they initiate the plots. Thus in *Poppies and Prefects*, the Guides staying in Marieux encounter small half-English Jeannine, whom they rescue from a hard-hearted aunt and a dreadful life working in a lace-school; brought back to school in England, she becomes the pivot of the story. *The New Girl at Graychurch* carries this integration furthest: half the book, with half the plot, is set in Switzerland.

Many of the motifs of these books are derived from Darch's experience of girls and their parents. As in real life, girls are the product of their homes: Heather (*Heather at the*

High School), who suffers from the snobbery of one of her classmates, still feels that 'one could not be expected to be friends with people like those dreadful, dirty Nixons from Marsh Cottage', and *The New School and Hilary* makes amusing play with Marigold's parroting of her parents' opinions:

> 'It's a nuisance having such a lot of [scholarship girls], as of course they are all quite common.'
>
> 'Would they be less common if they'd come without scholarships?' asked Hilary in an interested tone.
>
> 'Yes, because their people would be paying for them,' explained Marigold… Hilary looked at Mrs Marvell, expecting to hear her challenge this extraordinary remark, but she only said, 'Hilary, won't you really have some more cake?'…
>
> So perhaps Cousin Beatrice had not been attending to Marigold.

As so often in school stories, friendship is a key motif; but in Darch's books it is treated more realistically than usual. Darch is happiest with a calm, unemotional friendship between equals, but that ideal is rarely achieved before the end of a book; the vicissitudes of affection drive many plots. Darch is particularly wary of devotion given to an unworthy object. This may be the standard 'pash' of younger girl for older, such as Simone's love of Cynthia (*For the Honour of the House*), a relationship between contemporaries, such as Margaret's devotion to the beautiful but weak Rosamund (*Margaret Plays the Game*), or Susan's selfless but misguided care for her artistic twin sister Diantha (*Susan's Last Term*). In each case, glamour, beauty and brilliance are seen as of far less worth than the less exciting but more lasting qualities of the heroines—steadiness, thoughtfulness and humility.

There is little melodrama in Darch: girls rarely rescue each other from cliffs, bogs or fires. Tragedies are more often academic, with Chris (*Chris and Some Others*) removed from school to learn under an incompetent governess; Margery (*The Scholarship and Margery*) deprived of her scholarship by the wiles of a fellow-pupil; and Jean and Bride (*Jean of the Fifth*) forced to leave their school by financial problems. And it takes a High School mistress to create drama from some of the unpromising material which Darch works with: a wrong entry in a register (*Margaret Plays the Game*) or a Board of Inspectors' report leaked to a local newspaper (*The Head Girl at Wynford*). But out of these elements, Darch forges compelling and utterly credible plots with attractive characters; these, mixed with an English teacher's eye for precisely the right phrase, and a delightful sense of irony, make Darch's books among the best school stories ever written.

Further Reading
Folly 9, 10

Chris and Some Others, OUP (1920). Illus. Savile Lumley
Jean of the Fifth, OUP (1923). Illus. M D Johnston

Poppies and Prefects, OUP (1923). Illus. Charles E Brock
Cecil of the Carnations, OUP (1924). Illus. Mary Strange Reeve
Heather at the High School, OUP (1924). Illus. Charles E Brock
Gillian of the Guides, OUP (1925). Illus. M D Johnston
Katharine Goes to School, OUP (1925). Illus. M D Johnston
The New School and Hilary, OUP (1926). Illus. Mary Strange Reeve
Varvara Comes to England, OUP (1927). Illus. M D Johnston
Cicely Bassett: Patrol Leader, OUP (1927). Illus. M D Johnston
The Upper Fifth in Command, OUP (1928). Illus. M D Johnston
For the Honour of the House, OUP (1929). Illus. M D Johnston
The Fifth Form Rivals, OUP (1930). Illus. Mary Strange Reeve
The Lower Fourth and Joan, OUP (1930). Illus. M D Johnston
Margaret Plays the Game, OUP (1931). Illus. E Brier
The Girls of Queen Elizabeth's, OUP (1932). Illus. M D Johnston
The School on the Cliff, OUP (1933). Illus. M D Johnston
The Head Girl at Wynford, OUP (1935). Illus. Reginald Mills
Susan's Last Term, OUP (1936). Illus. Margaret Horder
Elinor in the Fifth, OUP (1937). Illus. Margaret Horder
Alison Temple—Prefect, OUP (1938). Illus. Gilbert Dunlop. Reprinted as *Alison in a Fix*, Spring ([1961]). Illus.
The Scholarship and Margery, OUP (1938). Illus. Margaret Horder
The New Girl at Graychurch, OUP (1939). Illus. Gilbert Dunlop

Jennifer David
Hilltop House, Victory Press (1969). Not illus.

Alan Davidson *see* A D LANGHOLM

H B Davidson
(Helen Beatrice Davidson)
1898-1998
Helen Beatrice Davidson, the fourth daughter of the Rev. Lionel Davidson, Rector of Stanton St John near Oxford, was born on 14 July 1898 and died on 18 January 1998 at Englefield Green, Egham, Surrey. Little is known about her life, but she was captaining a Guide company in Eastbourne in 1918 and in East Dean in 1920. She ran a Ranger company in Friston in 1920, and a Guide company in Polegate in 1923. She was running a Ranger company in Eastbourne in 1930, and was still there in 1933. Her brother, Lt-Cdr George Davidson RN is recorded in Eastbourne in 1915; in 1939 Helen too was living there, apparently with three of her sisters and another brother (she had at least five siblings); she is recorded as doing 'voluntary social work'; the others all had private means, so probably she did too. As one might expect, she was a fairly prolific writer of Guide and Brownie stories, but six of her books are set wholly or partly in girls' boarding schools, and thus qualify her for an appearance in this book.

Her second book, *Pat of Whitehouse*, sets the tone: this is a 'proper' school story, but the Guide movement has an almost redemptive power in uniting a divided school and leading unsatisfactory girls (those who don't like fresh air and hockey) to repentance. Guiding here takes the place of Christianity in evangelistic books. *The Guides Make Good* explicitly links Guides and games; the two things change a poor school to a good, keen, growing institution, rather as one sees in **SIBYL B OWSLEY**'s work: but Davidson's characterisation is fuzzier and her approach more that of the pedagogue than Owsley's. Many of her chapters have notes appended directing Guiders or Patrol Leaders to Guide publications, or recommending a game played by her characters as 'excellent preparation for camp'. Her attempts at drama are half-hearted: the sinister Fred Ardice (*The Ardice Fortune*) or the 'little black man' who attempts to steal the aeroplane plans in *Billy Goes to Camp* are drawn in a perfunctory manner, and cookpots clearly excite her more than kidnappings. Only *Peggy's School Pack* (despite its title) focuses on the normal concerns of school life: whether Peggy will be chosen as the Captain of the Junior House is of more moment than her ability to draw a Union Jack. And it is noticeable that all her school stories and partial school stories were written fairly early in her writing career; as she grew in experience, she sensibly left out the school-story veneer and wrote 'pure' Guide and Brownie stories.

1   *Peggy Pemberton, Brownie**, Sheldon Press ([1923])
    Pat of Whitehouse, Sheldon Press ([1924]). Illus. Savile Lumley
2   *Peggy's School Pack*, Sheldon Press ([1925]). Illus. Savile Lumley
    The Guides Make Good, Sheldon Press ([1925]). Illus. W H Birch
    The Ardice Fortune (part school), Sheldon Press ([1926]). Illus. R B Ogle
    How Judy Passed her Tests* (school setting), Sheldon Press ([1936])
    Billy Goes to Camp* (initial school setting), Sheldon Press (1937)

Many other Guide and Brownie stories

E M de Foubert
(Edith Mary de Foubert)
1873-1957

Edith Mary de Foubert was born on 11 July 1873 in Cork, daughter of Walter Edward de Foubert (a clerk in the employment of the Cork Steam Packet Company, in which he rose to be managing director) and his wife Mary Downey. She had at least one full brother and sister (Madeline) and one half-sister (Barbara). We do not know where she had her secondary education, but she was awarded a third-class BA honours degree in English at Bedford College, London, in 1896. By 1901 she was teaching at Corran Collegiate School, Watford, and in 1907 went to be Second Mistress and head of Sixth Form at St

George's School in Edinburgh, where she also taught English and History until 1916. During part of that time she shared a house (5, Roseburn Cliff) with **ETHEL TALBOT**, to whom her first book was dedicated and who remained a lifelong friend. She left to take up gardening and poultry-keeping near Pitlochry, and lived in Keswick for a time. By 1929 she had moved to London, and seems to have remained there until her death on 4 March 1957, at some point moving from Maida Vale to Ealing.

De Foubert's books are standard fare as regards plots: kidnapped babies, hidden jewels, lost heirs and missing wills abound, although she has fewer gallant rescues than one might expect. Nevertheless, her books are not entirely conventional. Her characters are far more solid and life-like than usual, and she has a trick of putting them against a background which accentuates their idiosyncrasies: Marty Vries, the effusive, outgoing South African, is sent to a school of superlative refinement and English reserve (*The Girl from Back-of-Beyond*); Hilary Sherlock, penniless but fiercely proud, goes to St Truda's, where the girls pride themselves on running their own finances (*First Term—Worst Term*); and Sally Denby, who has an excess of physical 'pluck' but little will-power, is contrasted with Alix, the 'funk' who abounds in moral courage (*Sally's Sporting Chance*).

There is a strong romantic streak in de Foubert which feeds upon Ruritanian material (*The League of the Links*), the ancient Russian aristocracy (*The Fighting Fourth*) and even the May Queen ceremony (*Queen of the School*)—which may seem Oxenham-like but was actually derived from the ceremony at Cork High School for Girls, instituted by the Head, a former student of Whitelands. At the same time, she can be utterly down-to-earth: financial difficulties, the problems of concealing a hated school uniform, and even the discomfort of riding in a car full of trunks and boxes of hens are all treated with realism and humour. She tells a story with great energy. The openings of her books are never conventional; she launches straight into the story without introduction, and lets us pick it up. As one might expect, she is excellent at creating suspense, not only in the books which contain 'adventures', but equally in relationships between her characters. Friendship is very important in de Foubert's books, but it is always a source of tension, seen as fragile and vulnerable, and having to be worked at.

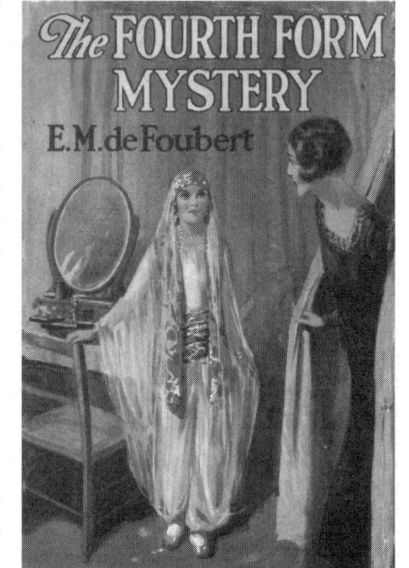

De Foubert, though, is not universally liked. The mysteries which she sets up are too easily penetrated—though not by her heroines, who are infuriatingly slow to see what any half-attentive reader realises by the end of page two. There's a strong correlation in de Foubert between naivety and niceness: villains, by contrast, are worldly wise. Her style too (possibly influenced by Ethel Talbot's writings) is somewhat idiosyncratic: she has a habit of narrating the story via her characters' meditations in indirect speech, and using abbreviations such as *'twould* and *'tis* which are presumably meant to be colloquial, but actually sound self-consciously quaint, and, when taken together with her habit of punctuating with dashes, appear slightly breathless.

Nevertheless, at her best she is a writer worth reading for the vividness of the characters she creates and the intensity of the emotions she communicates.

Sources: St George's School records; Sarah Burn; Barbara de Foubert; Griselda Fyfe

Every Girl's Book of Hobbies*, T C & E Jack (1924)
That Term at the Towers, Cassell (1927). Illus. 'C Morse'
Queen of the School, Cassell (1928). Illus. P B Hickling
The Girl from Back-Of-Beyond, Cassell (1929). Illus. 'A B Mi...'
The Fourth Form Mystery, Cassell (1930). Illus.
First Term—Worst Term, OUP (1932). Illus. M D Johnston
The Fighting Fourth, OUP (1934). Illus. Reginald Mills
For the Sake of Shirley*, Nelson ([1935]). Illus. A M'Whor
Two on their Own (college story), Hutchinson ([1935]). Illus. K Duke
The League of the Links, OUP ([1936]). Illus. Margaret Horder
Sally's Sporting Chance, OUP (1938). Illus. Margaret Horder
The Vac at St Verda's* (holiday at school), Nelson ([1938]). Illus. E E Brier
Penny in Search of a School, OUP (1939). Illus. Margaret Horder

Nancy Delves
(Annie Myfanwy Delves Fitzhugh)
1905-1959
Annie Myfanwy Delves was born on 3 September 1905 in Hoylake on the Wirral, the daughter of John Edwin Delves, an accountant, and his wife Sarah Catherine Williams. She had one sister and two brothers, one of whom died young. The family later moved to Deganwy in Caernarvonshire, which she uses as the setting for several books. She attended a day school, though we do not know where. She married Godfrey Edmund Fitzhugh, of Plas Power in Wrexham, on 18 November 1931, and had one son. She served with the ATS during World War II. She and her husband divorced in 1948, and she moved to County Cork, where she died in 1959.

Despite the assumptions of many critics of school stories (few of whom have actually read the books they castigate), **ANGELA BRAZIL**'s influence on her contemporaries was very limited as far as style is concerned. Nancy Delves, however, is clearly a disciple. Her six school stories (all unrelated) are full of merry madcaps and jolly japes. 'Swotting' is abhorrent, and several books reprobate the unpleasant prig who, like Maudie Heywood in Brazil's *The Madcap of the School*, works too hard and 'sets the pace' for the rest of the form. Even her slang is reminiscent: 'Oh, jubilate!' two of her characters exclaim. Her plots are frustrating: most of her books initiate ideas—boarders versus day-girls in *Rebel of the Fifth*, spoilt Anglo-Indian girl in *The Fourth Form*—which are simply forgotten after the first couple of chapters, when the story slips back to the standard material of games, mischief and false accusations. There is no attempt to analyse character or motivation: in *Fifth Form Rivals*, for instance, Doria Smith, who falsely takes credit for a heroic deed, is simply a cowardly sneak. Admiration is directed towards Jane, the physically confident and 'plucky' practical joker. Unsurprisingly, there is a good deal of emphasis on games, with hockey, lacrosse, tennis, rowing and even squash matches described in detail. Delves' style is bright: her girls don't just 'say', they 'laugh', 'carol', 'snigger', 'chuckle', 'giggle' and 'chirrup'. One very positive feature is a strong sense of place, particularly in Wales, where two of her books are set, and a third takes girls for a holiday; she clearly loved the Principality in which she grew up.

Source: Godfrey Fitzhugh, Nancy Delves' son

The Fourth Form, Sampson Low ([1929]). Illus.
Well Played, Scotts!, Sampson Low ([1930]). Illus. 'MLP' [Mary Louise Parker]
Fifth Form Rivals, Sampson Low ([1931]). Illus.
The Rebel of the Fifth, Sampson Low ([1933]). Illus.
Trouble in the Fourth, Sampson Low ([1934]). Illus.
Thrills for the Lower Fifth, Sampson Low ([1935]). Illus. 'Wilson'

Muriel Denison
(Jessie Muriel Goggin Denison)
1886-1954

Muriel Denison was born Muriel Goggin in Toronto but raised in Regina; she was educated at Havergill College, Toronto; Edgehill School, Windsor, Nova Scotia, and the Royal Conservatory of Music, Toronto. She married the playwright Merrill Denison in 1926 and died in 1954.

Her charming Canadian series about small Susannah, who lives for a period with the Canadian Mounties, is included here because the third book, *Susannah at Boarding School*, sends the heroine to England, and to a boarding school in Windsor. The book seems partly autobiographical, and is placed with a nice exactitude in the last year of Queen Victoria's reign. Period detail is occasionally slightly obtrusive, but more often fascinating: the account of the taffeta petticoats, and the difference it made to the girls' hockey, is both amusing and utterly convincing.

1 *Susannah of the Mounties**, Dodd, Mead & Co. (Canada, USA, 1936), Dent (London, 1938). Illus. Marguerite Bryan
2 *Susannah of the Yukon**, Dodd, Mead & Co. (Canada, USA, 1937), Dent (London, 1939). Illus. Marguerite Bryan

3   *Susannah at Boarding School*, Dodd, Mead & Co. (Canada, USA, 1938), Dent (London, 1940).
    Illus. Marguerite Bryan
4   *Susannah Rides Again**, Dodd, Mead & Co. (Canada, USA, 1940), Dent (London, 1942).
    Illus. Marguerite Bryan

Dorothy Dennison
(Dorothy Emily Dennison Golden)
1899-1978

Dorothy Dennison was born on 14 September 1899 in London, the daughter of Charles Dennison, a dried-fruit merchant. She was educated at the North London Collegiate School, and worked for the Scripture Union for some time. She married Gerald Newton Golden, an orthopaedic surgeon, in 1931, and had one daughter ('Jill') and one son ('Geoff'). She lived for a time in Sutton, and then in Haslemere in Surrey, and died on 3 March 1978 of leukaemia.

Dennison is very clearly a Protestant evangelistic writer. However, it would be unfair to dismiss her as one of the legion of Victory Press/Pickering & Inglis read-alikes: she is a thoroughly competent writer who generally manages to integrate conversion with school life more comfortably than most.

She is conscious of the potential for embarrassment and exaggeration, and usually avoids it. Rosemary (*Rumours in the Fourth Form*) gets converted, but does not go on to convert the rest of the school and staff. In *The Trio of Grangecourt School*, the 'nice' mistress talks to the girls about Christ, but only in passing, and they get converted 'offstage', so to speak, in the gap between *Trio* and its sequel, *The Odd House of Grangecourt*. She is not always so careful: in *The Rival Schools of Trentham* almost the whole of the Sixth Form is converted in one fell swoop. And she is apt to settle into the classic pattern found in many school stories, particularly evangelistic ones: her protagonist makes a good beginning, but matters go downhill to a nadir of awfulness before she gives herself to Christ, when everything starts to get better.

Nevertheless, to write her off as a competent evangelist misses one very important point: although her worst books (avoid *The Historic Third* if you can) can be dreadful, at her best she overflows with vitality and humour. The delightful account of the first netball match in *The Odd House of Grangecourt* ('Isobel played netball much as a large bear might play it, and every bit as cheerfully') is a fine example of set-piece comedy which also reveals more about the characters and their relationships. And the chapters in *The Rebellion of the Upper Fifth* which describe the competitive knitting of tiny vests for African babies combine suspense (will the Upper Fifth win?) with laughter. She also has the gift of not only bringing her characters alive, but making her 'good' characters really attractive—a necessary quality, but one not always achieved by other writers.

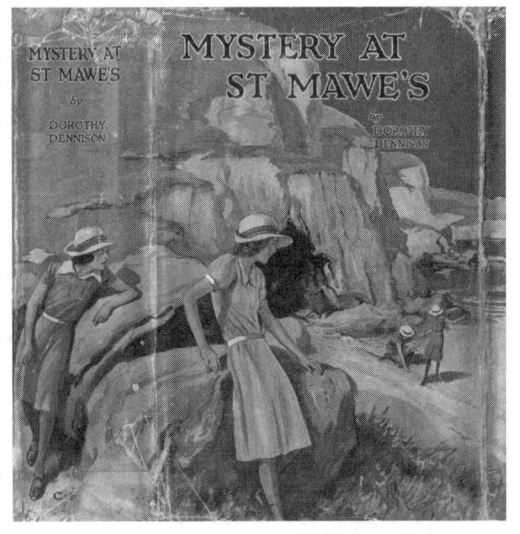

See also **EVANGELISTIC SCHOOL STORIES**

Rumours in the Fourth Form, RTS ([1925]). Illus. Arthur Twidle
Paddy the Pride of the School, Every Girl's Paper ([1928]). Illus. Laurence East
Chronicles of the Lower Fifth, Every Girl's Paper ([1929]). Illus.
The Rebellion of the Upper Fifth, Every Girl's Paper ([1930]). Illus. W Spence
The Sixth Form Goes Abroad* (holiday abroad), GOP ([1931]). Illus. Ellis Silas
1   *The Trio of Grangecourt School*, RTS ([1932]). Illus. Norman Sutcliffe
The Historic Third & Other Stories, CSSM ([1933]). Illus. [Norman] 'Sutcliffe'
2   *The Odd House of Grangecourt*, RTS ([1934]). Illus. [Norman] 'Sutcliffe'
The Rival Schools of Trentham, CSSM ([1934]). Illus. 'A Lambe'
Mystery at St Mawe's, CSSM ([1936]). Illus. [Norman] 'Sutcliffe'

NB All Dennison's non-CSSM books are RTS/GOP/Every Girl's Paper, depending on what the incarnation was at that point. We follow the title page each time.

Also adult novels, children's fiction and Christian manuals for girls, including the non-school series *The Courtney Chronicles* with her daughter Gillian Golden

Oscar Denton
The Sarah Ogden Prize consists of nine unconnected short stories of annual type, using standard themes—new heads, snobbery, identical twins and so on.

The Sarah Ogden Prize, Vawser & Wiles (1946). Illus. 'EMW'

Anne Digby
(Pseudonym)
Anne Digby's ancestry is Cornish. She was born in Kingston-upon-Thames, and educated at the North London Collegiate School. Having begun writing at nine, she worked as a magazine journalist for five years and contributed to *School Friend* and *Girl*. She lived in Paris for a time, and then moved to Oxford as Oxfam's press officer. Her first full-length novel was published in 1976. She is married to Alan Davidson, with three daughters and a son, all now grown-up. She lived near Sherborne for eighteen years, and currently lives in Sussex. She is now best known as the writer of the extremely popular Trebizon series; her Jill Robinson books, which have a secondary day school in the background, cannot really be thought of as girls' school stories, save perhaps the first of the series, *Me, Jill Robinson and the Television Quiz*; and the Jug Valley Juniors series (now restyled as the Out of School Detectives series) and other books for younger children have a background of mixed junior school which sets them outside the scope of this book.

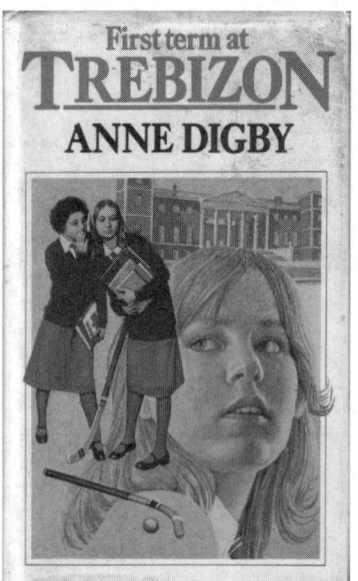

Anne Digby's work is interesting: she was the first post-

1960s writer to have written a really lengthy series of girls' boarding-school stories, the longest one to date. She has said that she wanted to write a modern school-story series which would have 'an enclosed setting, with plenty of scope for stories within a small self-contained world' (*Folly* 13). Trebizon is certainly modern, both externally (Rebecca's fees are paid by her father's firm when he's assigned to Saudi Arabia; the girls are in jeans or disco wear as often as uniform; and boys are quite specifically boyfriends, not just 'chums') and in its ethical focus. The central motif of pre-war school stories was 'honour', and its dilemmas; in the 80s and 90s, the girls worry far more about external problems—examinations and careers, and even (in the later books, especially) boyfriends. They (like Nicola in *The Cricket Term*—**ANTONIA FOREST**) will lie, albeit guiltily, if they feel it's really necessary (*Fourth Year Triumphs at Trebizon*). When a girl feels an injustice has been done and someone is Falsely Accused, far from agonising about the morality of sneaking, she informs the entire school (*First Term at Trebizon*). They are, in fact, less idealised and thus, perhaps, more credible than their predecessors to modern readers.

The plots, however, bear more resemblance to their antecedents. *First Term at Trebizon* is made in the classic mould: new girl Rebecca, initially miserable and isolated at her large boarding school, gradually makes friends, learns to enjoy games and has a clash with a dishonourable prefect, ultimately expelled. Interestingly, Digby says she has only ever read one school story (**A M IRVINE**'s *The Girl Who Was Expelled*), but her plot devices fit well into the tradition. She uses the named-handkerchief-left-at-the-scene-of-the-crime (*Boy Trouble at Trebizon*) and the falsely-accused-of-going-to-party (*The Tennis Term at Trebizon*), though in both cases she gives considerably more rationale for suspicion than her predecessors. Sometimes the framework is traditional and the details modernised: we are well acquainted (in life as well as in fiction) with the girl who has frittered away her time on games and finds her academic work falling behind; Rebecca's playing for the county junior team in tennis, and the offer (*Fifth Year Friendships at Trebizon*) of a contract—rejected, but causing much heart-searching—fit well into this tradition. Clearly these motifs spring organically from the school setting.

As in many older school stories, we also have a mystery in every book after the first. Sometimes this is a standard detective-style puzzle, such as the riddle of the theft of Mr Slade's car (*Boy Trouble at Trebizon*); sometimes we have an unexplained personality change. Why does Tish behave in such an odd way in *Second Term at Trebizon*? Why does Rebecca's French pen-friend Emmanuelle suddenly neglect Rebecca and her friends (*The Unforgettable Fifth at Trebizon*)? The plotting is very well executed, intricate without over-complexity, and relying on character to create the mysterious events. There are no missing wills, no fathers returning from the dead (only from Saudi Arabia) and not a secret passage in sight.

Digby has utilised the experiences of her daughters at school, and has put in some painstaking research. Tennis coaching, hockey games, sailing and surfing incidents are convincingly described. Academic work is important: portions of lessons are recounted, homework is specified, and one could almost reconstruct syllabuses from the GCSE work described. Adults might feel that the 9-12 age group for whom these books are intended would be put off by this, but the books' sales refute this.

The major irritant of these books is more likely to bother English teachers than their pupils: Digby's style becomes progressively more like the teenage magazines also pored over by this age group. *First Term at Trebizon* flows quite smoothly; but by *The Unforgettable Fifth at Trebizon* we have paragraphs like this:

> Back for the Sixth. Two more years at Trebizon. First year in Willoughby, second year in Parkinson. Lovely houses, both of them. Lots more privileges now!

Nor is it just the style which is heavily teen mag (though it must be acknowledged that this incident is not representative):

> Suddenly he, too, was holding her very tightly and he was kissing her, trembling like a leaf. They both were. She made him coffee in the kitchen and for an hour they talked in low voices about all the trials and tribulations of the last two terms and also how much they meant to each other.

And almost from the beginning of the series, she has a pernicious habit of telegraphing the action: 'It was something very different when they came back' (*Into the Fourth at Trebizon*) … 'In time they might be sorely tempted to revise their opinion' (*The Unforgettable Fifth at Trebizon*). This is presumably meant to arouse anticipation or ensure the reader is in the right mood, but it does tend to kill suspense.

Despite these criticisms, Anne Digby's books were understandably popular during the last two decades of the 20th century, and she was widely translated (there is even a Japanese version); she is a fascinating example of the way a genre can be revitalised. In recognition of this, Hodder commissioned six books from her as continuations of **ENID BLYTON**'s Naughtiest Girl series: an interesting match between one of the most popular writers of 1940s and 1950s school stories and her modern equivalent.

Given the widespread revival of the girls' school story in the last 20 years, for which Digby may take some credit (*see* **MODERN SCHOOL STORIES**) it is fitting that Egremont UK reissued the first ten Trebizon titles in 2016-17.

Further Reading
Folly 13

1   *First Term at Trebizon*, W H Allen (1978). Not illus.
2   *Second Term at Trebizon*, W H Allen (1979). Not illus.
    The Big Swim of the Summer (sport), Dennis Dobson (1979). Not illus.
3   *Summer Term at Trebizon*, W H Allen (1979). Not illus.
4   *Boy Trouble at Trebizon*, Granada (1980). Illus. Gavin Rowe
5   *More Trouble at Trebizon*, Granada (1981). Illus. Gavin Rowe
6   *The Tennis Term at Trebizon*, Granada (1981). Illus. Gavin Rowe
7   *Summer Camp at Trebizon**, Granada (1982). Illus. Gavin Rowe
8   *Into the Fourth at Trebizon*, Granada (1982). Illus. Gavin Rowe
    Me, Jill Robinson and the TV Quiz (part school), Granada (1983). Not illus.
9   *The Hockey Term at Trebizon*, Granada (1984). Not illus.
10 *Fourth Year Triumphs at Trebizon*, Granada (1985). Not illus.
11 *The Ghostly Term at Trebizon*, Swift Books (1990). Not illus.
12 *Fifth Year Friendships at Trebizon*, Swift Books (1991). Not illus.
13 *Secret Letters at Trebizon*, Straw Hat (1993). Not illus.
14 *The Unforgettable Fifth at Trebizon*, Straw Hat (1994). Not illus.

For Digby's *Naughtiest Girl* continuations *see* **ENID BLYTON**

There are two omnibuses: *Rebecca's First Year* (Puffin 1992) and *Adventures at Trebizon* (Dean 1995).
   Also pony books, series set in mixed primary schools (*Jug Valley Juniors* and *Three R Detectives*) and the *Jill Robinson* series, mainly based round a youth club

Audrey Dines

Dines' two books are evangelistic: the first, a school story using classic themes (split friendship and jealousy among others) with one of the main characters converted before the book begins and the other at the end. The sequel is set at a Christian 'house party' on the Isle of Wight for 30 teenage girls; Dines had almost certainly run such a house party herself, and the details are convincing. There is a somewhat perfunctory mystery concerning hidden treasure: the real focus of the book is on conversion and the Christian life. The books are written with more liveliness and humour than is normal in evangelistic school stories.

1   *Pine Tree House*, Victory Press (1951). Not illus.
2   *The Secret of Lockerby Hall**, Victory Press (1955). Not illus.

Other Christian books for children

See also *The Encyclopaedia of Boys' School Stories*, **AUDREY DINES**.

Winifred Donald
(Winifred Wilson Donald)
1917-1999

Winifred Donald was born in Aberdeen on 31 July 1917, the daughter of a house-furnisher (which no doubt explains why at one point she was manager of a nursery furnishing business). A graduate of Aberdeen University, she taught English at two schools between 1940 and 1946, then turned to nursery furnishing, writing in her spare time. From 1955 to 1958 she was a lecturer in English at Jordan Hill training college, Glasgow, and from 1959 until at least 1970 was principal English teacher at Lansdowne House School, Edinburgh. She also worked for the educational department of Collins from 1963-65, apparently editing abridged versions of English classics. She died in Edinburgh in 1999. We know from a publisher's handout that she also wrote detective novels, presumably under a pseudonym as none has been recognised under her own name.

Source: contemporary publicity material from Hutchinson and information from Lin Murison

Linda—the Schoolgirl Detective, Hutchinson ([1949]). Illus. 'Gervase'
Linda in Lucerne*, Hutchinson ([1950]). Illus. 'Norman Meredith'
Linda and the Silver Greyhounds*, Hutchinson ([1952]). Not illus.
Linda in Cambridge*, Hutchinson ([1955]). Not illus.
Linda in New York*, Hutchinson ([1956]). Not illus.

Sarah Doudney
1843-1926

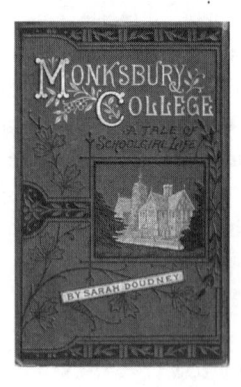

Only two of Sarah Doudney's many books were set in girls' schools, but all fit the standard late Victorian pattern of contrasting good girls and bad girls. The good are generally poor in worldly terms, but rich in the 'ornament of a meek and quiet spirit' (1 Peter 3: 4) and exercise all the Christian virtues, particularly towards the bad girls, who may be thoughtless and snobbish or self-righteous and hypocritical, but are converted in the end. The school stories also have the normal false accusations and the 'innocent schoolgirl friendship, so romantic, and yet so pure and true' (*Monksbury College*). Sarah Doudney has all the moral imperative of L T Meade with more theology and less energy, but is interesting as one of the pioneers of a genre the later developments of which would probably have appalled her.

Monksbury College, Sunday School Union ([1878]). Illus.
When We Were Girls Together, Hodder & Stoughton (1885). Illus.

Approx 65 other books, mainly adult religious novels

Olive C Dougan
(Olive Constant McMicken Dougan)
1904-1963

Olive Constant Dougan was born on 16 October 1904 in Highbury, London, the daughter of John Nathaniel Major McMicken, a Scottish letter-sorter, and his wife Annie Sarah Williams. Her secondary education is unknown, but she attended University College, London School of Librarianship from 1923. In 1929 she married a fellow-student, Robert Ormes Dougan; there were no children of the marriage. The young couple lived initially in Crouch End and then moved to Arnos Grove in north-east London. Her first writing success was *The Bendon Bequest*, which won a competition for new school-story writers organised by Hutchinson. At the outbreak of World War II, her husband was posted to Perth, where she joined him, living in Scone till the end of the war, when they moved to Balbeggie. In 1952 Robert took up the post of Librarian at Trinity College, Dublin; Olive did not join him until after the deaths of her mother and mother-in-law, for whom she was caring. In 1957, she accompanied Robert to California, where he became Librarian of the Huntington Library at San Marino. Her health deteriorated, and she died on 4 January 1963. Her husband donated her books and papers to Scripps College, Claremont, California.

Olive C Dougan was in no way a prolific writer: seven books in thirteen years is not a large output. Of those books, only four are purely girls' school stories. (*Schoolgirls in Peril* begins in a Belgian *pensionnat*, but is, like *The Schoolgirl Refugees*, a war story.) But in them, she makes her mark as an original and thought-provoking writer.

From the beginning there is an eschewing of melodrama, which makes her books unusual. The mischief is down-to-earth and well observed: laziness, hiding things, breaking bounds, giggling with boys—nothing spectacular, but very recognisable to anyone who has had anything to do with adolescent girls. The characterisation is subtle but definite: not only the heroines but many of the supporting cast are well-drawn. There are certain prejudices: maths teachers are always unpleasant, and protagonists (save Greta, who is half Norwegian) always partly Welsh, often living in a household where the Welsh are despised. Indeed, the underlying theme in all four school stories is that of the outsider, and her fight for acceptance.

In *The Bendon Bequest*, her earliest and most conventional book, she is feeling her way. The plot is formulaic: an orphaned, half-foreign new girl, resented by her form, finds purpose in devotion to Doris, the Head Girl, the only girl who is kind to her, and fails a scholarship examination for Doris's sake. But the book is more interesting than this bald summary might imply. Most school stories of this type imply that the outsider, by not fitting in, is inferior to her contemporaries in the ways that really matter, and must assimilate; here, we are made to *like* Greta's differences. We see almost everything through Greta's eyes: her isolation, unsympathetic surroundings and hostile form and her urge to sacrifice herself for the beloved. It is interesting to contrast Dougan's attitude with that of **NANCY DELVES**: both create girls who 'set the pace too high' and make the rest of the form work harder; but in Dougan, Va resent this because they are lazy, and in Delves, Doria only works hard because she is a nasty sneak.

In the ten years between *The Bendon Bequest* and Dougan's next school story, she seems to have consciously moved away from standard plots. *Tubby of Maryland Manor* focuses on a fat girl—a type common enough in school stories, but rarely pre-eminent. *Tubby* inverts the cliché of the merry, popular 'fatty'.

> 'I'm just a miserable worm, a hanger-on,' thought Lindsay bitterly, and she kicked at a bit of stone with her shabby shoe. 'I don't like them much, yet I'm too scared to snap my fingers at them. No one really wants me. I'm just one huge joke to them all. I amuse them, and as long as I make them laugh, I'm OK. But how sick I am of everything. How I loathe being the school joke!'

Dougan's craft lies in the juxtaposition of Lindsay's (aka Tubby) thoughts with the way in which schoolmates, staff and friends see her—as a popular jester and self-mocker, always good for a laugh; as an obstinate, sullen rebel; as a talented girl hindered by her size. Dougan gives Tubby a home environment (an elderly and restrictive great-aunt) which clearly generates many of her problems; yet the connection is never forced down our throats. Tubby's initial over-eating and obesity and the semi-anorexic state into which she moves can both be explained as the attempt to take control of a life managed by others—but Dougan is content to tell the story, providing clues for the sensitive reader to pick up. The sequence describing Tubby's loss of weight and subsequent weakness and misery is full of pathos, possibly the most moving thing Dougan wrote. It takes one right inside the fat girl, to the thin girl longing to get out, and then unable to cope with what she has become.

In *Nancy Finds Herself*, the outsider again tries to become the insider by becoming something she isn't—this time, wild, careless and rebellious. The analysis is excellent: Nancy's urge to win the friendship of the glamorous and undisciplined Louie Hamilton is clearly a function of her own self-contempt. Here is Nancy reacting to an accusation of being weak and 'easily led'. 'Nancy felt she *was* two people. She was CB [Cry-Baby—an unwelcome nickname]. Shy, nervous, thin-skinned, retiring CB. She was also a Nancy who could push that desperate other self into scenes and happenings that were beyond CB.' Dougan does not give Nancy any easy way out of the problems which surround her. Most school stories would allow Nancy to rescue someone from a fire, win a scholarship or star in the school play, thus redeeming herself. Here she is forced to face up to her selfishness and egocentricity, and doesn't change overnight: even at the end of the book she's the same person—careless, forgetful and dreamy. But she has learnt something from her mistakes, and can make a self-abnegating choice.

In *Princess Gwyn*, the theme of outsidership is treated in a completely different way. The protagonist this time appears to be an insider—pretty, well-dressed, brilliant at work and games, the star of the school and (apparently) the petted granddaughter of a Welsh aristocrat. But she is secretly terrified by the consciousness that she would be rejected were her friends to discover her real background: her dead father had been cast off by his family when he married, and Gwyn has been brought up by her working-class mother and grandmother who keep a boarding house in Finsbury Park. Paradoxically, at home with her family she is a complete outsider, despising her relatives and embarrassed by her circumstances. She is contrasted throughout the book with Evelyn, the new girl who is both *nouveau riche* and American in her speech and behaviour. In a conventional school story, Evelyn would be the outsider who has to be brought into the fold; here, though the reader is irritated by her vulgarisms, her thoughtless and often cruel actions and her tactlessness, it is made clear that she has an essential honesty which Gwyn lacks and must learn. The comparison is always there, but never forced.

Dougan, then, is using the form of the school story to study real problems in a way which we might associate with **JOSEPHINE ELDER, MARY K HARRIS, ANTONIA FOREST, ANN PILLING** and such writers. It has to be said that she is not as skilful with words as these; her vocabulary is more restricted, and she tends towards simpler sentences and more exclamation marks. But she is well worth reading for all that.

Source: Robert Dougan

The Bendon Bequest, Hutchinson ([1934]). Illus.
The Schoolgirl Refugee*, Blackie (1940). Illus. H Coller
Schoolgirls in Peril (small part school), Blackie ([1944]). Illus. John de Walton
Tubby of Maryland Manor, Blackie ([1945]). Illus. D L Mays
Princess Gwyn, Faber (1946). Illus. Marjorie Owens
Nancy Finds Herself, Blackie ([1947]). Illus. E Spring-Smith
The Forbidden Holiday*, Faber (1948). Illus. Marjorie Owens

Also: *Shadows and other Poems* (ed. Robert C Dougan), Carol Cockel (Arcadia, California, privately printed, 1963)

Castleden Dove

No details are known about this writer, save that he/she was presumably Australian. *Lowanna* is an emotional but skilful study of the relationship between two girls in Elaroo College in Sydney: brilliant, popular, egocentric Lowanna and shy, talented Joan, whose integrity gradually moves Lowanna to affection and respect. The book is clearly aimed at a late adolescent readership; Joan's brother Philip is introduced as Lowanna's future husband—possibly an acceptable heterosexual substitute for the real object of desire.

Lowanna (Australia), OUP (1925). Illus.

C M Drury
1900-1990

(Clara Constance Maria Drury Hoskyns-Abrahall) Clare (as she was always called) Drury was the daughter of Richard and Gertrude Drury; her father was a civil engineer, who eventually settled in Dawlish, Devon, after a career spent partly abroad. She was born in London on 31 January 1900 and educated at St Helen's School, Abingdon, and the Royal College of Music. In 1925 she married Sir Theo Chandos Hoskyns-Abrahall; there were one son and one daughter of the marriage, which was dissolved in 1944. After living for some time in Essex, she died in St Albans on 29 November 1990.

The plot of Clare Drury's first book, *Kit Norris, Schoolgirl Pilot*, splits into two sections, connected only by their protagonist. The first half is pure school story, using the common motif of a girl's promotion (here, to Head Girl) splitting up friendship when she tries to reform the school; the second is a flying melodrama even less believable than most, with Kit absconding with the aeroplane belonging to machine-gunning gangsters and ending up as a national heroine. There are few technical details to compensate for the implausibility, though there are plenty of (unintentionally) amusing moments, as when a gangster reveals his true nature to an unsuspecting lady by 'saying in a rather common voice that he was "pleased to meet her."'

Chris of Crighton's, published 27 years later, is, as one would expect, considerably more mature, and avoids melodrama, preferring a comparatively realistic story of a girl struggling to find her place in a new school.

As C M Drury
Kit Norris, Schoolgirl Pilot, Juvenile Productions (1937). Illus. 'C Leslie'

As Clare Abrahall
Chris of Crighton's, Max Parrish ([1964]). Not illus.

Several other children's books, including historical stories and biographies

Olive Duhy
Esme and the Smugglers, Bruce Publishing Co. [1945]). Not illus.

Swapna Dutta
(Swapna Sen Dutta)
Swapna Sen was born in Patna, India, on 17 May 1943, the elder of the two daughters of textile engineer Benoy Bushan Sen; her mother, Dr Jyoti Sen, was an anthropologist. She was educated at Mount Carmel Convent, Hazaribagh, run by nuns of the Apostolic Carmel congregation, the establishment depicted in her

three school stories. After reading English Literature at Lady Brabourne College, Calcutta, and gaining an MA from the University of Calcutta, she taught for some time (initially at her own old school, and then at college), subsequently moving into writing and editing: she worked as Deputy Editor for the *Encyclopaedia Britannica* (India). On 10 August 1967 she married Swapan Chandra Dutta, who worked in the Government Service until retirement as Director General (Posts). They have two daughters.

Swapna Dutta's three school stories, based on the author's own experience of Mount Carmel Convent, are consciously within the British and Commonwealth school-story tradition. The three books cover Juneli Chaudhuri's first year at St Avila's at Ranjipur, with the normal round of friendships, enmities and activities. While the plots and characters are quickly recognisable, the setting gives them an exotic fascination for the non-Indian reader, with its mixture of commonplace and *outré*: the irritable singing master is fairly standard, but when an otherwise standard eccentric is teaching the girls *sargam* and criticising their 'hoo-hoo sort of English singing', it is very appealing. Dutta has read many girls' school stories, and one can trace their influence in these books: the style is Blytonesque and the climax of *Juneli's First Term* reminiscent of *The Girls of the Hamlet Club*. Overall, these gentle, charming books are worthy additions to the canon.

Source: information from author

Juneli's First Term, Indus (HarperCollins, India), (1992). Illus.
Juneli at St Avila's , Indus (HarperCollins, India), (1992). Illus.
An Exciting Term, Indus (HarperCollins, India), (1992). Illus.

The Juneli stories were first published in the Indian English-language magazine *Children's World* from 1984-5.

Also books for young children

Vera G Dwyer *see* **ADULT SCHOOL FICTION**

THE BICYCLE FLEW BETWEEN THE HEDGES

page 127

Frontispiece from *Philippa at School* by S K Ensdaile

E

Grace M Easton
(Grace Mary Easton)
1895-1980
Grace Easton, almost certainly born and married abroad, seems to have attended the Church Missionary School, after it moved out to Surrey (where it became St Michael's School, Limpsfield, closing in 1996). Her husband was in holy orders but his career has not been traced; it is likely that he was a missionary, though they spent their retirement in England. Her only school story has a rather old-fashioned air about it, despite the father of Carol and Ruth, the heroines, being captured by Chinese Communist brigands (sic). It is set at a school for the children of missionaries, and judging by the foreword, is based on the author's own school memories. The school takes girls from 10 to 17 and boys of prep- and pre-prep age (though the viewpoint is entirely feminine) and is marked by a firmly evangelical Anglican piety.

Merry-All-the-Time*, John Ritchie, Kilmarnock, (1936)
The School on the Hill, Pickering & Inglis ([1940]). Illus.

W W Eastways/W E Eastways
No details are known about this writer, not even sex! The name may possibly be a pseudonym. The three school stories form an unusual chronological sequence. *Greycourt* covers a term and a half, focusing on motherless fourth-former Joan ('Jill') Winter, who loses her soldier father at the start and takes the rest of the book to cope with her depression. *The Girls of Greycourt* follows on, taking Jill and her friends Dolores and Mary up to the end of their sixth-form career. There is then a hiatus of about six years: *Christine of the Fourth* introduces to the reader to a completely new set of girls, with Dolores appearing as a married Lady

Bountiful and Jill, offstage, writing a pageant for the current Greycourtiers. The books are credible and undramatic, emphasising character development—in every book outsiders are reformed by kindness and affection—but they are rather pedestrian in style.

1   *Greycourt*, Harrap (1939). Illus. T H Robinson
2   *The Girls of Greycourt*, Collins (1944). Illus. Heade
3   *Christine of the Fourth*[1], Collins ([1949])

[1] Author's name is given as 'W E Eastways', but the book is part of the Greycourt series.

Marion Eden

Success for Jane clearly aims to be a 'different' type of school story: certainly its rambling, repetitive and pretentious narrative (the entire book is centred on a girl who 'already felt the multiplicity of herself') cannot have attracted many schoolgirl readers. *Felgarth's Last Year* has a stronger plot, very reminiscent of **ELSIE J OXENHAM**'s *Rosamund's Tuckshop* (1937) and *The Abbey Girls* (1920); but even with three potentially interesting subjects—Rosamund starting up in business for herself, finding a long-lost grandfather, and a school preparing to leave its historic premises—Eden cannot grip her readers. Jane and Rosamund are writers, probably alter egos of their author; but Eden did not have her creations' genius.

Success for Jane, A & C Black (1936). Illus.
Felgarth's Last Year, Warne (1938). Illus.

Josephine Elder
(Pseudonym of Olive Gwendoline Potter)
1895-1988

'Josephine Elder' was the pseudonym of Dr Olive Gwendoline Potter, who was for 60 years in general practice in Sutton, Surrey. She was born in Croydon on 5 December 1895, the daughter of Albert William Potter and his wife Ellen Wakefield; she had one younger brother. She attended Croydon High School because her father, an accountant with Lever Bros, insisted on the best available education for his clever daughter and encouraged her to take up medicine instead of the journalism to which she half inclined. She certainly made a very good doctor, but never lost the desire to write which eventually gave her a second career.

She read medicine at Girton College, Cambridge, following this with hospital appointments and eventually setting up in general practice in Sutton; but in 1923 patients were slow to patronise a woman doctor, and Olive turned to 'Josephine Elder' to supplement her income. She began prolifically with short stories for annuals, but soon added full-length books. These suited her better, with their scope for developing character over a longer period (sometimes over several fictional years), and are always interesting. One of them, *Evelyn Finds Herself*, ranks among the finest of the genre.

Her first book, *Erica Wins Through*, is a fairly conventional story of a tomboy going to school, getting off on the wrong foot and gradually falling into step. What is entirely characteristic of Elder is the way she depicts Erica's early getting into trouble—she is not 'naughty' for the sake of it, but because her ideas do not conform to her surroundings. And only an Elder heroine would be found dissecting a dead cat to see how its muscles work.

The Scholarship Girl is set at the same school, but some years later, when Erica is Games Captain. Monica comes from a council school with a scholarship to the public school Greystones, handicapped not so much by her background as by the mistaken advice of her old Headmistress to concentrate on academic work and not to fritter her energies away on games and such-like trivia. This naturally leads Monica into difficulties; fortunately she is befriended by gentle Francesca from a scholarly Cambridge background who sorts out her tangles, teaches her about *mens sana in corpore sano* and brings her into happy conformity with the school ethos. Their college careers are dealt with in the sequel, *The Scholarship Girl at Cambridge*, which takes them to 'Girnham', but is based firmly and with great detail on Olive Potter's own Girton memories.

It seems likely that Elder was able to draw on the boarding-school experience of her closest school friend, who had gone into teaching after Cambridge and eventually became a headmistress; but with her fourth book she turned to her own High School background. *Thomasina Toddy* has much more of the real Olive Potter in it than the first books, and is all the better for it. Veronica (nicknamed 'Tom Toddy' from babyhood because she is so small, with a big head) is as physically small as Dr Potter herself, and she is equally a fighter. The book begins with her struggle to get into a proper hockey team, not just the despised Third Eleven; in the process she becomes friendly with a new girl, Stella, partly because her two previously inseparable friends are taller and have achieved greater games status. Only gradually do we realise that Stella is not the Good Thing she seems; even more gradually, Veronica does too. By the end of the book she has not only won her fight to be judged on merit, not size, but has also learned not to be obnoxious in the process. The relationships of the book, perhaps a little awkwardly handled, in fact foreshadow the similar problems of *Evelyn Finds Herself*.

Like most of Elder's books *Evelyn Finds Herself* follows its heroine through a substantial portion of her school career, but Evelyn is older than most—just Upper Fifth when we meet her, rising to Head Girl with her Cambridge scholarship secure at the end. This enabled Elder to portray her growth to maturity, rather than simply showing her combating her problems, and for that reason the book is Elder's most successful. The resolution is one of developing character, not just of plot. Evelyn's situation is palpably derived from Elder's own—High School, hockey, influential botany mistress, Cambridge, medicine—but it is equally clear that the book is not pure autobiography. The details are real but the story is fiction. Elder was able to use her ingredients to write a perceptive account of a girl's 'finding herself'—finding her individuality—and as she does so altering in relation to those about her. Friendship is always important in a Josephine Elder story (just as friends were important to Olive Potter), and Evelyn's intellectual career is pointed at every turn by her relations with Elizabeth. They appear at the beginning as long-established and inseparable friends; at the end they are preparing to go up to Cambridge together, though not to the same college. But in the years between, there has been a time when they have barely been on speaking terms, an estrangement partly resulting from the coming of Madeleine, whom Elizabeth likes and Evelyn does not, but partly because Madeleine is the instrument which makes them realize that they are two different people, not one. Plot, background and characters are all superbly integrated in *Evelyn Finds Herself*, and its excellence has been justly appreciated by critics and other authors alike.

Perhaps because she put so much of herself into Evelyn, Elder never quite achieved the same heights again. *Barbara at School*, which followed it, is another boarding-school story with another younger heroine, another new girl getting off to a bad start, but this time staying there for much of the book. It is perceptive and has well-drawn characters, but it is very grim. Barbara is too young to achieve Evelyn's maturity, and her sufferings are too acute for comfort. *The Redheads* saw Elder back on day-school ground, and dealt with the intertwining fortunes of four new girls entering at various stages of the school (including staff), but it is too diffuse for real success. Elder's clear eye for character sometimes betrayed her into a lack of sympathy.

Probably Elder realised that she had exhausted her school-story vein for the moment, for she turned next to adult novels (written under the pseudonym 'Margaret Potter'): one was a hospital story, *Sister Anne Resigns* (rather good) and the other a thriller, *The Mystery of the Purple Bentley* (rather bad). Not for seven years did she go back to school, and then it was to a completely different kind. This time she gave it a solid background, that of her grandparents' Kentish farm, but placed on this a school which was ideal and not actual. By now she seemed to have grown out of her devotion to Croydon High School and had evolved a vision of what education ought to be like. The Farm School, to which Annis Best is sent from her London High School for health reasons, is co-educational, very small, very informal and very practical, with pupils learning what they need for their own talents to come to fruition and otherwise only what they need for general culture. Their teachers are not only exceptional as teachers, they also all have something 'special' about them as well. In short, the Farm School, for all the well-drawn characters there, is a little too good to be true, unlike Elder's other schools, which are mostly a little too true to be comfortable. It is possible that Elder herself realised this, as the third of the trilogy, *Strangers at the Farm School*, which sees the school enlarged to take far more pupils, including a pair of Jewish refugees, also brings it slightly closer to conventional patterns of education. But overall, the trilogy is gentler than the earlier books and has an almost lyrical quality. In part, it was an elegy for the beloved family farm which had been swallowed up by expanding Maidstone, and even though there is a realistic amount of muck and hard work, one wonders how long it would be economically viable.

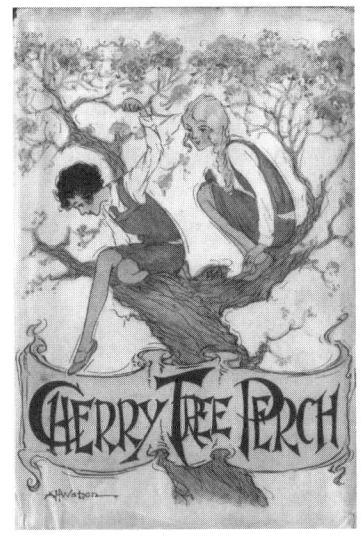

Strangers at the Farm School was published in 1940, by which time Dr Potter was running two practices as well as her own, and had no more leisure to write. After the war she turned to writing adult novels, which are interesting, though not outstanding, and wrote no more school stories. She retired twice from being a GP, the second time in 1983, when she moved to Somerset and took enthusiastically to village life; she died on 24 July 1988, having crammed every one of her 92 years with at least twice as much as most people. 'Josephine Elder' had been only one aspect of her; she is the example par excellence of the school-story writer who pursued a full and vigorous career elsewhere. Her books are all worth reading and none is negligible. There are not enough writers for children of whom one can say the same.

Sources: Mrs Joy Welch, Dr Potter's secretary and long-time friend; Girton College, Cambridge

Further Reading
Folly 11
Introduction to *Evelyn Finds Herself*, Girls Gone By (2006)

S1 *Erica Wins Through*, Chambers ([1924]). Illus. Nina K Brisley
S2 *The Scholarship Girl*, Chambers ([1925]). Illus. Rosa C Petherick
S3 *The Scholarship Girl at Cambridge*, Chambers ([1926]). Illus. Enid Warne Browne
    Thomasina Toddy, Chambers ([1927]). Illus. T J Overnell
    Evelyn Finds Herself, OUP ([1929]). Illus. M D Johnston
    Barbara at School, Blackie ([1930]). Illus. Gordon Browne
    The Redheads, OUP (1931). Illus. M D Johnston
    Sister Anne Resigns* (as 'Margaret Potter'), Selwyn & Blount (1931)
    The Mystery of the Purple Bentley* (as 'Margaret Potter'), Selwyn & Blount (1932)
    Fifty-Two School Stories for Girls, Hutchinson ([1935]). Illus. Noel Syers & A M'Whor. Stories

all written under a variety of pseudonyms and identified as Elder's on stylistic grounds. Presumably originally in annuals.

F1 *Exile for Annis*, Collins (1938). Illus.
F2 *Cherry Tree Perch*, Collins (1939). Illus. A H Watson
F3 *Strangers at the Farm School*, Collins (1940). Illus. NB: The Children's Press editions of F2 and F3 are abridged; F1 remains the same.
Lady of Letters* (adult novel), Lutterworth Press (1949). Not illus.
The Encircled Heart* (adult novel), Lutterworth Press (1951). Not illus.
The Doctor's Children* (adult novel), Lutterworth Press (1954). Not illus.
Fantastic Honeymoon* (adult novel), Robert Hale (1961). Not illus.

S = Scholarship Girl series
F = Farm School series

Edith L Elias
(Edith Lea Morice Elias)
1879-1952

Edith Lea Morice was born on 2 May 1879, the daughter of John Lumsden Morice, a ship's chandler, and his wife Mary Ann Lea (sister of John Lea, 1850-1927, Liverpool colliery owner, coal merchant and local politician, Lord Mayor of Liverpool 1904-5); there were at least one son and two other daughters of the marriage. Edith was educated at the School for Girls, Grove Street, Liverpool, and then at Liverpool University (as it became in 1903), where she gained her BA in English Literature, Latin, English and French in 1899, and her MA in English Language and Literature in 1902. A professional author, she wrote books ranging from children's fairy tales to accounts of polar exploration, a great interest. She married Frank Elias (see *The Encyclopaedia of Boys' School Stories*, **FRANK ELIAS**), and they settled in Felixstowe; there seem to have been no children of the marriage. After the death of her husband in 1949, she moved back to Merseyside. She died at West Kirby, Wirral, on 15 February 1952. Her collection of books on polar exploration was bequeathed to the Scott Polar Institute in Cambridge.

Elias's school stories avoid melodrama, but focus on the intensity of relationships, both positive and negative, which can occur in an enclosed community between girls of different ages. Her villainesses are very unpleasant, but in both cases their rebellion is understandable and believable; and she is careful to avoid a clear black-and-white ending, with the villainess expelled. Her heroines are intelligent, shy and endearing; and both books stand out from the common run, although the plot material is not particularly unusual. We may regret that, despite her reasonably full output, Elias only wrote the two school stories.

Elsie Lockhart, 3rd Form Girl, RTS ([1925]). Illus. J Finnemore
Deanholme, Harrap (1926). Illus. 'Waudby?'

Also many other children's books, literary and historical readers for schools

Lydia S Eliott *see* **Lydia S Graham**

Winifred Ellams
The Girls of Lakeside School, L Orridge ([1949]). Not illus.

E E Ellsworth
(? Edith Ellen Bennett Ellsworth)
?1886-1956
The only Edith Ellen Ellsworth to be found was born Edith Ellen Bennett on 2 July 1886; she married Alvah Edgar Roy Ellsworth (a Canadian) in 1917 and lived with him in Hastings and St Leonards-on-Sea before dying on 12 June 1956. This makes her rather older than one might expect, but she was a school teacher, both before her marriage and in 1939; she had two sons and a daughter.

Doctor Noreen, Lutterworth Press ([1945]). Illus.

Many other young children's books

Beatrice Embree
(Beatrice Mary Embree Ashton)
1884-1952
Embree was born in Ontario on 20 September 1884, the daughter of a school teacher of Scottish descent; she herself became a teacher. In 1920 she married Major Edward James Ashton, a widower who had been quite badly wounded in World War I, and acquired three stepchildren; she went on to have two daughters of her own. This probably explains why she only produced one book. She died in Ottawa on 29 April 1952.

Beatrice Embree dedicates *The Girls of Miss Clevelands'* 'To Canadian School Girls—Past and Present'. Her style is easy, merry and slangy (though her characters do give up slang for Lent). Set chiefly in Toronto, *The Girls of Miss Clevelands'* mildly resists the traditional school-story ethic and reflects her own experience: there is a slight identification with Miss Dewson, a young, pretty and sympathetic teacher. Certainly she has no interest in 'school spirit', declares that school discipline will do less good than a spirit of 'charitable leniency' among the teachers; and implies that the moral improvement of girls at boarding school will come (if at all) more from the spontaneous interactions of the girls than from any efforts of the staff. Mischievous Babs, who unexpectedly takes over the book, instigates most of the girls' sporadic attempts at self-improvement, half in a spirit of fun.

Margot Louis

The Girls of Miss Clevelands' (Canada), Musson Books (1920). Illus. E Elias

Natalie Joan Engleheart *see* **NATALIE JOAN** (under N)

Esther E Enock
(Esther Ethelind Enock)
1874-1947
Esther Enock was born on 13 June 1874 in Edgbaston, one of the eight children of Arthur Henry Enock, who eventually turned from mercantile work to being a landscape artist; by 1891 the family had moved to Devon. Enock was a paid companion in 1911 but by 1939 described herself as 'author'; she was then living in Exeter, where she died on 5 June 1947.

Four Girls and a Fortune (part school), Pickering & Inglis (1935). Illus.

S K Ensdaile
(Pseudonym of Anne Treneer)
1891-1966
S K Ensdaile has now been identified as the pseudonym of the Cornish writer Anne Treneer, best known for her evocative autobiographical works, particularly *School House in the Wind* (1944). Born on 30 January 1891, she was the youngest child (with four older brothers and one sister) of Joseph and Susan Treneer; he was the schoolmaster of Gorran, Cornwall. Anne was educated at her father's school and then at the Pupil Teachers' Centre in St Austell (later the St Austell County School). She went on to teacher training at the Diocesan Training College in Truro and then taught at the Treverbyn Council Mixed School and, from 1912, at Exmouth Church School. Later she was able to go to University College, Exeter, and gain an external degree from the University of London, after which she taught English at Camborne County School (1919-29). She submitted a thesis on George Meredith for a London MA, and then spent a year as a research fellow at Liverpool University writing *The Sea in English Literature*. From 1929 she had two happy years at Lady Margaret Hall, Oxford, working for a B Litt. After this she became Senior English Mistress at King Edward's High School, Birmingham, where she stayed until 1948; all her life she seems to have been rather unenthusiastic about teaching, although it was presumably financially necessary. In 1948 she returned to the south-west to live in Exmouth near her beloved sister Susan, and in 1956 they finally moved back to Cornwall, Anne continuing to write and broadcast; she became a bard of the Cornish Gorsedd in 1945, with the bardic name Flogh Plu Woran (Child of Gorran). She died on 22 August 1966.

Her identity as S K Ensdaile was known only to her family and close friends. Presumably she wrote her school stories to eke out her income; they date from the period before her 'real' writing took off. In *School House in the Wind* she says of her childhood 'I read no girls' school stories', but relates a longing for one, *For the Sake of a Friend*, which she did not get but which later inspired her: 'I am sure that one reason why my first published books consisted of four girls' school stories was *For the Sake of a Friend*. I wrote in my age what I was unable to read in my youth'.

Her output comprises a number of short stories in annuals, and the four full-length school stories, unconnected with each other—probably (together with a dearth of reprints) why she is collected only by the cognoscenti. Her weakness lies in the plots; the first three books in general consist of incidents connected only by their protagonist, and *Puck of Manor School* (where she seems to be consciously attempting to construct a much tighter story) is marred by an implausible, if familiar, plot about an 'orphan' (she is fond of orphans) actually stolen as a baby, and her best friend, kidnapped in error.

Nevertheless, 'Ensdaile's' books are well worth reading. Their heroines are in general lively and charismatic girls, who run into trouble through an overflow of high spirits: they are intelligent, but despise work, and would far rather be dashing around on the hockey pitch until (only too plausibly) they reach the stage where careers and qualifications are in view, when they regret their misspent youths. They are original, too, in their mischief, if 'mischief' is the right word (there are always excellent reasons for their behaviour): Philippa and her cronies are good examples of this when they try to make money by making and selling ice-cream during a very hot summer. In general, though, the focus is on relationships between girls, and occasionally between girls and mistresses; and the books are far better written than the majority of girls' school stories, with touches of irony and sardonic humour which the adult reader will perhaps relish more than their intended audience

Further Reading
Treneer, Anne *School House in the Wind*, Cape, 1944; *Cornish Years*, Cape, 1949; *A Stranger in the Midlands*, Cape, 1952. (These three books of memoirs were published in one volume, *School House in the Wind*, by the University of Exeter Press, 1998, introduction by Patricia Moyer and Brenda Hull, including a biographical sketch.)

Philippa at School, A & C Black (1928). Illus. 'J H Hart'
Marceline Goes to School, Partridge (1931). Illus.
Discipline for Penelope, Warne (1934). Illus. 'Castell'
Puck of Manor School, Warne (1938). Illus.

A Erskine
Kath of Kinmantel, Oliphants (1958). Illus.

Evelyn Everett-Green
1856-1932
Evelyn Everett-Green was born on 17 November 1856, the daughter of G P Everett-Green, an

artist, and his wife Mary Anne Everett Wood, a historian. Educated at home till she was twelve, she went on first to school, then to Bedford College, which was followed by a spell at the Royal Academy of Music. Her intention of making a home for her brother in India was prevented by his death, after which she took up social service, then trained as a nurse, as well as writing well over 300 books between the 1880s and 1930s. She died on 23 April 1932.

Several of Everett-Green's romances for teenage girls and young women have school-story elements: *Miss Greyshott's Girls* (1905), for instance, though it deals with young women rather than girls, is set at the home of the Misses Greyshott who have taken in boarders for many years, and focuses largely on the enmity of one snobbish resident towards a newcomer. *Dickie and Dorrie at School* has a small girl who accompanies her brother to his prep school, though she does not attend the school herself. However, only *Queen's Manor School*, published late in Everett-Green's writing career, can be classified as a school story: it describes the relationship between American Hulda (sic) Damer, new, serious and rich (seriously rich) and Anglo-Indian Laura Wyon, poor, brilliant but unstable. It is notable mainly for being the only school story of the period, as far as we know, where one girl drugs another's coffee to prevent her winning a prize. Though published in 1921 and set at a large modern school, it has a curiously Victorian air (there is an exemplary senior student called Ursula who dies in the odour of sanctity) and presumably represents Everett-Green setting an elderly toe on a bandwagon which rolled on without her.

Further Reading
Clare, Hilary, 'Evelyn Everett-Green' in *The Oxford Dictionary of National Biography*, OUP (2004)

Queen's Manor School, Stanley Paul (1921). Illus.

Also over 300 other books, comprising books for children of all ages, girls' fiction, adult romances and historical novels; some collaborations; also wrote (from 1909 onwards) as 'Cecil Adair'

See also The Encyclopaedia of Boys' School Stories, **EVELYN EVERETT-GREEN**

Mrs Ewing
(Juliana Horatia Gatty Ewing)
1841-1885

See **EARLY SCHOOL STORIES**

'It's beastly, being so little,' she said crossly.

The frontispiece from *Thomasina Toddy* by Josephine Elder

VIVIEN SHOUTED AND WAVED DESPERATELY

The frontispiece from *The Best Term Ever* by Cecilia Falcon

F

M Fahy
St Clement's, George Allen & Sons (1910). Illus. 'Art+Craft'

Mary Alice Faid
(Mary Alice Faid Dunn)
1899-1990
Mary Alice Faid, the elder daughter of Robert Faid, a butcher, and his wife Mary Margaret Beck, was born in Greenock on 21 January 1897; she had at least one younger sister. Both girls were married on 3 July 1923, Mary Alice to Alexander Carson Dunn, a school teacher (of English); as the ceremony was according to the form of the Primitive Methodist church, this presumably represents the family religious background. Mary Alice Dunn had at least one daughter, and died in Helensburgh on 14 January 1990.

The Trudy series comprises ten evangelistic books, all set in Scotland, which follow the fortunes of Trudy from the age of fifteen, through a (short) primary teaching career, to her becoming the materfamilias. In the meantime, she converts most people whom she meets, including several of her college chums. There is little school interest (although *Trudy Takes Charge* does show the heroine at school), but the fourth in the series is set at a teacher training college.

1 *Trudy Takes Charge* (part school)*, Pickering & Inglis (1949). Illus.
2 *Trudy's Island Holiday**, Pickering & Inglis (1950). Illus.
3 *Trudy's Uphill Road**, Pickering & Inglis (1951). Illus.
4 *Trudy's College Days* (college story), Pickering & Inglis (1953). Illus.
5 *Schoolma'am Trudy**, Pickering & Inglis (1955). Illus.
6 *Trudy on her Own**, Pickering & Inglis (1957). Illus.

7   *Trudy's Small Corner**, Pickering & Inglis (1959). Illus.
8   *Trudy Married**, Pickering & Inglis (1961). Illus.
9   *Trudy in Demand**, Pickering & Inglis (1964). Illus.
10 *Trudy and Family**, Pickering & Inglis (1970). Not illus.

Cecilia Falcon

Nothing is known about this writer, and the name may well be pseudonymous, possibly concealing a male author. Her (?) two full-length school stories are very much in the **MAY WYNNE** mould, with the interest firmly on thriller elements—missing wills, boxes containing silver daggers, mysterious 'Chinamen' and so on. Her fifteen- to sixteen-year-old heroines are far more interested in solving mysteries than in school, although there is some hockey interest in *Deborah's Secret Quest* and swimming plays a large part in *The Best Term Ever*.

Deborah's Secret Quest, Thames Publishing Co. (1950). Illus. "Mold"
The Best Term Ever, Thames Publishing Co. (1952). Illus. Nat Long

Penelope Farmer *see* **HISTORICAL AND FANTASY SCHOOL STORIES**

Gwendoline Featherstonehaugh
(Gwendoline Winifred Featherston(e)haugh Oliver, later Taylor)
1912-2000

Despite the evidence of the book jacket of *Caroline's First Term*, Gwendoline Featherstonehaugh (the surname is sometimes spelt Featherstonhaugh) appears to have been born on 24 January 1912, not 1913, but we have no reason to suppose that the event did not take place, as is given, in Charlottenburg, Berlin, to an English father and Irish mother. However, two of her four elder sisters may in fact have been half-sisters, children of her mother's first marriage. Her father's mother, Caroline Brook Hill, came of a theatrical family; he, Albany Newry Salis Featherstonehaugh, was a language teacher. Unsurprisingly, the family left Germany on the outbreak of the First World War, and Gwendoline was educated at boarding schools in Devonshire and Gloucestershire. In 1939 she was living with her family in London and working as a bank clerk; in 1949 she married Harold Oliver, with whom she had a son. After his death in 1965 she married Walter Headley Taylor (d. 1992) and herself died in Kingston-upon-Thames in 2000.

No more details of this writer are known, though the story of the Dutch science mistress (of course suspected of being a Nazi spy) in her only school story, *Caroline's First Term*, is so movingly described that it suggests some autobiographical input; the book itself is surprisingly competent, despite a bulk order of clichés (everything from buried treasure to identical twins). It is redeemed by an unexpected deftness of characterisation and a slightly ironic narrative: most of the clichés are, if not stood on their heads, at least made to look slightly foolish.

The Romance of a China Doll*, Golden Galley Press (1946). Illus. Tom Kerr
Caroline's First Term, Golden Galley Press (1947). Illus. 'Mates' (?)

Ellenor, Lady Fenn
(Ellenor Frere Fenn)
1743-1813
See **EARLY SCHOOL STORIES** and *The Encyclopaedia of Boys' School Stories*, **ELLENOR, LADY FENN**

Kathleen Fidler
(Kathleen Annie Fidler Goldie)
1899-1980

Kathleen Annie Fidler was born on 10 August 1899 in Coalville, Leics, and educated at Wigan Girls' High School. She trained as a teacher at St Mary's College in Bangor. She was Headmistress of Scot Lane Evening Institute from 1924 to 1930 and taught at St Paul's Girls' School, Wigan, between 1925 and 1930, when she married J H Goldie; they had one son and one daughter. Apart from her many children's books, she also wrote scripts for the BBC, and received the Moscow Film Festival Award in 1967. She died in 1980.

Kathleen Fidler, a prolific writer, did not write many books which could be classified as girls' school stories; although her Mr Simister series is largely set at a mixed school, the books are not intended for girls alone. *School at Sea*, set on a school cruise ship with 800 sixth-formers from schools all over Britain, only scrapes into this book, but since it uses the traditional plot of Rebellious Girl (Myrtle, over-fond of boys and contemptuous of rules) set on the right path by her schoolfellows, it may be classed as an honorary school story.

A full bibliography of Kathleen Fidler may be found in *Twentieth-Century Children's Writers*.

School at Sea, Epworth Press (1970). Illus. David Grice

Margaret C Field
(Margaret Cecile Field Sheminant)
1903-1974

Margaret Field was born in 1903 in India, daughter of the Rev. Claud Herbert Alwyn Faure Field, a Church Missionary Society missionary stationed at Peshawar, 1892-1903. She was educated in private schools and became an Associate of the London Academy of Music and Dramatic Art, presumably while living with her family: her father took up a curacy at St Paul's, Onslow Square in 1903, and at Holy Trinity, Lincoln's Inn Fields, 1905-6. Evidence from her writing would suggest that she was experienced in drama and elocution, but her knowledge of music seems rudimentary. Apart from the fact that she was living in Brighton with her family during the 1930s, so far we know little more for certain about her, though her books indicate that she was very interested, and probably involved, in the Guide movement. She married Henry T Sheminant, in 1930 and apparently had several children; the family appears to have adopted the surname Field. Certainly when she died in Brighton on 15 July 1974 she was known as Margaret Field.

Her school stories are unrelated, but share certain themes. A favourite is girls who are outsiders, for various reasons—Field clearly likes individuality, though the outsider is always finally accepted by the group. Her plots are fairly standard, with the usual sprinkling of rescues, secret passages and buried treasure; Guides are generally mentioned, though only occasionally are they central. *Freda at School* is aimed at seven- to ten-year-olds; the rest at the twelve to sixteen age group. Her writing is adequate, if undistinguished, but she could have done with a more competent copy editor.

The Taming of Teresa, Warne (1926). Illus.
A Strange Term, Warne (1927). Illus.
Freda at School, Warne (1927). Illus. P E Paul
Cecile at St Clare's, Warne (1929). Illus. 'LRB'?
Hilary of Taunton, Newnes ([1931]). Illus.
A Risky Term, Hutchinson ([1930s]). Illus. D Osborne
Madelaine of the Middle Fourth, Mellifont Press, Pocket Library edition (1934). Not illus.
The Franklin Mystery*, Warne (1935). Not illus.
The Rival Schools, Mellifont Press, Pocket Library edition (1936). Not illus.

May Fielding *see* **ERNEST PROTHEROE**

Bertha Mary Fisher

An Unpopular Schoolgirl concerns identical twins, one sweet, gentle and scholarly and the other aggressive, non-academic and brilliant at acting, singing and all sports, who change places several times during the course of the term. The tale is ingenious but telegraphs its punches to such an extent that few girls could have been deceived.

*Honour and Dishonour** (school?). Not traced
*The Player**, Henry J Drane ([1911])
An Unpopular Schoolgirl, Partridge ([1913]). Illus. C E Rhodes

Lucy Gladys Fitzpatrick

Fitzpatrick's only book, *Sonia's First Term*, brings a twelve-year-old American orphan heiress to a boarding school in Liverpool, where she becomes devoted to the junior mistress, voluntarily taking the blame for the latter's misdeeds—caused by the persistent demands of a drunken Irish mother. The book is undistinguished, save in its risibility.

Sonia's First Term, GOP ([1927]). Illus. 'G Barker'?

Penelope Fletcher

The Jewel of Kasr-ed-Shendi, Arthur Stockwell (1973)

Rosemary Ford

Trio Fights Back, a spy thriller, sneaks into this volume because one of the eponymous Trio is at school, where her counter-espionage activities land her in hot water. Unfortunately, Ford equates complexity with profundity; *Trio Fights Back* is quite baffling, and *The Joy School* rather embarrassing, with lengthy analyses of emotional and psychological traumas—the book seems unsure whether it wants to be *The Madcap of the School* or *Regiment of Women*. Ford also has an obsession with something called 'Free Discipline', which produces balanced and independent individuals (apart from the ones that get expelled) but we're never told what it is. Well worth avoiding.

The Joy School, Gerald Swan (1947). Not illus.
Trio Fights Back, Gerald Swan (1947). Not illus.

A Ruby Forde

Forde's only known book may have been produced by a vanity publisher, and is a slight tale of an Irish boarding school to which comes a Canadian schoolgirl (Cherry) who turns out in the end to be Bunny Longfield, best-selling schoolgirl writer of wonderful girls' school stories (wish-fulfilment on the writer's part, possibly), and cousin/pen-friend to Jocelyn, her chief enemy (until Cherry rescues her from drowning, naturally).

Cherry Jam at Glencastle, Dawson Publications (Dublin, 1945). Not illus.
   The title page gives her as 'Author of Long, Long Ago; Fairy Honesty (Broadcast)'.

Antonia Forest
(Pseudonym of Patricia Guilia [sic] Caulfield Kate Rubinstein)
1915-2003

Antonia Forest was the granddaughter of a Russian-Jewish emigrant who was sent to France as a boy, and arrived in England via Ireland. Her mother was an Ulster Protestant, brought up in Dublin. She herself was born in Hampstead in north-west London (an area featured in *The Thursday Kidnapping*), on 26 May 1915, and was an only child, though with the friendship of a neighbouring large family. She was educated at South Hampstead High School, where she enjoyed netball and cricket, and then at University College, London, from where she obtained a Diploma in Journalism (with distinction in English Literature) in 1936. Brought up in the tradition of Reform Judaism, she converted to Catholicism in 1946. From 1939 she lived in Bournemouth, where she died on 29 November 2003.

Antonia Forest is widely regarded as one of the best—if not the best—writers of girls' school stories; yet paradoxically wrote only four, and at a time when the genre was virtually defunct and might well have been supposed to be completely exhausted.

Her four school stories (*Autumn Term*, *End of Term*, *The Cricket Term* and *The Attic Term*) are part of an eleven-book series about the Marlow family. Two (conceived as one but split for reasons of length) relate to an Elizabethan ancestor, but the rest follow one another in a chronological sequence of school and holiday stories. But the school stories can be read on their own, and, as they are the ones which eventually became Puffin paperbacks, increasingly are; they are also the ones which, because of the conventions of boarding-school life, have dated less rapidly. It is interesting that *The Thuggery Affair* was spot-on in its use of language to reflect social class and age when published in 1965, but the teenage slang (some real, some invented by Forest) and current pop music means it is now the one least accessible to the modern reader.

Autumn Term was written as a deliberate attempt to get a book—any book—into the hands of a reputable publisher so that the author could then go on to write 'real' novels. Yet it is not a mere exercise in school-story form. The conventions are there—a traditional boarding school of the very grandest kind, the large family of sisters, the twins whose failures to do the 'proper' thing according to family tradition are the mainspring of the book—but these conventions are deployed with a delicate irony which reminds us that they are both conventions and realities.

In Antonia Forest, literary ability combines with a mastery of plot and an acute delineation of character. Every episode contributes to the whole, every chapter builds up to the final resolution. Nor is it possible to guess from the opening chapter what the last one will reveal. Even in *Autumn Term*, the most conventional of the four, we might guess that Nicola and Lawrie will eventually triumph, but not how, or after what vicissitudes. The plays in *Autumn Term* and *End of Term*, the final match in *The Cricket Term*—a match that will grip even the most cricket-illiterate reader because of the relationships between the opponents—are not simply set-pieces which display literary virtuosity, but vital climaxes to the books in which they occur.

And it is not simply by deft plot handling that Antonia Forest scores. What really marks her out is her remarkable gift for character. If we come to know Nicola inside out (quite literally, for it is Nicola who is the focus for most of the books), the rest of the Marlows and their friends are instantly recognisable and perfectly distinguishable. Lawrie, Tim, Miranda, Esther and their satellites are uniquely themselves, not only sharply drawn, but also perfectly related to their backgrounds. Antonia Forest is one of the very few writers who relate boarding-school girls to their homes and parents, not crudely, but within the narrow spectrum of the professional middle classes. If Nicola and Lawrie are the plausible products of a Naval Service background (even Lawrie, for all her dithers and panics, can rise to an occasion), Miranda is superbly the intelligent, wealthy Jewish child, Tim the off-beat Bohemian (gloriously inappropriate for the Headmistress's Niece, yet utterly believable) and timid Esther the anxious product of her parents' divorce. The one person whose background we do not know is Lois Sanger, the older girl, ultimately prefect and Games Captain, who crosses the twins' path from their earliest schooldays and is both saviour and antagonist. We do, though, know Lois's inner workings: exactly why she dislikes Nicola and how she justifies to herself her persecution. Similarly the dismal Marie Dobson, memorably dreary in *Autumn Term* and spectacularly, if offstage, dead in *The Cricket Term*, is as recognisable and as instantly real as any schoolfellow we have ever disliked for her mediocrity.

Antonia Forest's characters are individualised not only by their actions and their thoughts, but by their extraordinarily vivid dialogue. Rowan's relaxed irony, Lois's pointed sarcasm, Miranda's flashing rejoinders, Tim's conscious parody of Girlish Dialogue ('Just from things Me Auntie says, I don't think They'd go too much on the sweep-the-lowlies-behind-the-pavilion bit. So—p'raps Lois didn't think she'd—bother—Craven about it—you know?' *The Cricket Term*,) and Lawrie's mumbling grievances: there is rarely any need for the speaker to be indicated. Perhaps at times these girls are wittier and more articulate than their real-life equivalents, but they are most convincing. The staff are equally distinctive, even in reported speech. Here is Upper IVA's form mistress, Miss Latimer, relaying the Head's disapproval of their contribution to the Carol Service:

'Miss Keith feels you didn't altogether grasp what was needed. Not so much a performance, more a contribution to a quasi-religious service … In this particular case, Miss Keith feels you were not quite in tune with the occasion.'

Upper IVA gazed at her in collective dejection.

'I was asked to mention this to you and I've therefore done so.' Miss Latimer leaned back in her chair and smiled her slow, lazy smile. 'On the other hand, some of us were distinctly grateful to you for providing a welcome break from all that predictable, worthy, but oh-so-ineffably-dull vocalizing …' (*The Attic Term*)

And Miss Cromwell's *bon* (if terrifying) *mots* are common currency among lovers of Antonia Forest ('You must look for [Meg's physics notes] later. Or I shall be obliged to define for you the difference between legitimate and morbid curiosity.' *The Cricket Term*).

That Antonia Forest produced four school stories of equal merit is a tribute to her skill and perhaps derives from the fact that the books sprang from separate ideas and not from the mere need to write a sequel. Second books are notoriously disappointing, but *End of Term* is better than *Autumn Term* and *The Cricket Term* perhaps best of all. *The Attic Term* is no less good, but because it is a sadder book does not in general inspire the same affection as its predecessors. Each book has its own flavour, but uses the same ingredients, and in Nicola Marlow has a heroine whose fortunes we care about desperately. The only real criticism one can make of Miss Forest's books is that there are not enough of them: thirteen books in nearly fifty years was not an enormous output. But then, had she produced a book a year, one may doubt whether the result would have been as absorbing.

Further Reading
Book and Magazine Collector 160
Folly passim, especially 15, 39 and 41
Ang, Susan, section in *The Widening World of Children's Literature*, St Martin's Press, 1999
Watson, Victor, chapter in *Reading Series Fiction*, Routledge, 2000
Forest, Antonia, Introduction printed in all Girls Gone By reprints, first issued in *Falconer's Lure*, 2003

Sims, Sue, 'The Life and Fiction of Antonia Forest', *Children's Literature in Education,* March 2005, Vol 36, issue 1, pp 69-82

Clare, Hilary, 'School Stories Don't Count: The Neglected Genius of Antonia Forest', in *Out of the Attic: Some Neglected Children's Authors of the Twentieth Century,* ed. Pat Pinsent, Pied Piper Publishing Ltd, Shenstone, 2006

Copson, Belinda, 'Patricia Giulia [sic] Caulfield Kate Rubinstein' in *The Oxford Dictionary of National Biography,* 2007

Heazlewood, Anne, *The Marlows and their Maker: A Companion to the Series by Antonia Forest,* Girls Gone By, 2007

Hicks, Laura, (ed.) *Celebrating Antonia Forest: The Papers of the Bournemouth Conference* Girls Gone By 2008.

M1   *Autumn Term,* Faber (1948). Illus. Marjorie Owens
M2   *The Marlows and the Traitor*,* Faber (1953). Illus. Doritie Kettlewell
M3   *Falconer's Lure*,* Faber (1957). Illus. Tasha Kallin
M4   *End of Term,* Faber (1959). Not illus.
M5   *Peter's Room*,* Faber (1961). Not illus.
     The Thursday Kidnapping,* Faber (1963). Not illus.
M6   *The Thuggery Affair*,* Faber (1965). Not illus.
M7   *The Ready-Made Family*,* Faber (1967). Not illus.
P1   *The Player's Boy** (historical novel about Marlow ancestor), Faber (1970). Not illus.
P2   *The Players and the Rebels** (as above), Faber (1971). Not illus.
M8   *The Cricket Term,* Faber (1974). Not illus.
M9   *The Attic Term,* Faber (1976). Not illus.
M10 *Run Away Home*,* Faber (1982). Not illus.

Forest Continuation by Sally Hayward
M11 *Spring Term,* Girls Gone By (2011). Not illus

M = Marlow series
P = Players pair

Maude S Forsey
(Maude Sarah Forsey Lane)
1885-1974

Maude Forsey is now known to have been the sister of George Frank Forsey (1889-1974), Professor of Classics at Southampton University; this identifies her as the Maud Sarah Forsey born in Stockwell in 1885 to George and Sarah Stockwell, the youngest of nine children of whom several died in infancy. Her father was a carpenter and her mother, in the 1901 census, was listed as a 'grocer and confectioner'; Maud herself in this year, aged fifteen, was a pupil teacher; in 1911 she was an elementary school teacher with the London County Council, like one of her elder sisters. In 1925, aged 40, she married Herbert Percy Lane, a widower and librarian at the Guildhall School of Music; there were no children. He died in 1947 and she in March 1974 in Weymouth.

Maude Forsey's two school stories are competent enough to make one wish that she had written more: *Mollie Hazeldene's Schooldays* is a gentle but very amusing first person account of a London girl's two years at a boarding school in the country; *Norah O'Flanigan, Prefect* follows Norah's year as form prefect to the Fourth Form of a day school, and details both Norah's scrapes and her ultimate good influence. Neither book has a great deal of plot; perhaps for that reason, both carry more conviction than the majority of school stories.

Southampton University library holds an unpublished manuscript of hers, *Partly a Prig*, dated 1945.

Mollie Hazeldene's Schooldays, Nelson ([1924]). Illus. W Bryce Hamilton
Norah O'Flanigan, Prefect, Nelson ([1937]). Illus. (W) Lindsay Cable

Also a book for young children and some short children's plays

Olivia Fowell
(Agnes Olivia Fowell)
1876-1953

Olivia Fowell was born on 16 June 1876 in Margate, the daughter of William John Fowell, a minister in the Methodist Church, and his wife Agnes Gregson Aspinall. We know little else so far save that she lived in Worthing for all her adult life and died there on 19 June 1953.

'Now, Pat, don't go and say you've seen the ghost, too.'
'I'm not quite dotty!'

Told that this passage of dialogue dated from 1906, many would guess that it came from the earliest stratum of **ANGELA BRAZIL**. But there were several writers, contemporaries or precursors of Brazil, who helped to transform the girls' school story, and Fowell was one of them. Though only five in number, her school stories, like those of **MRS GEORGE HORNE DE VAIZEY**, **MAY BALDWIN** and **RAYMOND JACBERNS**, mark the transition from the Victorian moral tale set in a small family-style school to the bracing public-school story of the post-war period; and are particularly interesting, in that they show, quite independently of Brazil, the colloquial dialogue and use of slang and of humour which Brazil is often said to have initiated.

Fowell's school stories come in two pairs, with one unrelated book in between. The first two, set at Marcot Grange, a boarding school with around 50 pupils, focus chiefly on Pat Temple, a former Wild Irish Girl now at the top of the school, and her relationships with a variety of fellow pupils. *Her First Term* uses the characteristic Victorian device of false accusation; Pat is deliberately 'framed' by the unpleasant Minnie Perkins who has been stealing money from purses. However, Fowell rejects the standard Victorian dénouement, where the villainess repents on either her own or her victim's near-death-bed (the sequel to *Her First Term* uses this device). She manages Pat's exoneration using a technique which recalls later writers such as **BRUCE**: a devoted junior called Joan (the eponymous 'Her') tracks down the real culprit, and helps to expose her.

In *Patricia's Promotion*, set a year later, Patricia is forced to befriend Helen Molyneux, a new girl whose dead mother (a friend of the Head) made a mésalliance with a bookseller—albeit a very gentlemanly one—and whose presence at this exclusive school puts up the backs of her better-born and worse-mannered schoolfellows. Using this situation, Fowell again rejects her literary predecessors; the introduction of pupils not 'ladies' by birth into 'schools for the daughters of gentlemen' would become a central theme for the next generation of school stories, and can still be seen as late as 1956 in **ELINOR M BRENT-DYER**'s *A Problem for the Chalet School*.

Fowell's interest in change does not stop here. Marcot Grange, we are told in *Patricia's Promotion*, has altered even within Patricia's memory:

> There were so many more 'visiting masters', *so many games* [my italics], separate bedrooms, and a sitting-room for the older girls; all these Pat had seen added to the old arrangements.

We are seeing, in fact, the gradual transformation of the small private 'ladies' seminary' into a modern pseudo-public boarding school. And five years later, *The Doings of Dorothea* presents us with a school established by 'some gentlemen [who] felt that a school of this sort was needed at Moreton Bay', who built the house and 'engaged a lady as head-mistress'. We are on the way to the fully fledged girls' public school.

Admittedly we aren't yet there in *The Doings of Dorothea*, which has, ironically, a more old-fashioned air than any of Fowell's other school stories; the thirteen-year-old heroine is sweet and gentle, the Head Girl so honourable it hurts, and the narrator rather too inclined to take the reader into her confidence ('You may imagine that Dorothea had many and wonderful dreams that night'). But Dorothea's friend, the impish Peggy, enlivens the book, and saves it from becoming over-sentimental.

Why there is a gap of fourteen years separating *The Doings of Dorothea* from Fowell's second pair of school stories we do not know; but during these years, the majority of school stories made the transition which we can see in Fowell. By 1926, the standard background is the girls' public school; and her two tales of Lestholme College are perfect examples of the genre. *The Girls of Tredennings* follows the fortunes of Shirley Stainer, installed as head of undisciplined Tredennings House, in her ultimately successful efforts to transform it; *The Latimer Scholarship* introduces a Welsh scholarship girl, despised by the more snobbish elements of the house, who ultimately turns out to be the long-lost cousin of Eve Latimer, the American girl whose father has established the scholarship. The books, well-written and vivid though they are, would not in themselves be outstanding; but when one sees them in context, they become a fascinating index of change—social, educational and literary.

M1 *Her First Term*, Marshall Brothers ([1906]). Illus. 'Richard Tod'
M2 *Patricia's Promotion*, Marshall Brothers ([1907]). Illus. 'Richard Tod'
    The Doings of Dorothea, Blackie (1912). Illus. Frank E Wiles
    Brave Girls All*, Jarrold & Sons ([1912]). Illus. Elizabeth Earnshaw
    The Mystery of Barwood Hall*, Harrap (1920). Illus.
T1 *The Girls of Tredennings*, OUP (1926). Illus. 'M D Johnston'
T2 *The Latimer Scholarship* Blackie ([1929]). Illus. 'H L Bacon'

M = Marcot Grange pair
T = Tredennings pair

Cecily Fox
That New Girl Anna is a reasonably standard Royalty-at-School tale: in this case, the thirteen-year-old Queen of Sarnavia, taking refuge at Beechwood Hall from her enemies. Here her true identity is hidden from all save the discerning reader, who suspects that any girl whose maid covers her hand with kisses is not quite your normal British schoolgirl. However, the story is told with a lightness and sense of irony which compensates for a good deal of Ruridiocy.

That New Girl Anna, Nelson ([1930]). Illus. E Brier
Eve Plays her Part*, Nelson ([1934]). Illus.

A couple of other miscellaneous books

Dora B Francis *see* DORA CHAPMAN

Joy Francis
(Pseudonym of Olive Sarah Hill Folds)
1888-1978

Olive Sarah Folds lived in Welwyn, Herts; she was born Olive Sarah Hill, the youngest of the three daughters of Frederick Hill, a straw plait and briar merchant, later grocer, of Breachwood Green, Herts, on 1 November 1888. In 1915 she married Francis Walter John Folds (whose Christian name presumably suggested her pseudonym) and eventually had two daughters. She died on 25 April 1978.

Of her five school stories, the first two cover consecutive terms at Greystone Manor School; the others are unrelated, even the two St Anne's having different Heads, girls and locations. The books are good middle-of-the-road examples of the genre, only unusual in her liking for first person narrative (unmarked by the rather irritating self-consciousness adopted by most school-story writers when inventing 'schoolgirl authors') and her comparative lack of new girls in the foreground.

Francis's protagonists are, in general, form prefects or sub-prefects, very keen that their form should win the form prize on offer. They are honourable and upright, disliking any kind of dishonesty; this tends to get them into trouble when, as happens in *The Greystone Girls* and *The Girls of the Rose Dormitory*, they wrongly suspect dishonesty in a mistress or classmate. They have a distressing tendency to get into trouble while acting with the best of motives. However, truth will out, and they end up receiving the plaudits of their comrades, being painted on to the Honours Board, or even (as in *Rosemary at St Anne's*) seeing a scholarship for needy girls established in their name. They are brave as well: though Francis doesn't let them perform any gallant rescues, they do catch burglars!

The school backgrounds of Francis's books are more realistic than many and she may well have been a teacher (one of her sisters certainly was); her use of mischievous five-year-olds in three of her books might indicate bitter experience of that age group as well. Mind you, she also has a *tendre* for reuniting sundered families, which is less true to life!

1. *The Greystone Girls*, Blackie ([1928]). Illus. Stanley Lloyd
2. *Biddy at Greystone*, Blackie ([1929]). Illus. Stanley Lloyd
   The Girls of the Rose Dormitory, Blackie ([1930]). Illus. John Campbell
   Rosemary at St Anne's, Blackie ([1932]). Illus. Comerford Watson
   Patsy at St Anne's (unrelated), RTS/GOP ([1936]). Illus.

Cicely Fraser

Cicely Fraser's only known school story, *Feuds and Friendships*, is a slightly rambling and episodic tale centred on fifteen-year-old Natalie Bridgeforth, clever, good at games and a natural leader, who is continually at odds with authority. The story has a realistic background and the writing is competent.

Feuds and Friendships, Harrap (1935). Illus. Eileen Soper
First—The Infant* (on nurseries and nursery schools), Pitman (1943). Illus.

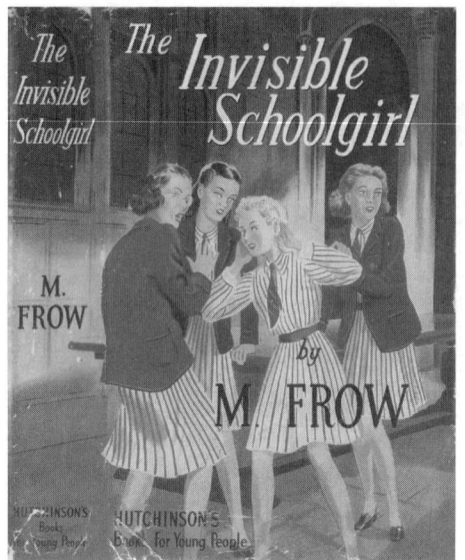

M Frow
(Marion Frow)

A publisher's handout states: 'Marion Frow was educated at Manchester University. She went to live in France, where she did some teaching. Writing and hockey were her twin passions for years. She is married to an army officer and has one son. She travels a lot and hopes one day to see Australia and New Zealand.'

Marion Frow's only school story is written in a style somewhat resembling **ETHEL TALBOT**'s in its mixture of breathlessness and reflection; the plot, which must be one of the silliest even in a genre renowned for silly plots, concerns St Monica's School in Wales and new girl Meg, daughter of a film star. Meg encounters Ceridwen, an apparent foundling, who is haunting the secret passages in this former convent, but who turns out to be the Head's long-lost niece. With all its daftness, the book is curiously readable.

The Invisible Schoolgirl, Hutchinson ([1950]). Illus.

Also children's adventure stories, including the Intelligence Corps sequence

Leonora Fry
(Leonora Fry Oswin)
1913-1999

Leonora Fry was born on 10 July 1913, the daughter of **BERTHA LEONARD**. In 1939 she was described as 'authoress', and living with her parents. She made a late marriage, in 1975, to Norman Oswin, and died in Brighton in 1999.

For the School's Sake, Shaw (1934). Illus. 'Arthur'?

Also other children's fiction, and much educational non-fiction

Agnes Furlong
(Agnes Holroyd Furlong)
1907-1988
Agnes Furlong was the wife of Norman Furlong of the Training College, Ashton Road, Lancaster, later of Canley, Coventry, and ultimately of Silverdale, Lancashire.

The School Library Mystery (part mixed school), Blackie ([1951]). Illus. Eric Winter

Also other children's fiction

Muriel Fyfe
(Jane Muriel Stirling Nisbet Fyfe)
1908-1990
Muriel Stirling Nisbet (she seems always to have used her second name), the daughter of a solicitor, married James Gabriel Fyfe, a publisher's editor, on 27 January 1931 and lived with him in Glasgow in the 1930s; later she lived in Kippen (where James died in 1949) and Greenock; she died in 1990.

Sally Travels to School, Blackie (Summit Library, [1937]). Illus.

Also many readers, abridgements of classics, etc

The prospect of thirty years of premenstrual tension was too horrid to contemplate.

The frontispiece from *First Term for Ziggy* by R E Warfe

ADULT SCHOOL FICTION

The difficulty of defining the limits of the girls' school story is intensified when it comes to looking at its adult equivalent. This is partly because the adult 'school story' is not simply a grown-up version of the girls' form: whereas the girls' school story is, from the late 19th century onwards, perceived by writers as a genre with its own themes, motifs and expectations, adult novels set in girls' schools are *sui generis*. The writers have different motivations, different aims and different methods, and there is no point in even attempting to discuss them under the same heading. Can one classify part one of *Gulliver's Travels* and *The Borrowers* as part of the 'miniature people genre'?

However, a book such as this, which attempts to look at the whole range of British and Commonwealth girls' school stories published in book form, is going to be challenged if it omits readers' favourite 'school story'—and if that happens to be *Frost in May* (see **CONVENT SCHOOL STORIES**), judged by the somewhat partisan Elizabeth Bowen to be 'the only school story to be ... a work of art', or *The Getting of Wisdom*, so much the worse for the book's compilers. Hence this article. It does not attempt to define 'adult school fiction': if the original publishers bound and marketed the novel for an adult audience, we have accepted their judgement. Admittedly, the rise of the Young Adult novel has complicated matters somewhat, but these are discussed in **MODERN SCHOOL STORIES**: here, we're sticking to the grown-ups. As in most of the other topic articles, we're only listing stories set in girls' schools and women's colleges: boys, whether in single-sex or mixed establishments, are out of bounds, as are primary schools.

Though readers and collectors of girls' school stories have always made a conscious or unconscious distinction between the books aimed at girls and those targeted at an adult audience, this does not seem to have been the case in the field of boys' school stories. Isabel Quigly, Jeffrey Richards and others have discussed *Tom Brown's Schooldays* and *The Hill* cheek by jowl (*see* **THE CRITICAL**

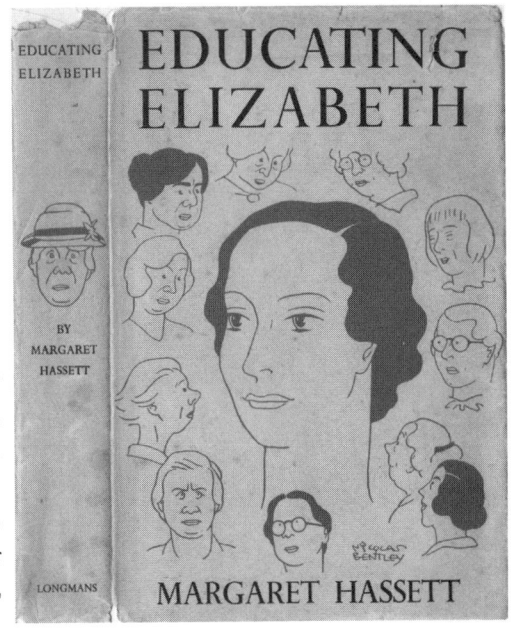

RESPONSE); critics of girls' school stories do not, in general, consider *The School at the Chalet* alongside *Regiment of Women*. There may be many reasons for this: the one which leaps to the eye, however, is the difference in men's and women's attitudes to the schools they write about. The adult novel set in a boys' school is far more likely to have a nostalgic, even affectionate tone, even when critical in places (as with Alec Waugh's *The Loom of Youth*—see *The Encyclopaedia of Boys' School Stories*); the novel set in a girls' school tends to express what Gillian Avery describes as a 'smouldering resentment about past injustices' (*The Best Type of Girl*). This is clearly a very wide generalisation: some novels, like Elizabeth North's *Dames*, exhibit a certain sardonic fondness for parts of the institution; but on the whole the attitude to girls' schools has not changed a great deal since the 18th century, when they were conceived as places to which no careful parents would send their daughter. 'Look Back in Anger' might be a suitable subtitle for many of the serious novels mentioned here.

Everyone will remember one early account of a girls' school: Charlotte Brontë's swingeing attack in *Jane Eyre* (1847) on her old school of Cowan Bridge (rechristened 'Lowood') is written in vitriol, and burns its way into the reader's memory. The appalling physical privations of Lowood, from burnt porridge to typhus fever, cannot easily be paralleled elsewhere in girls' school fiction; the humiliations suffered by the young Jane most certainly can. The contrast between the two teachers, Miss Scatcherd and Miss Temple, is another common motif: in book after book, mistresses are polarised between the angelic and the demonic, and one of the motifs which mark out the adult novel from the girls' school story is often the relationship (ranging from mild admiration to a full-blown affair) between student and teacher. The Lowood sequence in *Jane Eyre* can in many ways be seen as a pattern for a large number of later novels.

One repeated factor in many of *Jane Eyre*'s successors is their unsurprising tendency to be based on the writer's own schooldays. This may be why comparatively few adult stories with real school interest were published during the 19th century: school was not a universal experience for middle-class girls. Charlotte Brontë used her experiences teaching at a *pensionnat* in Brussels for both *The Professor* (1857) and *Villette* (1853); but these books are largely love stories, and seen through the eyes of the adult protagonists throughout. Christabel Coleridge's *The Green Girls of Greythorpe* (1890) is similarly focused on her schoolmistress heroine, who comes to a charity school and attempts to make radical changes: the school itself, full of cloddish, unwanted girls, is an infinity away from the world of the girls' boarding school. The story is at least partially a romance. The Australian writer Vera G Dwyer's *A War of Girls* (1915) has a similar blend of romance and school, concerned as it is with the blighted love affair of the beautiful schoolmistress Vieve Stockley; since her suitor is the brother of the headmistress of a rival school, the two sets of pupils become involved. Neither Coleridge nor Dwyer is particularly interested in school for its own sake.

Between Coleridge and Dwyer, however, comes the first generation of writers to have been educated in High Schools and public schools. They are very interested in school; and very critical. The detachment conferred by rechristening their heroines and using the third person is clearly not enough to create objectivity, and many of their books demonstrate a passionate disapproval of the system or the personalities to which they were subjected. **NETTA SYRETT**'s *A School Year* (1902) is on the borderline between girls' and adult fiction, and is discussed in the alphabetical entries, but she is clearly recalling her time at the North London Collegiate School, and should thus be mentioned here. Ethel Florence Lindesay Robertson, née Richardson, one of Australia's best-known writers, who used the pseudonym 'Henry Handel Richardson', is another early writer in this field. *The Getting of Wisdom* (1910) recounts Laura Rambotham's time at 'The Ladies' College, Melbourne' is based firmly on Florence's own time at the Presbyterian Ladies' College there. The cold school, 'just like a prison', Laura's terror that the girls might discover that her mother had to work for a living; the chilly, remote Headmistress—all are mercilessly exposed, and the conclusion reached: 'the unpardonable sin is to vary from the common mould'. A story intended for girls would have ended with this misfit happily absorbed: but writers of adult fiction tend to pride themselves on their distinctness from the common throng.

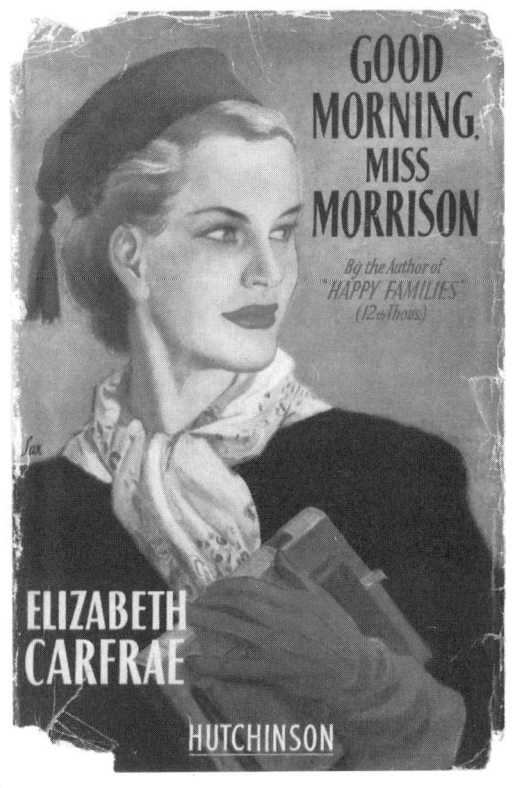

The outsider theme in adult school stories also appears in those books which focus on staff-room politics, with girls mainly having walk-on roles. Eleanor Scott's 1928 title *War among Ladies* sums up this type of novel. The most common theme in these books is the clash between the protagonist—an outsider in that she is young, charming and progressive—and an older, more traditional mistress. *Gildersleeves* (E M Wilmot-Buxton, 1921), for instance, pits newly qualified Margaret Alison against middle-aged Miss Costerton; Winifred Lear's *Shady Cloister* (1950) has the added twist that the older teacher has a sister at the school who is devoted to the younger, charismatic mistress. In *Educating Elizabeth* (1937), Margaret Hassett raises the bar by making her eponymous heroine the newly appointed Headmistress, foiled at every stage by 'the Beezer', who detests all modern innovations; the plot is also characteristic of this sub-genre by producing a deus ex machina in the form of an attractive man who extracts the heroine from her difficult situation by marrying her. Kathleen Barratt's *To Fight Another Day* (1947) reverses the standard situation by making the new headmistress the villainess—young, charming, progressive and evil—while the heroine is fighting hard for tradition; but the dénouement once again is escape via marriage (as we also see in *Gildersleeves* and *Shady Cloister*).

Numerically, however, there are considerably more books where the outsider is a schoolgirl. The intense religious culture found in convents can doubly exclude the child who cannot or will not assimilate (*see* **CONVENT SCHOOL STORIES** for further discussion), but there are plenty of secular schools that have the same effect. While not all adult school fiction is autobiography, writers often draw from their own schooldays, even when the plot is entirely invented. Only a tiny part of *The Constant Nymph* (1925) is set at school, but Margaret Kennedy uses memories of Cheltenham Ladies' College in portraying the agonies of the Sanger sisters at 'Cleeve College'; children are merciless to those who do not fit in. Elizabeth North, whose *Dames* (1981) interweaves the schooldays and later lives of a group of girls at the eponymous school, has constructed a careful picture of her old school, Downe House, whose charismatic founder, Olive Willis, hovers over the book (under the epithet 'The Founder') despite being dead before the book begins. Elizabeth Bowen, an older girl of Downe House, had recreated her school in *Friends and Relations* exactly 50 years earlier in 1931 as 'Mellyfield'; the characteristic intellectual atmosphere of the place is identical in both novels.

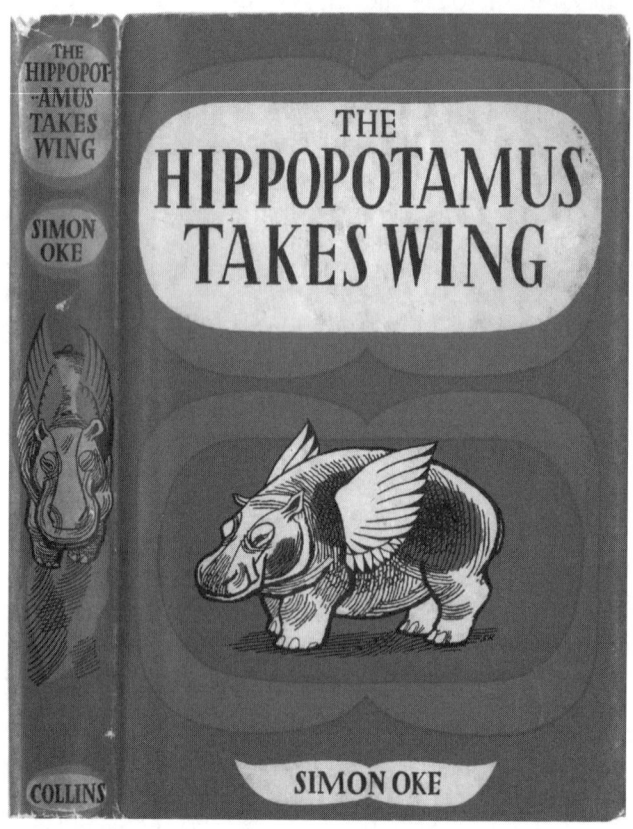

It is difficult to define the point at which one says of a fictional school: 'This is a real place'; but the feeling of recognition is unmistakeable. One has it in Rosemary Manning's *The Chinese Garden* (1962), with its portrait of Bampfield and its extraordinary Headmistress ('Chief'), Anne Valery's *The Edge of a Smile* (1977) and Priscilla Johnston's *The Narrow World* (1930). Johnston's 'Laykington' is emphatically school as seen from the pupil's point of view; any mistress would regard it as extremely subversive. We read about ragging in class, reading forbidden novels, avoiding cricket practices—all the things which in the majority of school stories are only practised by rotters, are here regarded as normal and natural. In its conclusion ('School is only a few years of your life, an incident'), it resembles **LUCY KINLOCH**'s (or Kinlock: the publishers couldn't make up their mind) *A World within a School*; one wonders why Duckworth put *The Narrow World* on to their adult list and Warne targeted *A World within a School* at girls. The books resemble each other in another area as well: both deal with passionate friendships between the protagonist and a more senior girl. Nora's relationship with Roberta in Kinloch's book is paralleled by the feelings of Joyce, the heroine of *The Narrow World*, towards prefect Alix. But the British schoolgirl is an inhibited creature: Joyce's passion can only be expressed tentatively, reading poetry with Alix and touching her hand just once, at the very end of the novel.

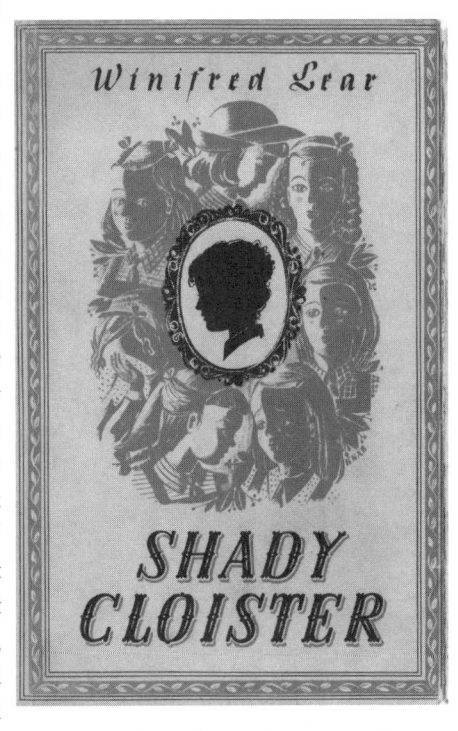

In general, women fictionalising their schooldays concur with this approach. Friendship between schoolgirls, however deep, is rarely expressed physically, and overt lesbianism is extremely rare; a fact which disappoints many readers. Fact, however, has never stood in the way of fiction. One may note that when Colette wrote *Claudine à l'école* (1900; English translation 1956), her husband Willy (who encouraged her to write so that he could publish it under his own name) told her not to be afraid of 'racy details'; and then, when they were complete, to 'hot … these childish reminiscences up a little … For example, a too passionate friendship …' (English translation by Antonia White, Secker & Warburg edition). Thus there is a whole sub-section of the adult school novel which, taking as its starting point the fact that schoolgirls very frequently indulge in violent adorations for senior girls or teachers (the 'pash', 'crush', 'rave' or 'GP'), goes on to depict passionate, homosexual love: less often between pupils than between pupil and teacher or (sometimes) two teachers. The first of these seems to have been Clemence Dane's *Regiment of Women* (1917), in which the magnetic Clare Hartill creates destruction in her wake, with Louise, the sensitive pupil who has adored her, ultimately committing suicide by throwing herself from a window. Dane was writing at a period when society was being encouraged to view 'spinster schoolmistresses' as 'predatory lesbians' (*see* Rosemary Auchmuty's *A World of Girls*). There is an interesting parallel with the German writer Christa Winsloe, whose play *Krankheit der Liebe* was produced in 1932 in London as *Children in Uniform*. In that play (and in *Das Mädchen Manuela*, Winsloe's novel on which she based the play), Manuela kills herself in precisely the same way as Louise, though whether because incipient lesbians have a fatal attraction for windows, or because Winsloe had read *Regiment of Women* is hard to tell. *Olivia* (1949), by Dorothy Strachey Bussy, sister of Lytton Strachey, who published it as 'by Olivia' and kept herself anonymous, tells a similar story in the first person, from the girl's point of view, rather than the teacher's: here, the setting is a finishing school in France and the object of Olivia's devotion is Mademoiselle Julie, the charismatic joint principal.

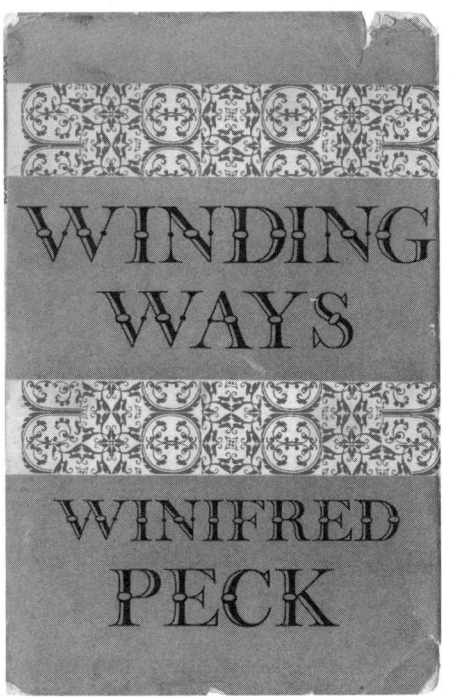

Later books which treat sexual or incipiently sexual relationships between pupils tend to focus on a separate problem: suspicion in the minds of Authority that something is wrong. While this book can't (for reasons of space as well as accessibility) generally discuss American authors, there are a few books which stand out, Madeleine L'Engle's 1945 *The Small Rain*, the first part of which was adapted for British girls as *Prelude* (1970), among them. In this novel, L'Engle sends her American heroine Katherine, a pianist of potential genius, to an English boarding school in Switzerland. Any similarities with Nina Rutherford (*A Genius at the Chalet School*) are not only coincidental but deceptive. Motherless Katherine, who detests the continual silliness and noise of her fellow pupils, is befriended by Sarah; but the staff interpret their (completely innocent) fellowship as lesbianism, and the friendship is broken. In Paula Neuss's *All Girls Together* (1979), there is a further twist: the relationship between dreamy Hetty and the brilliant Ellen is being attacked by Clarissa Embleton-Smith, the Art Mistress, on the grounds of its danger—but we (and several of the characters in the novel, including Ellen herself) realise that Miss Embleton-Smith is in love with Ellen and sees Hetty as a rival.

All these books treat sexuality with various degrees of objectivity: even *Olivia* is interested as much in the consequences of passion—jealousy, manipulation, deceit—as in the passion itself. The same cannot be said for Rosalind Wade's *Children, Be Happy* (1931). This rare book (all copies were recalled by the publishers after two libel actions by Rosalind Wade's London day school) is unintentionally hilarious in its attempt to show that girls' schools are a hotbed of unnatural (and admittedly a fair amount of natural) vice. The problem lies in the fact that Rosalind Wade, only 20 when she wrote the book, still had the outlook of an adolescent, for whom sex (and, to a much smaller degree, religious doubt) are all-absorbing. Unfortunately she transferred these obsessions to every major character in the book, so that from the Headmistress downwards, everyone thinks constantly about sex, either with frustration (the spinster staff), longing (the younger, pretty mistresses), disgust (the Head) or intense curiosity (the girls). Nor is sexual activity all in the mind: seventeen-year-old Joyce sleeps with Harry, who then deserts her; Sylvia, the heroine, has an affair with a mistress, who discards her greasy fiancé for Sylvia's sake; Sylvia's friend Anna catches her father cuddling his mistress in the drawing room; fat, ugly Janie heads towards psychosis by growing to believe in her imaginary lover; the blowsy maid, Ada, who spends most nights on the Heath with her boyfriend, gets pregnant and tries to bring on an abortion; finally Miss Nares, the really warped teacher (all the others are just relatively warped), denounces everyone in sight and then hangs herself in the girls' cloakroom. As Miss Hether reflects: 'It had been almost too much for the most iron nerves, to find a fellow-schoolmistress hanging from the bracket in the ceiling.' There are one or two non-sexual happenings, just to enliven matters: Miss Lines, the deputy Headmistress, develops a fatal cancer, and Matron is dismissed for watering the milk.

However, Wade's youth accounts for much of this: it is interesting that the novel which most resembles *Children, Be Happy* is also, apparently, by an adolescent. The American novel *Schoolgirl*, published in 1930, a year earlier than Wade's book, was (according to its introduction), written by Carmen Barnes at the age of sixteen, and is autobiographical. If the introduction is telling the truth, one can only assume that American girls at 1920s boarding school were somewhat different from their carefully guarded English counterparts, as these girls not only smoke and drink, but have passionate sexual encounters with each other ('Her lips met Janet's in wild longing … [her] timid fingers caressed Janet's white throat and the dear, intimate curves of her breast') and 'go the limit' with boys who pick them up from school in 'scarlet roadsters'. But the steamy style, liberally scattered with exclamation marks, and the adolescent obsession with sex and bodies, link the two books with each other, if not with any real-life school or sequence of events.

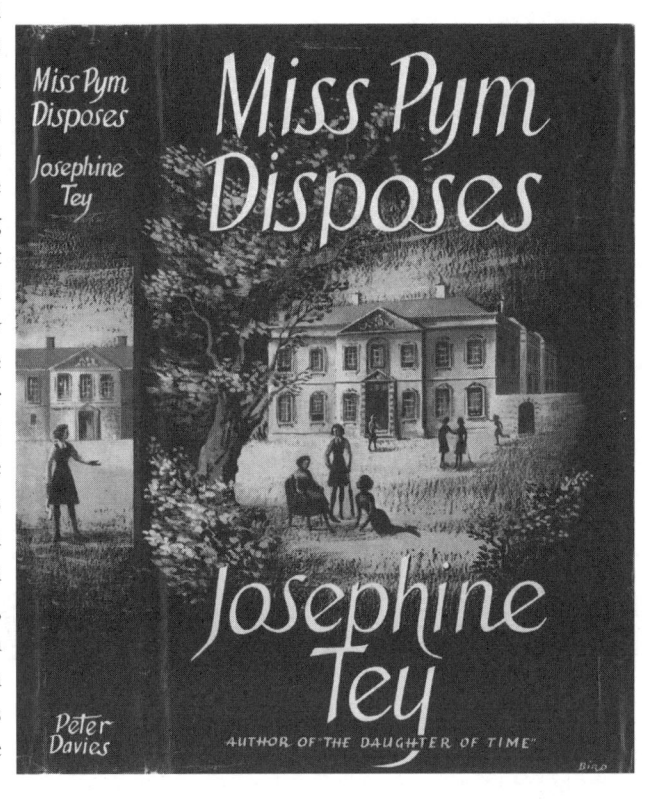

These books are hardly pornography, although *Schoolgirl* brushes the edge of that genre once or twice; but the idea of groups of females enclosed together is a staple of pornography, whether in a school or a convent. Readers who wish to pursue this further will need to make their own inquiries, as the authors of this *Encyclopaedia* are neither interested in nor knowledgeable about the field. But it may be useful in this context to mention a handful of curiosities. The first of these, a novella by Lord Berners, was privately printed in 1936 for his own somewhat dubious circle of friends. *The Girls of Radclyff Hall* (an obvious reference to the author of the lesbian novel *The Well of Loneliness*), by 'Adela Quebec' (another obvious parody) features heroines in black rubber macs and a Head who likes to 'form young people'; it reads somewhat like a perverted version of Arthur Marshall. Philip Larkin, as an Oxford undergraduate, wrote two 'school stories' using the pseudonym 'Brunette Coleman', *Michaelmas Term at St Bride's* and the unfinished *Trouble at Willow Gables*: these *jeux d'esprit*, which mix clever pastiche with sado-masochistic sexuality, were published in 2002 with a fascinating critical apparatus by Dr James Booth, revealing Larkin's enjoyment of authors like **DORITA FAIRLIE BRUCE**. Susan Swan's *The Wives of Bath* (1993) is not pornography, but the combination of school story, Gothic horror and perverted sexuality (the climax—there is certainly no pun here—is likely to make many readers feel physically sick) makes it appropriate to mention at this point.

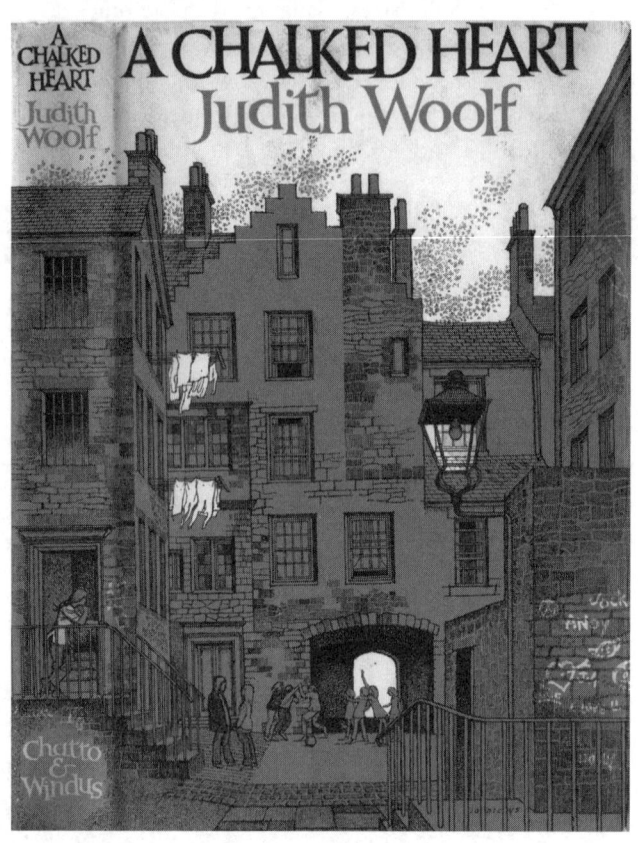

Any body of work which has developed formulae, of course, invites pastiche and parody, and as with Larkin, the girls' school story is no exception. Arthur Marshall is renowned for his send-ups of the school story, but he is by no means the only one. **PETER GLIDEWELL**'s books about St Ursula's are dealt with in the alphabetical section, as the publishers used their children's imprint; but *Poison for Teacher* (Nancy Spain, 1949) is an over-the-top detective story which also giggles shamelessly at the most beloved conventions of the school story. Simon Oke's *The Hippopotamus Takes Wing* (1952) is, like the pair of books by Eric Shepherd (*see* **CONVENT SCHOOL STORIES**), a detective story set in a convent school, but is designed as pure farce (indeed, the epithet on the title page is 'A Farrago').

Australian writer R E Warfe produced a more contemporary parody, in *First Term for Ziggy* (1997): its subtitle, *Sex Scandal at Greyfriars*, is slightly unfair to the book, which concentrates almost equally on drugs, AIDS and environmentalism. The author has clearly read plenty of school stories: quite apart from the mistresses' names (Miss Brent-Dyer, Miss Oxenham, Miss Brazil and Miss Potter—this is Australia), the whole plot centres on the ingenuous new girl who comes to school expecting everything to be like her favourite school story, *Paradigm Towers Wins Through*. Much of the humour stems from Ziggy's naivety, though Warfe also enjoys outrageous incongruity, as when Miss Blyton, the Head, aims to turn the new gymnasium into a sado-masochistic brothel. However, the book tries rather too hard to amuse, and the flavour is more boys' locker-room graffiti than successful parody.

It would be unfair to classify as pastiche Jenny Colgan's *Class* (2008), *Rules* (2010) and *Lessons* (2020) (the first two originally published under the pseudonym 'Jane Beaton'): there is plenty of originality in these gently humorous romances. Nevertheless, the story of working-class Scottish teacher Maggie Adair, who leaves her inner-city Glasgow comprehensive for Downey House, an excessively posh girls' boarding school, has been heavily influenced by the school stories Colgan enjoyed as a child, and which she acknowledges in her introduction. Downey House is on the Cornish coast, has a tower at each corner, and there is a carefully planned trick (I almost wrote 'treek') played on the staff, but there are other intertextual nuggets for the aficionado, such as the prominent new girl whose name is Alice Trebizon-Woods.

On the same lines is the series by Debbie Young set at St Bride's (*Secrets at St Bride's*, 2019, and *Stranger at St Bride's*, 2020). Like Colgan's protagonist, Gemma Lamb is an outsider in the well-heeled girls' boarding school where she takes a post as English teacher while fleeing from an abusive boyfriend. While influenced by the classic girls' school story tradition, Young also draws on her experience working for many years at a well-known girls' boarding school in the south-west of England, and her books are full of affectionate humour at the idiosyncrasies of girls and teaching staff.

Two works written for the stage should also be mentioned here. *Daisy Pulls it Off*, Denise Deegan's popular 1983 play, is full of tropes from the classic girls' school story: Daisy, the scholarship girl at Grangewood School for Young Ladies, has to battle snobbery while she excels at hockey, hunts for hidden treasure, saves the lives of her enemies in a classic cliff-top rescue, and is eventually reunited with her not-actually-dead father. A similar approach, with extra lesbianism, appears in the musical *Crush* (2015) by Maureen Chadwick and Kath Gotts. In both cases, 'pastiche' is probably a more appropriate word than 'parody': there's affection, perhaps even celebration, here.

There is no doubt, though, that the most famous mockery of all is the name which (aided by the film versions) still leaps to the lips of most British men if asked to name a fictional girls' school—St Trinian's. Ronald Searle, confined in a Japanese POW camp, had drawn the sweet English Rose schoolgirl mixed up with the brutality around him. On his return, he found that his cartoons touched a nerve in the public. St Trinian's is the subversion both of frilly femininity and of the public school ethos. His girls look like apes, murderers and the worst type of passport photographs. They wield hockey sticks as though they were Kalashnikovs and keep stores of liquor in the dormitories; they hang unpopular mistresses from the nearest tree, and roast entire pigs at their midnight feasts. They are far more visual than verbal: the one St Trinian's novel, written by D B Wyndham Lewis using the pseudonym 'Timothy Shy' and illustrated by Searle, has some excellent one-liners which one could envisage below a cartoon ('"Five split infinitives in your English essay once again. How many a's in 'bastard?"'), but between each of these, there are several paragraphs on the lines of 'Down the corridor thundered a crowd of English Roses of every size, fresh from prep and ripe for devilry, laughing, fighting, howling, and playing a thousand merry pranks'. For the real St Trinian's, one needs the cartoons, originally published in various magazines, but collected in volumes such as *Hurrah for St Trinian's* (Macdonald, 1948) or *Back to the Slaughterhouse* (Macdonald, 1951).

It is possible to subvert the girls' school story without resorting to pastiche or hyperbole, as we see in *The Passion-Flower Hotel*, published in 1962 by 'Rosalind Erskine' (a pseudonym for Roger Erskine Longrigg, creative director of an advertising agency, who went on to write 55 more novels under eight different names, including two rather lacklustre non-school sequels to the original *The Passion-Flower Hotel*). The fifteen-year-old schoolgirls who decide to run their own brothel for the benefit of the local boys' school are about as far from the Chalet School as one can get. They are not even obsessed with sex: certainly they want the experience, but they are even more charmed by the thought of making money from the venture. The cleverness of the novel is revealed in the final twist: these hard-nosed, ostensibly sexually experienced girls ultimately admit that, once in the *boudoir* with their boy, they are too nervous to do anything except talk, and later claim a passionate bout of love-making. In the end the novel undermines even its own cynicism.

These books all work by turning the school story on its head to create laughter, particularly by attacking the connotations of innocence implied by the image of the schoolgirl. The school detective story uses another aspect of the girls' school to create its effects: the safe enclosure, where girls are protected and guarded from anything sordid or hostile. Probably the best-known book of this type is Agatha Christie's *Cat among the Pigeons* (1959), but there are many others. Sarah Campion, whose teaching experience in girls' boarding schools was initially utilised in her 1935 novel *If She is Wise*, published *Unhandsome Corpse* in 1938, making it possibly the earliest murder mystery set in a girls' boarding school. There are several more recent books of this type: books like Val McDermid's *Report for Murder* (1987), set in a girls' public school in Derbyshire, and Iona McGregor's 1989 novel *Death Wore a Diadem* (which is also semi-historical) put murder in an unexpected context; Nayana Currimbhoy's *Miss Timmins' School for Girls* is interesting as well for its setting, an English missionary school in 1970s India. Several of these later school murder mysteries exploit the all-female society to introduce a lesbian theme.

The potential of this type of background is intensified when the institution is a convent school, a setting not known in real life for homicide but very effective in fiction. (For further discussion, see **CONVENT SCHOOL STORIES**.) Authors are reluctant, however, to cast a mistress or (even worse) a nun as murderer, though several are victims: even when the villains are female, as in *Gaudy Night* or *Cat Among the Pigeons*, they are normally outsiders. In making a student the murderer, Josephine Tey breaks ranks, delighting, as ever, in ignoring convention.

The shock of murder (or attempted murder) in an apparently secure environment is also noticeable in the college detective stories. The most famous of these, of course, is Dorothy L Sayers' Oxford novel *Gaudy Night* (1935), where the disruptive effect of crime is all the greater in the cloistered severity of the academic life. Not as well known (perhaps unfairly) are Gladys Mitchell's college stories such as *Laurels are Poison* (1942) and Josephine Tey's delightful *Miss Pym Disposes* (1946), set in a physical training college. Ruth Dudley Edwards' cynically amusing *Matricide at St Martha's* (1995) should also be mentioned here, though the detective element of the book is less memorable than the satire on political correctness. It's also a rarity in the modern world: with fewer and fewer colleges now reserved for women, most fictional college crime is well and truly mixed.

The trend towards mixed colleges has also largely killed that more sophisticated relative of the girls' school and college story, the Oxbridge novel. The period between the two World Wars was notable for the number of Oxbridge women graduates who felt compelled to publish their experiences to the world; a handful of those novels are still read today, largely due to the gallant work of the publishers Virago, who have brought them back into print. Rosamund Lehmann's *Dusty Answer* (1927) and Vera Brittain's *The Dark Tide* (1935) are probably the best known of these books, but there are scores of novels which re-create the experience of women at Oxford—and to a lesser extent at Cambridge—during the period when women still had to struggle for acceptance at the two oldest British universities. Such books cannot really be covered here, but are listed in the bibliography below.

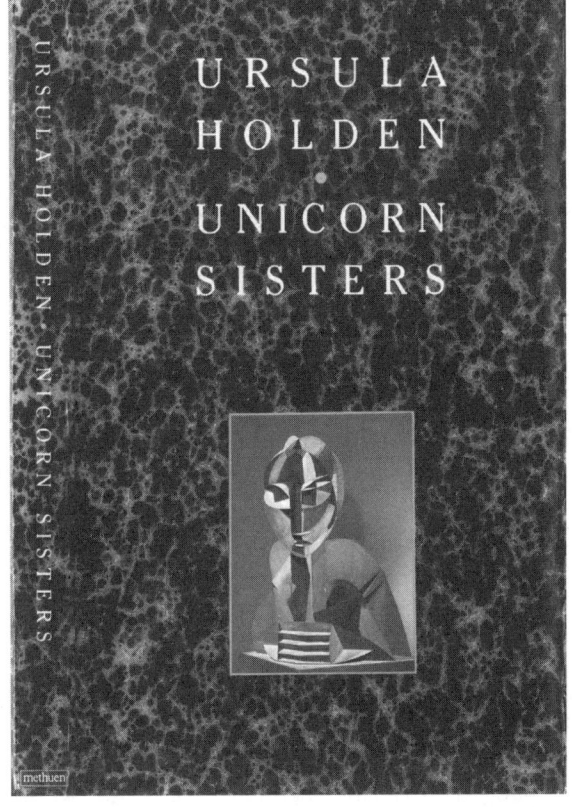

Finally, there is a handful of adult school fiction which is almost unclassifiable, but which needs to be mentioned for its originality, ingenuity or sheer charm. Muriel Spark's *The Prime of Miss Jean Brodie* (1961) needs no recommendation here: the eponymous Edinburgh schoolmistress (apparently based at least in part on Spark's own teacher at James Gillespie's School for Girls, Christina Kay) is one of the great characters of fiction. Angela Thirkell's *The Headmistress* (1944) has all that author's ironic humour. Eleanor Scott, herself a teacher, shows in *War Among Ladies* (1928) the real problems which affect teachers and is particularly memorable for its depictions of an appalling School Inspector. *Secret Places* (Janice Elliott, 1981) brings a cosmopolitan refugee into an English girls' school, with memorable results. *No Talking After Lights* (Angela Lambert, 1990) is an anarchic look at boarding school life in the 1950s, complete with menstruation and pupils 'playing horses' in the dormitory; and Mary Bell's *Summer's Day* (1951) is simply an excellent picture of the life of pupils and staff in a normal school: or perhaps not 'simply', as the skill and ease with which the story is told occurs too rarely, in school fiction or outside it.

Our thanks to Sarah Sneddon, part of whose PhD thesis has been unashamedly cribbed in compiling this article, to Scott Thompson, whose blog Furrowed Middlebrow (http://furrowedmiddlebrow.blogspot.com/) has been invaluable in suggesting titles to investigate and to Lyn Dodd, whose collection of adult school fiction has both expanded and illustrated this article.

Bibliography

Listed below are the books mentioned in the article above; some other adult novels wholly or partly set in girls' schools or colleges (though the list makes no claim to comprehensiveness); and a selection of books which may be felt to be in some way significant, even though only a small part may have girls' school or college interest. As with the main section of this volume, books set in boys' or co-educational schools are omitted, as are books set in primary schools (which means that the books by Miss Read are excluded) as well as short stories and articles, such as those in *The Girl's Own Paper*. Books which are overtly autobiographical (such as Molly Hughes' *A London Girl of the Eighties* (1946) or Winifred Peck's *A Little Learning* (1952), though extremely valuable sources for the history of girls' education, are not fictional, and are thus not included. Those which, though heavily autobiographical, are fictionalised, at least to the extent of third-person narrative and a change of nomenclature (such as *Frost in May*) are included.

Non-British books are here given with their British publisher, where appropriate, and date of first British publication.

P B Abercrombie (Patricia Barnes), *The Little Difference*, Gollancz ([1959])
Barbara Anderson, *Girls' High* (New Zealand), Secker & Warburg (1991)
Carmen Barnes, *Schoolgirl* (USA), T Werner Laurie (1930)
Kathleen Barratt, *To Fight Another Day*, Chapman & Hall (1947)

Jane Beaton, *see* Jenny Colgan
Sally Beattie, *Small Rebellious Acts*, Andre Deutsch (1986)
Mary Bell, *Summer's Day*, Collins (1951)
Clara Benson, *The Trouble at Wakeley Court* (detective), self-published (2016)
Charity Blackstock (Ursula Torday), *The Briar Patch*, Hodder & Stoughton (1960)
Elizabeth Bowen, *Friends and Relations*, Constable (1931)
The Little Girls (part school), Jonathan Cape (1964)
Dorothy Bowers, *Fear and Miss Betony*, Hodder & Stoughton (1941)
Vera Brittain, *The Dark Tide* (college), Richards (1935)
Charlotte Brontë, *Jane Eyre* (part school), Smith, Elder & Co. (1847)
The Professor (Belgium), Smith, Elder & Co. (1857)
Villette (Belgium), Smith, Elder & Co. (1853)
Sarah Campion (Mary Rose Coulton Alpers), *If She is Wise*, Peter Davies (1935)
Unhandsome Corpse (detective), Peter Davies (1938)
Elizabeth Carfrae, *Good Morning, Miss Morrison*, Hutchinson (1948)
Agatha Christie, *Cat Among the Pigeons* (detective), Collins (1959)
Douglas Clark, *Golden Rain* (detective), Gollancz (1980)
Christabel Coleridge, *The Green Girls of Greythorpe*, National Society's Depository ([1890])
Colette (Sidonie-Gabrielle Colette), *Claudine à l'école*, Ollendorff (1900). As *Claudine at School* (trans. Antonia White), Secker & Warburg (1956)
Jenny Colgan, *Class*, Sphere (2008, as 'Jane Beaton'; reissued under real name 2016) and its sequels *Rules*, Sphere (2010, as 'Jane Beaton'; reissued under real name 2016), *Lessons*, Sphere (2020)
Ivy Compton-Burnett, *More Women than Men*, Heinemann (1933)
Catherine Cookson, *The Devil and Mary Ann* (part convent), Macdonald (1958)
Honoria Renée Minturn Croome, *The Mountain and the Molehill*, Chatto & Windus (1955)
Amanda Cross (Carolyn Heilbrun), *The Theban Mysteries* (USA, detective), Gollancz (1972)
Nayana Currimbhoy, *Miss Timmins' School for Girls* (Indian, detective), Harper Perennial (2011)
Clemence Dane (Winifred Ashton), *Regiment of Women*, Heinemann (1917)
Betty De Sherbinin, *Monkey Puzzle*, Putnam (1952)
Ruth Dudley Edwards, *Matricide at St Martha's* (college, detective), St Martin's Press (1995)
Vera G Dwyer, *A War of Girls* (Australia), Ward Lock (1915)
Janice Elliott, *Secret Places*, Hodder (1981)
Rosalind Erskine (Roger Erskine Longrigg), *The Passion-Flower Hotel*, Jonathan Cape (1962): the two sequels, *Passion-Flowers in Italy* (1963) and *Passion-Flowers in Business* (1965) aren't set in school
Cherry Evans (Jean Cherry Drummond of Megginch, 16th Baroness Strange), *Love from Belinda*, Hodder & Stoughton (1962)
Margaret Forster, *Miss Owen-Owen is at Home*, Secker & Warburg (1969)
Antonia Fraser, *Quiet as a Nun* (convent, detective), Weidenfeld & Nicholson (1977)
Tana French, *The Secret Place* (convent, detective), Hodder & Stoughton (2014)
Kathleen Gibberd, *Vain Adventure*, John Lane (1927)
Stella Gibbons, *Pure Juliet* (part college), posthumously published by Vintage Digital (2016)
Caroline Glyn, *Don't Knock the Corners Off*, Gollancz (1963)
Gwethalyn Graham, *Swiss Sonata*, Jonathan Cape (1938)
Henry Martineau Greenhow, *Leila's Lovers* (college), Digby, Long & Co (1902)
Diane M Greenwood, *Holy Terrors* (detective), Headline (1994)

Daphne Greer, *Finding Grace* (Canadia, convent school), Nimbus (2019)
Sally Griffiths, *Winter Day in a Glasshouse*, Hutchinson (1968)
Sheila Hancock, *Miss Carter's War*, Bloomsbury (2014)
Elizabeth Hargreaves, *The Miss*, Hutchinson (1955)
Margaret Hassett, *Educating Elizabeth*, Longmans, Green & Co (1937)
Beezer's End (sequel to above), Longmans, Green & Co (1949)
Ian Hay, *Little Ladyship*, Hodder & Stoughton (1941)
Mavis Doriel Hay, *Death on the Cherwell* (college), Skeffington & Son (1935)
Renée Haynes, *Neapolitan Ice* (college), Chatto & Windus (1928)
Rose Marie Hodgson, *Rosy-Fingered Dawn* (college), Constable (1934)
Ursula Holden, *Unicorn Sisters*, Methuen (1988).
Hazel Holt, *Delay of Execution* (detective), Macmillan (2001); reissued by Signet in 2002 as *Mrs Malory and the Delay of Execution*
Victoria Holt (Eleanor Hibbert), *The Time of the Hunter's Moon*, Collins (1983)
Winifred Holtby, *South Riding*, Collins (1936)
Leslie Howarth, *Ladies in Residence: a Novel of Cambridge* (college), Hodder & Stoughton (1936)
Frances Huish, *Selina Triumphant*, Hutchinson ([1940])
'J G G', *From Doubt to Faith: the Story of a Newnham Girl* (college), Marshall Bros., [1896]
Fanny Johnson, *In Statu Pupillari: a Story of Girls at College* (college), Swan Sonnenschein & Col (1907)
Priscilla Johnston, *The Narrow World*, Duckworth (1930)
Margaret Kennedy, *The Constant Nymph* (part school), Heinemann (1925)
Madeleine L'Engle, *The Small Rain* (USA, part Swiss school), New York (1945); first part adapted as *Prelude* in Britain, Gollancz (1970)
Elizabeth Lake, *The First Rebellion* (convent), Cresset Press (1952)
Angela Lambert, *No Talking After Lights*, Hamish Hamilton (1990)
Philip Larkin, *Trouble at Willow Gables* & *Michaelmas Term at St Bride's,* in *Trouble at Willow Gables and Other Fictions*, edited by James Booth: Faber (2002)
Winifred Lear, *Shady Cloister*, Macmillan (1950)
Rosamund Lehmann, *Dusty Answer* (part college), Chatto & Windus (1927)
Elizabeth Lemarchand, *Death of an Old Girl* (detective), Walker & Co (1967)
Joan Lindsay, *Picnic at Hanging Rock* (Australia), Cheshire (1967)
Christine Longford, *Making Conversation* (part school, part college), Stein & Gollancz (1931)
V I Longman, *Harvest* (college), Kegan Paul & Co (1913)
Sheena Mackay, *Dust Falls on Eugene Schlumberger*, Gollancz (1964)
Helen McCloy, *Through a Glass Darkly* (detective), Gollancz (1951)
Val McDermid, *Report for Murder* (detective), Women's Press (1987)
Iona McGregor, *Death Wore a Diadem* (detective), The Women's Press (1989)
Catriona McPherson, *Dandy Gilver and a Bothersome Number of Corpses* (detective), Hodder & Stoughton (2012) (Adult detective; no. 7 in ongoing series)
Rosemary Manning, *The Chinese Garden*, Jonathan Cape (1962)
Margaret Masterman, *Gentlemen's Daughters*, Ivor Nicholson & Watson (1931)
Gladys Mitchell, *St Peter's Finger* (convent, detective), Michael Joseph (1938)
Laurels are Poison (college, detective), Michael Joseph (1942)
Spotted Hemlock (college, detective), Michael Joseph (1958)
Convent on Styx (convent, detective), Michael Joseph (1975)

Diana Morgan, *Delia*, Hutchinson (1974)
Anne Morice, *Murder in Outline* (detective), Macmillan (1979)
Clare Morrall, *After the Bombing*, Hodder (2014)
Betty Neels, *A Christmas Wish*, Mills & Boon, (1994)
Paula Neuss, *All Girls Together*, Duckworth (1979)
Marjorie Norrell, *Nurse Lavinia's Mistake*, Mills & Boon (1968)
Elizabeth North, *Dames*, Jonathan Cape (1981)
Kate O'Brien, *The Land of Spices* (convent), Heinemann (1941)
Simon Oke, *The Hippopotamus Takes Wing* (convent), Collins (1952)
Olivia (Dorothy Strachey Bussy), *Olivia*, Hogarth Press (1949)
George Orwell, *A Clergyman's Daughter* (part school), Gollancz (1935)
Winifred Peck, *Winding Ways*, Faber & Faber (1951)
Wendy Perriam, *Michael, Michael*, Harper Collins (1993)
Adela Quebec (Lord Berners), *The Girls of Radcliff Hall* (parodic *roman à clef*), privately printed (1936)
Jill Roe, *Angels Flying Slowly* (convent), Hodder & Stoughton (1995)
Henry Handel Richardson (Ethel Florence Lindesay Robertson), *The Getting of Wisdom* (Australia), Heinemann (1910)
Dorothy L Sayers, *Gaudy Night* (college, detective), Gollancz (1935)
Eleanor Scott, *War Among Ladies*, Ernest Benn (1928)
Renée Shann, *Never Again*, Collins (1967)
Eric Shepherd, *Murder in a Nunnery* (convent, detective), Sheed & Ward (1940)
More Murder in a Nunnery (sequel to above: convent, detective), Sheed & Ward (1954)
Nan Shepherd, *The Quarry Wood* (part college), Constable (1928)
Carole B Shmurak, *Deadmistress* (USA, detective), Sterlinghouse (2004)
Timothy Shy (D B Wyndham Lewis) and **Ronald Searle**, *The Terror of St Trinian's*, Max Parrish (1952)
Barbara Silver (Ellen Barbara Sturgis), *Our Young Barbarians, or: Letters from Oxford* (college), Macmillan (1935)
Violet Simpson, *Occasion's Forelock* (part college), Edward Arnold (1906)
Frank Smith, *Fatal Flaw* (detective), Constable (1996)
Herbert Maynard Smith, *Inspector Frost and Lady Brassingham* (detective), Ernest Benn (1940)
Nancy Spain, *Death before Wicket* (detective), Hutchinson (1946)
Poison for Teacher, Hutchinson (1949)
Muriel Spark, *The Prime of Miss Jean Brodie*, Macmillan (1961)
D E Stevenson, *Charlotte Fairlie*, Collins (1954)
Jill Staines, *A Knife at the Opera* (detective), Bodley Head (1988)
Monica Stirling, *Dress Rehearsal*, Gollancz (1951)
Alice Stronach, *A Newnham Friendship* (college), Blackie (1901)
Mary Sturt, *Be Gentle to the Young* (college), Hodder & Stoughton (1936)
Susan Swan, *The Wives of Bath* (Canada), Granta Books, (1993)
Netta Syrett, *A School Year*, Methuen (1902), republished in 1934 by Mellifont Press, Dublin, as *Girls of the Sixth Form*
Alison Taylor, *Child's Play* (detective), Heinemann 2000
Domini Taylor (Roger Erskine Longrigg), *Suffer Little Children*, Hamilton (1987)
Gertrude Winifred Taylor, *The Pearl* (college), Blackwell (1917)

Josephine Tey (Elizabeth MacKintosh), *Miss Pym Disposes* (college, detective), Peter Davies (1946)
William M Thackeray, *Vanity Fair* (small part school), Bradbury & Evans (1848)
Angela Thirkell, *The Headmistress*, Hamish Hamilton (1944)
June Thomson, *Rosemary for Remembrance* (detective), Constable (1988)
Sylvia Thompson, *The Hounds of Spring* (part college), Heinemann (1926)
Nicola Thorne, *The Little Flowers* (convent), Severn House (2004)
Tivoli (Horace William Bleakley), *Une Culotte or A New Woman: An Impossible Tale of Modern Oxford* (college), Digby, Long & Co ([1894])
Gertrude Eileen Trevelyan, *Hot-House* (college), Martin Secker (1933)
Frances Turk, *The Summer Term*, Wright & Brown (1965)
Anne Valery, *The Edge of a Smile*, Peter Owen (1977)
Rosalind Wade, *Children, Be Happy*, Gollancz (1931)
Doreen Wallace, *A Little Learning* (part college), Ernest Benn (1931)
R E Warfe, *First Term for Ziggy* (Australia), Hodder & Stoughton (1997)
Antonia White, *Frost in May* (convent), Harmsworth (1933)
Ethel Lina White, *The Third Eye* (part school), Collins (1937)
Mary Wilkes, *The Only Door Out* (part college, part convent school), Faber & Faber (1945)
Ethel Mary Wilmot-Buxton, *Gildersleeves*, Sands & Co (1921)
Christa Winsloe, *The Child Manuela* (Germany), Chapman & Hall (1934)
Margaret Woods, *The Invader* (college), Heinemann (1907)
Judith Woolf, *A Chalked Heart*, Chatto & Windus (1972)
June Wright, *Faculty of Murder* (Australia, girls' hostel at university), John Long (1961)
Sara Yeomans, *Miss Bugle Saw God in the Cabbages*, Piatkus (1998)
Debbie Young, *Secrets at St Bride's*, Hawkesbury Press (2019), and its sequel *Stranger at St Bride's*, Hawkesbury Press (2020)